The Pre-Raphaelites

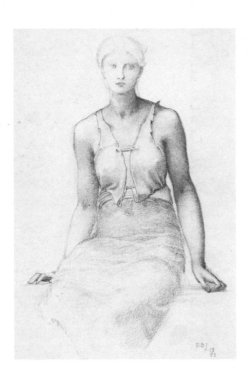

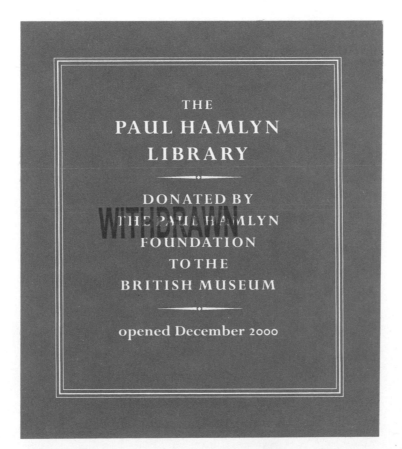

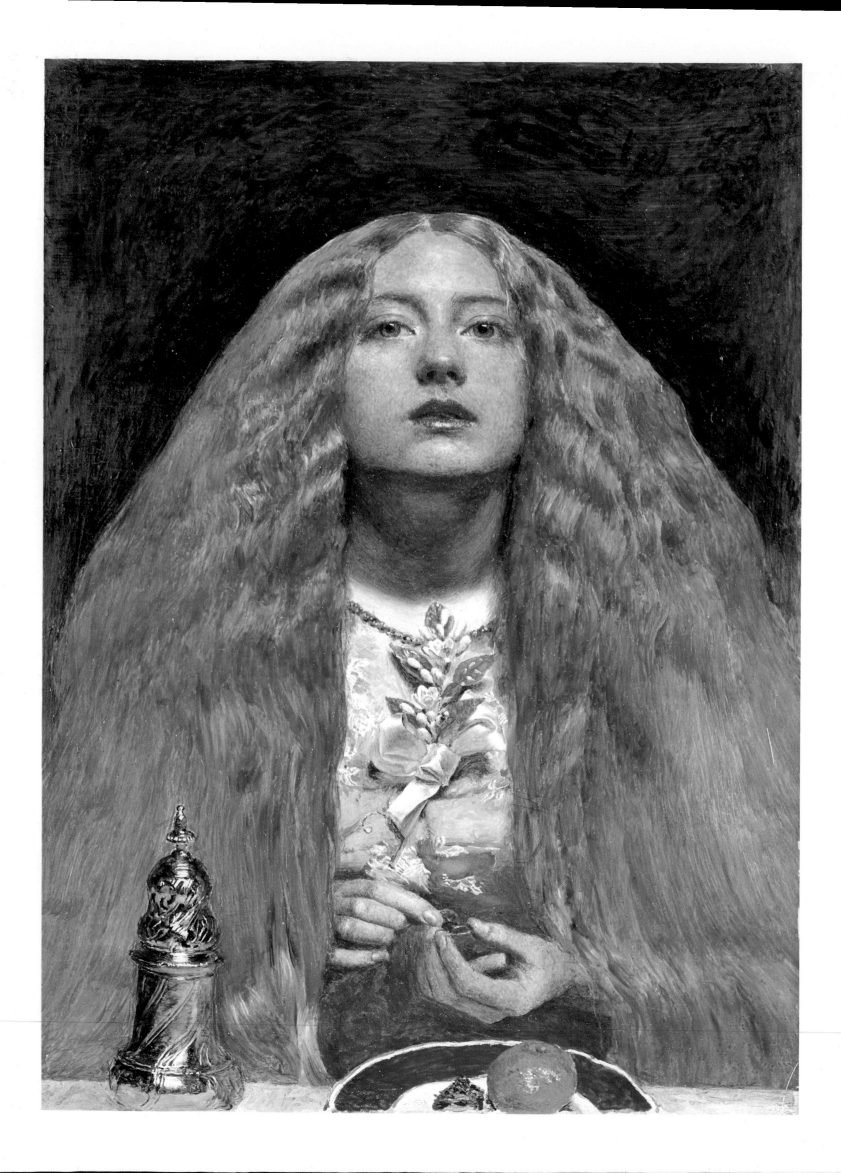

The Pre-Raphaelites

Christopher Wood

 PHOENIX ILLUSTRATED

Copyright © Christopher Wood, 1981

First published in 1981 by
George Weidenfeld & Nicolson Ltd
Second Impression 1983
Reeissued in hardback 1994

This paperback edition first published in 1997 by
Phoenix Illustrated
Orion Publishing Group, Orion House
5, Upper St. Martin's Lane
London WC2H 9EA

British Library Cataloguing-in-Publication Data
A catalogue record for this book is available from
the British Library

ISBN 0-75380-242-2

Designed by Jonathan Gill-Skelton
Typeset by Keyspools Ltd, Golbourne, Lancs
Printed in Italy

PICTURE CREDITS

NB: In-text page references relate to colour plates only and
appear with the first mention of a painting in each section.
For all black and white illustrations, refer to the index.

Black and White Illustrations
Ashmolean Museum, Oxford: 22, 98 (left); Birmingham
City Art Gallery: 12 (below), 34 (above), 84, 116 (both);
Reproduced by Permission of the Syndics of the
Fitzwilliam Museum, Cambridge: 2, 6; Forbes Magazine
Collection; 144 (above); Glasgow City Art Gallery: 120;
Guildhall Art Gallery, London: 9, 61; Harris Museum and
Art Gallery, Preston: 78; Lady Lever Art Gallery, Port
Sunlight: 37 (far right); Manchester City Art Gallery: 10,
51 (right); National Portrait Gallery, London: 24 (far left),
30 (above), 40 (above), 45, 46, 52, 106, 112 (below), 126;
Private collections: 13, 95 (below), 96 (below), 98 (below),
112 (above); Russell-Cotes Art Gallery, Bournemouth: 95
(above); Southampton Art Gallery: 123 (all); Tate Gallery,
London: 1, 16, 24 (left), 30 (left), 34 (left), 37 (right), 40
(below), 51 (far right), 54, 57, 59, 66 (both), 71, 77, 90, 94,
101, 110, 118, 137 (all), 144 (below), 146, 150; Victoria and
Albert Museum, London: 12 (above); Walker Art Gallery,
Liverpool: 86, 96 (left).

Colour Plates
All locations are shown in the plate captions. All
photographs were supplied by the respective owners, but
special thanks to the following: The Bucentaur Gallery
(151, 154); The Cooper-Bridgeman Library (31, 43, 57, 62,
152); John Leigh (137); Sotheby's Belgravia (136); John
Webb (all Tate Gallery subjects).

Page 1: **Sir Edward Burne-Jones**, study for *King
Cophetua and the Beggar Maid*.

2: **Sir John Everett Millais**, *The Bridesmaid*,
signed with monogram and dated 1851. Panel
27×20 cm/$10\frac{3}{4} \times 7\frac{3}{4}$ ins. A typical Pre-
Raphaelite 'stunner', with long, wavy hair.
Millais explained that it depicted 'a bridesmaid
who is passing the wedding cake through the
ring nine times', a marriage custom still
prevalent in Victorian times.

6: **Sir John Everett Millais**, study for *Isabella*, 1849.

Contents

Acknowledgements

All the illustrations in this book are reproduced by kind permission of their owners. I can only thank them collectively, whether they be private collectors, trustees, curators of museums, auctioneers or dealers. Many of them have been especially patient and helpful in arranging to have their pictures photographed in colour, in particular the staffs of the Tate Gallery, Birmingham City Art Gallery and Manchester City Art Gallery, who between them own most of the major Pre-Raphaelite masterpieces. I am especially grateful to Russell Ash for his tireless zeal in arranging all the photography and for so closely following the production of the book at every stage, Jonathan Gill-Skelton for his work in designing it, and also to Jill Hollis for reading and editing the manuscript. My thanks also to Alexandra Moore and Joanna Millais who both had the difficult task of typing the manuscript amidst the distractions and disturbances of working in my gallery.

This book was mostly written during a summer holiday with my family on the coast of Northumberland in 1980. The location proved inspiring, but I did not spend as much time with my wife and children as a father should on holiday. If the reader enjoys my book he should therefore think with gratitude not only of the author, but also his wife Sarah, and Alexander, Laura and Henry.

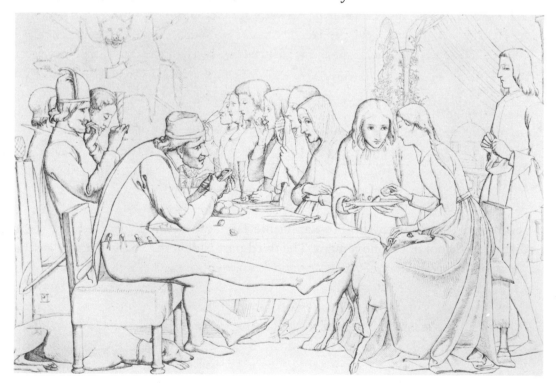

Introduction

The Pre-Raphaelite literature is already enormous, and threatens to become an industry. So why another book about them? I offer three reasons. Firstly, most of the books published about the Pre-Raphaelites have been small in format, and poorly illustrated. For the first time, this book sets out to illustrate many of the best-known Pre-Raphaelite masterpieces and a large number of lesser-known works in full colour of the highest quality. Secondly, most books have dealt mainly with the Pre-Raphaelite Brotherhood and the first phase of the movement, dealing only cursorily with the second, aesthetic phase. This is an unbalanced viewpoint, and I have therefore devoted over half the illustrations in this book to the second phase of Pre-Raphaelitism, carrying it right up to the end of the nineteenth century, and well into the twentieth. Thirdly, an extraordinary amount of Pre-Raphaelite literature has been devoted to the private lives of the artists concerned, in particular their love lives, and surprisingly little to their art. Some of these books are wildly prejudiced, and suffer from the pet hates and hobby-horses of their authors, which now makes them seem very dated. Others have sought to interpret the movement purely in political or social terms. I have attempted to provide a balanced, objective survey of the Pre-Raphaelites and their followers, concentrating more on their artistic achievements, and less on their personalities, fascinating though they may be. My text is not a long one, and the result can be no more than a survey, leaving the illustrations and captions to speak for themselves. Most of the artists mentioned need a separate monograph of their own and yet, surprisingly, there are still no good modern books about Holman Hunt, Millais or Madox Brown, to name only a few. I hope this book will make a useful contribution to this vast subject, and fill what is obviously a considerable gap.

The term 'Pre-Raphaelite' is in danger of becoming one of the most misused tags in art history. Some definition is needed, and I have therefore divided this book into three distinct parts. The first part deals with the Pre-Raphaelite Brotherhood and its close associates and followers; this covers the period from 1848 to about 1860. The second part deals with the Pre-Raphaelite landscape painters, who form a fairly distinct offshoot of the movement. The third part is devoted to the second, aesthetic phase of the movement, of whom the chief exponents were Rossetti and Burne-Jones. I have included here the numerous followers and disciples of Burne-Jones, and also such romantic painters as Waterhouse, Byam Shaw and Cadogan Cowper, who carried Pre-Raphaelitism well into the twentieth century. It is this third phase which is the most difficult to define. It is sometimes referred to as the Aesthetic Movement, or as 'Post-Pre-Raphaelitism'. Through William Morris it is linked to the Arts and Crafts Movement, and also had its followers among the architects of the Queen Anne Revival. It was a tremendously rich and highly eclectic period, and therefore produced art of infinite variety and diversity, in which Pre-Raphaelitism is only one element among many. But for most young English artists, even up to the 1890s, the example of the Pre-Raphaelites was still very much a living force, a symbol of high artistic endeavour, and a potent source of inspiration.

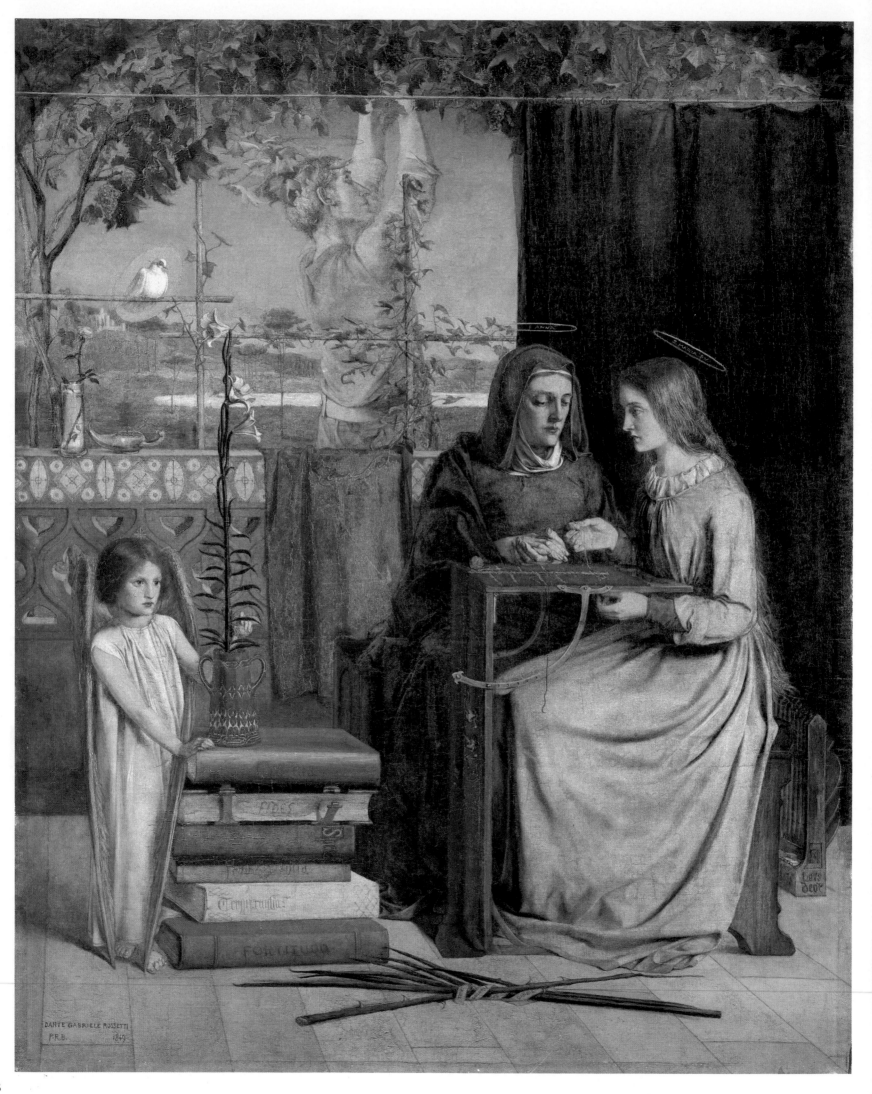

Dante Gabriel Rossetti (1828–1882)

The Girlhood of Mary Virgin

Signed and dated PRB 1849
Canvas 83 × 64 cm/32¾ × 25 ins
Tate Gallery, London

Rossetti's first major oil painting, and the first picture to be exhibited with the mysterious initials, 'PRB'. It was begun in 1848 and completed in 1849, with the help of both Madox Brown and Holman Hunt. The models for the Virgin Mary and her mother were Rossetti's sister Christina and their mother. The picture is full of symbolic references to the life of Christ. Mary Virgin and St Anne are shown embroidering a lily onto a crimson cloth. Before them stands a lily, symbol of purity, on a pile of books inscribed with the cardinal virtues, beside which there is a child-angel. On the ground lies a seven-leaved palm branch and a seven-thorned briar, tied with a scroll inscribed *tot dolores tot gaudia* ('so many sorrows, so many joys'), symbols of the Passion to come. Behind St Anne is a cross entwined with ivy, a crimson cloak, emblematic of the Robe of Christ, and a haloed dove, symbolic of the Holy Spirit. In the background St Joseph prunes a vine, a symbol of the True Vine and Great Sacrifice.

The origins of the Pre-Raphaelite Brotherhood

The year 1848 was a year of revolutions. All over Europe thrones and governments were toppling. In England political revolution was averted, but in that year three young Royal Academy students started a revolution in art that was to reverberate through the rest of the century. Their names were Dante Gabriel Rossetti, William Holman Hunt and John Everett Millais, founders of the Pre-Raphaelite Brotherhood, the most influential and controversial movement in the history of English art.

Before attempting to define the aims and artistic beliefs of the Pre-Raphaelite Brotherhood (or PRB as they are commonly called), it is important to realize two things. Firstly, the Brotherhood was a group of earnest, rebellious, high-spirited, and above all, very young men. Their artistic aims were inevitably rather confused. They all wanted change, but had very different ideas of how to bring it about. The results varied enormously from one artist to another. What they shared was their youth and their enthusiasm. Secondly, the Brotherhood, as a movement, was very short-lived. It was founded in the winter of 1848, and the first pictures to be signed with the secret initials PRB were exhibited in 1849. In 1853 Millais was elected an Associate of the Royal Academy, and Rossetti regarded this as the end of the Brotherhood. From then on its members, and their disciples and followers, went their very different ways. But in four years they had set in motion an artistic revolution that was to have momentous consequences. It is no exaggeration to say that the influence of the Pre-Raphaelites on English art and literature lasted until the very end of the nineteenth and even continued well into the twentieth century.

The story of the Brotherhood began in the summer of 1848, when Holman Hunt and Rossetti, both Academy students, became friends. Rossetti had seen and admired Hunt's picture *The Eve of Saint Agnes* at the Royal Academy Exhibition, and was studying oil painting with Ford Madox Brown, but quickly tired of the rigid disciplines imposed by the older man. He decided to share a studio with Hunt instead, and Hunt helped him to finish his first oil painting *The Girlhood of Mary*

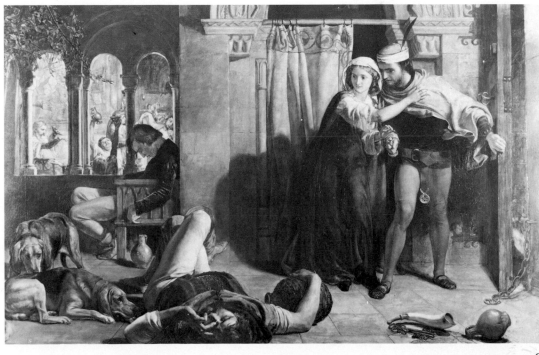

William Holman Hunt, *The Eve of Saint Agnes*, 1848.

Virgin (p. 8). Hunt was already a friend of Millais, an infant prodigy who had entered the Academy Schools at the age of ten. Hunt introduced Rossetti to Millais, and the three began to hold regular meetings, either at Hunt's studio in Cleveland Street, or at Millais' parents' house in Gower Street. Finding that they enjoyed each other's company, and also that their views about art coincided, they decided to form an artistic society of their own. All three of them already belonged to student or artistic societies of one kind or another, but this one was to be different. Probably at Rossetti's suggestion, it was to be a secret society, known only to its members. The conspiratorial aspect made it more exciting, and suggested a similarity to the revolutionary societies such as the Carbonari, which flourished in Italy at the time.

So what were they to call their new society? 'Pre-Raphaelite' was chosen because it reflected their admiration for the early Italian painters of the period before Raphael. None of them had actually been to Italy, but from their readings of Ruskin, and from a book of Lasinio's engravings of the fourteenth-century frescoes in the Campo Santo at Pisa, they decided that the honesty and simplicity of these primitive Christian artists was what they wanted to emulate in their own art. 'Brotherhood' was chosen because it reflected their desire to be a close-knit, secret band of brothers, dedicated to the pursuit of art. In this way they almost certainly wished to follow the Nazarenes, a group of German artists who had lived in Rome since 1810, and who had formed themselves into a semi-monastic order, dedicated to the rejuvenation of religious art, in the spirit of the early Italian and German painters.

Most fundamental changes in taste are a reaction against what went before, and in this the Pre-Raphaelites were no exception. They were all absolutely united in their opposition to the prevailing artistic establishment, and in particular the Royal Academy, 'which had for its ambition', Hunt was to write later, 'Monkeyana ideas, Books of Beauty, and Chorister Boys.' The Pre-Raphaelites were primarily rebels, in revolt against the tide of triviality and vulgarity which annually engulfed the Academy walls. They wanted to paint nobler, more serious pictures, such as 'turned the minds of men to good reflections', wrote Millais. They were crusaders, with an earnest desire to produce a better art, and to paint pictures that would inspire and uplift the spectator. They also condemned all academic tricks and conventional techniques such as they had been taught at the Academy Schools. All this was dismissed as 'slosh' and its high-priest, Sir Joshua Reynolds, derided as 'Sir Sloshua'. Instead of the artificial chiaroscuro of the Old Masters, they determined to paint their pictures with complete fidelity to nature, studying each figure from a model, and painting landscape on the spot, out-of-doors. They used pure colours over a white ground, a technique which makes their pictures still appear startlingly bright. In this they were mainly inspired by John Ruskin, who in a famous passage in his *Modern Painters* had exhorted young artists to 'go to nature in all singleness of heart ... rejecting nothing, selecting nothing and scorning nothing; believing all things to be right and good, and rejoicing always in the truth'. Ruskin had in fact been writing about Turner, whom one could hardly categorize as a Pre-Raphaelite. But although his technique and painterly approach were entirely different, he did share with the Pre-Raphaelites the determination to record every facet of nature with complete honesty. A later critic was to condemn Turner as 'the chief Pre-Raphaelite', and in one sense he was right.

The artistic ideas of the Brotherhood were not entirely new. Like most revolutionary movements in art, they represented a culmination as much as a new departure. What created the vital spark was the intensity and the determination with which these young artists put their beliefs into practice. Looking at the 1830s and '40s, the historian can find many antecedents and precedents for their ideas. Their admiration for early Italian art was not new. The writings of Lord Lindsay and Mrs Jamesone had already reawakened an interest in what they liked to call 'early Christian' art. Enterprising collectors, such as William Young Ottley and the Rev. John Sanford, had already begun to assemble collections of early Italian paintings.

Ford Madox Brown (1821–1893)
The Last of England

Signed and dated 1855
Panel, almost circular, 83 × 75 cm/32½ × 29½ ins
Birmingham City Museum and Art Gallery

The best known of all Victorian paintings on the theme of emigration. Brown first had the idea of painting it when he went to Gravesend to say goodbye to his fellow Pre-Raphaelite, Thomas Woolner, who was emigrating to Australia. The picture was begun in 1852, finished in 1855, and exhibited at the Liverpool Academy in 1856. The models for the two figures were the artist and his wife Emma, who had to sit for the picture out of doors in all weathers, even with snow on the ground. So painstaking was Brown's technique that the red ribbons on the bonnet took him four weeks to paint.

James Collinson, *Answering the Emigrant's Letter*, 1850.

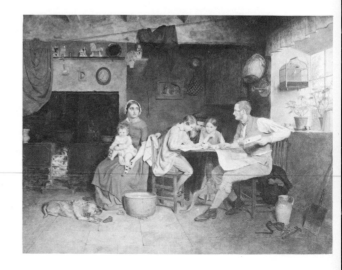

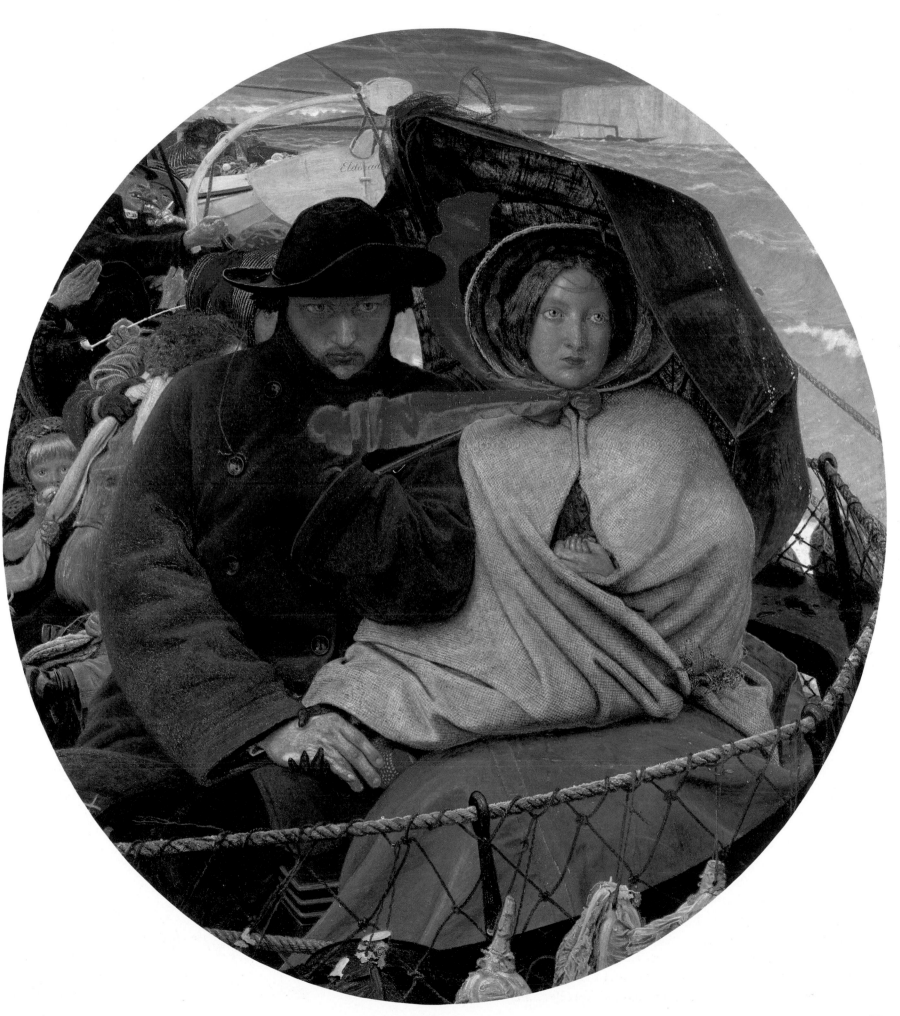

11

Another collector was Prince Albert. When the new Houses of Parliament were begun, it was decided in 1843 to decorate them with frescoes in early Italian style. Overbeck, one of the leaders of the Nazarenes, was approached, but refused. Competitions were therefore held, and Ford Madox Brown, a great admirer of the Nazarenes, returned to England in order to participate. Many English artists of the 1840s had been influenced by the Nazarenes, in particular William Dyce, William Charles Thomas Dobson, William Mulready, and John Rogers Herbert. In their religious pictures one can clearly see stylistic similarities with the early work of the Pre-Raphaelites.

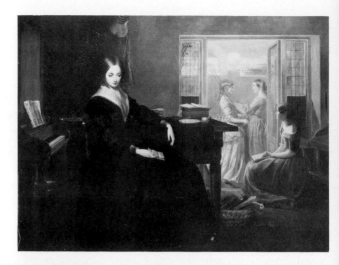

The techniques of the Pre-Raphaelites had also been anticipated by other artists. In particular, William Mulready was using the technique of painting in pure colours over a white ground in the early 1840s. Scrupulous attention to natural detail can be found in the fruit and bird's nest pictures of William Henry Hunt, whose statement that he felt 'really frightened' when beginning to paint a flower anticipated the Pre-Raphaelites' reverence for the minutiae of nature. The brilliant oriental scenes of John Frederick Lewis reveal that he too was using Pre-Raphaelite techniques long before the Pre-Raphaelites.

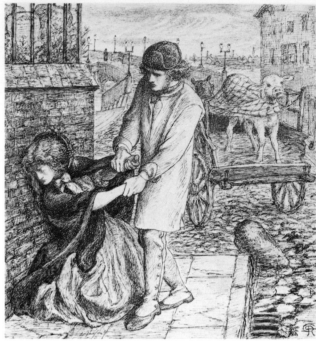

The Pre-Raphaelites were also extremely conscious of the social evils and injustices of the age. The 'hungry forties' was a turbulent and unsettled period, culminating in the great Chartist demonstration of 1848 which both Millais and Hunt witnessed. Although they were both highly patriotic, they found much to criticize in contemporary life, and were infected by the revolutionary spirit of the times. As a result, the Pre-Raphaelites were to paint a number of pictures on social themes, particularly that of the position of women in Victorian Society. In this they had been preceded by Richard Redgrave, whose famous picture, *The Governess*, was painted in 1844. In the 1840s Redgrave painted other pictures of exploited women – seamstresses, milliners, shop girls, unmarried mothers. The Pre-Raphaelites took up several of these themes, and Hunt was even brave enough to tackle the problem of prostitution in *The Awakening Conscience* (p. 42). Madox Brown made the biggest contribution to 'modern life' subjects with *Work* (p. 49) and *The Last of England* (p. 11); Rossetti struggled with *Found* which he never finished; Millais made a number of pen and ink drawings in the 1850s on social themes. Although such subjects constitute only a minority among Pre-Raphaelite pictures, they made a vital contribution to the development of modern-life painting.

Above: **Richard Redgrave**, *The Governess (The Poor Teacher)*, 1844. Below: **Dante Gabriel Rossetti**, study for *Found*, c1855.

But in all their pictures, even those based on medieval and literary themes, the Pre-Raphaelites were committed to painting with complete fidelity to nature. 'Absolutely without regard to the art of any period or country, I have tried to render this scene as it would appear', wrote Madox Brown of *The Last of England*. This remark might stand as a credo for the Pre-Raphaelite Brotherhood, and sums up their intense determination to make an absolutely fresh start,. They also subscribed wholeheartedly to the Ruskinian ethos that a good picture was a picture that conveyed a large number of ideas. Theirs was an intensely didactic, intensely moralistic art; it was also deliberately revolutionary – nothing else can explain its devastating effects on English nineteenth-century art. It is also a highly romantic art; the Pre-Raphaelites are unquestionably the Victorian heirs of the Romantic Movement. Ruskin revered Wordsworth; Hunt introduced the Brotherhood to Keats; many of their pictures were based on romantic poetry, and almost all of them deal with romantic or tragic love. The stories of their own lives are as romantic as any in art history.

The Pre-Raphaelite movement is a blend of romantic idealism, scientific rationalism and morality. This typically mid-Victorian mixture is, like so much in the Victorian age, full of paradox. How else can one explain a group of artists and intellectuals whose idea of modernity was to paint the Middle Ages? The Pre-Raphaelites were modern and medieval at the same time, and to understand them is to understand the Victorians.

The Brotherhood 1848–1853

And so in the autumn of 1848, the Brotherhood was formed. The question then arose of who else should be asked to join. In this matter the Pre-Raphaelites displayed a youthful perversity that has continued to astonish art historians ever since. The one artist who should have belonged – Ford Madox Brown – was opposed by Hunt on the grounds that he was too old and too steeped in the very academic conventions they wished to overthrow. Finally four other artists were invited to join the Brotherhood, making a total of seven. Of the four newcomers, only one – James Collinson – was actually a painter. Frederick George Stephens had never completed a picture, and he later gave up painting for writing. William Michael Rossetti was Gabriel's brother, and was not an artist at all, although he later became a well-known writer and critic. The seventh member was a sculptor, Thomas Woolner. He had at that time produced no sculpture that could be described as Pre-Raphaelite, and in 1852 he left England to seek his fortune in Australia. Just how this motley band of youthful rebels launched such an effective attack on the artistic establishment is one of the wonders of English art history. Never can such a momentous artistic movement have had such an unpromising beginning.

How did it happen? The story is now part of the Pre-Raphaelite legend, and can be quickly told. Through the winter and spring of 1848–49, the Brotherhood held regular meetings to discuss their ideas, the progress of their pictures, and occasionally to sketch together on a set subject. They also drew up lists of 'Immortals', heroes of art and literature whom they particularly admired. Their

William Holman Hunt, *Rienzi vowing to obtain Justice for the Death of his young Brother, slain in a skirmish between the Colonna and Orsini factions,* 1849. Hunt's first PRB painting, exhibited at the Royal Academy in 1849 where it hung next to Millais' *Isabella.* Rossetti modelled for the figure of Rienzi and Millais for the knight, Adrian, on the left. This was the first picture in which Hunt followed Pre-Raphaelite principles, painting the landscape direct from nature out-of-doors, 'abjuring altogether brown foliage, smoky clouds and dark corners...'

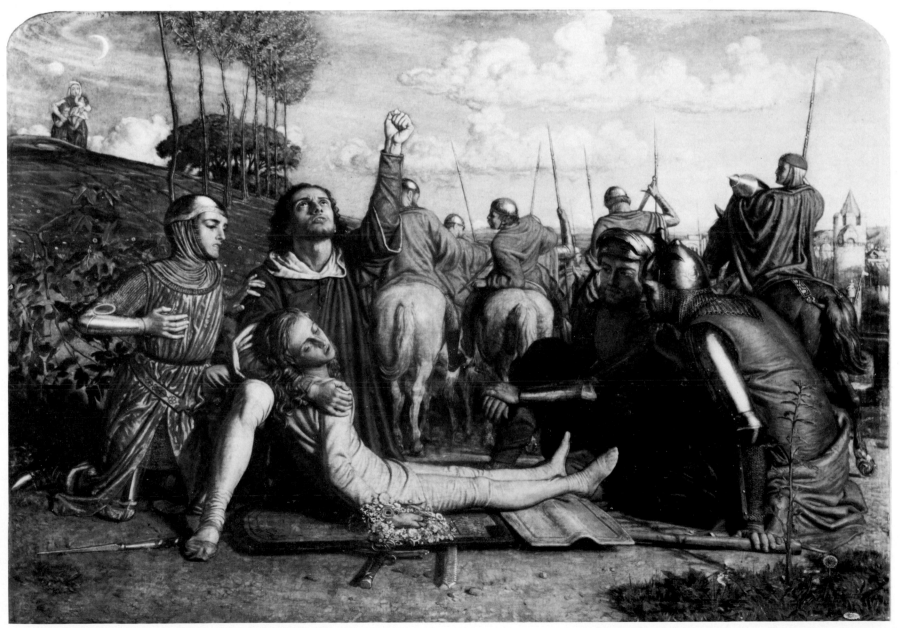

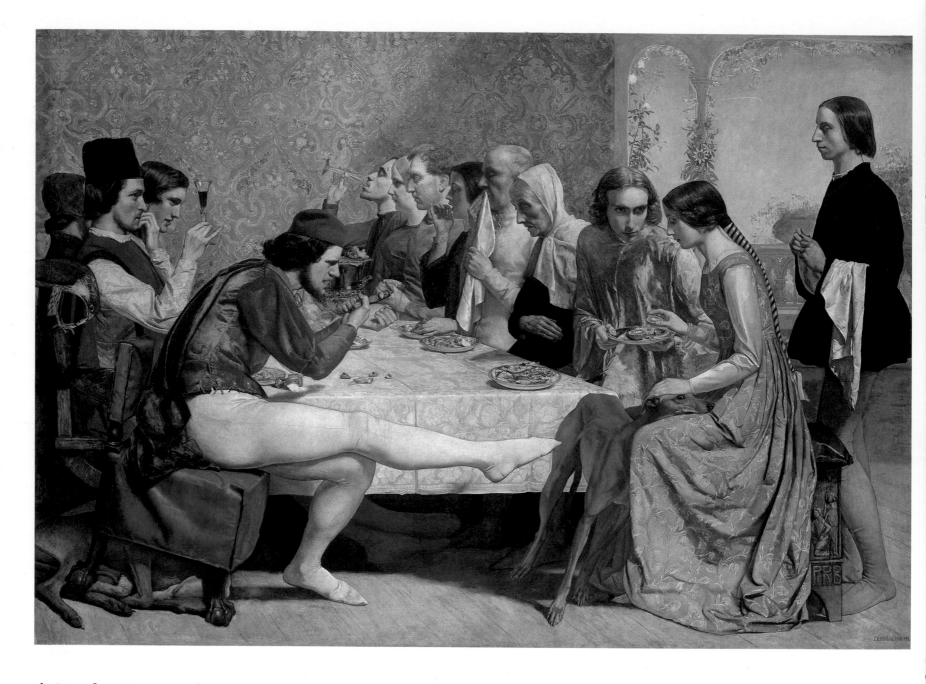

choice of names was almost as eccentric as the choice of members for the Brotherhood. Christ was at the head of the list; among the lower orders of immortals were Homer, King Alfred, Hogarth and Browning. By the summer of 1849 the first public manifestations of the Brotherhood took place. Rossetti was the first to exhibit. His first oil painting, *The Girlhood of Mary Virgin* (p. 8), was sent to the Free Exhibition about a month before the Academy opening. It owes a heavy debt to Madox Brown, and is plainly Nazarene in both style and subject-matter. It is, in fact, one of the few Pre-Raphaelite paintings which actually does attempt to revive the tradition of early Italian religious painting. It was favourably received by the critics.

A month later the first Pre-Raphaelite pictures appeared at the Academy. They were Millais' *Isabella* (above) and *Ferdinand Lured by Ariel*, and an Italian narrative subject by Collinson, *Italian Image-Makers at a Roadside Alehouse*. All three pictures were signed with the mysterious initials PRB, which seems to have passed completely unnoticed. The critics praised Millais' and Hunt's pictures as admirable attempts in the early Italian style, although the *Athenaeum* critic disliked the figure of the man kicking the dog in *Isabella*, which he described as 'absurd mannerism'. This strange image, together with the daring perspective and the awkward composition, were probably deliberate attempts to flout the conventions of academic correctness, and also, as Madox Brown later wrote, 'to touch the Philistine on the raw'. In England, it certainly takes courage to paint a picture of a man kicking a dog. Nonetheless the *Art Journal* praised the picture's 'feeling of the early Florentine school', and asserted that

14

Sir John Everett Millais (1829–1896)
Isabella

Signed and dated 1849/PRB
Canvas 103 × 143 cm/40½ × 56¼ ins
Walker Art Gallery, Liverpool

Millais' first Pre-Raphaelite picture, begun in 1848, and exhibited at the Royal Academy in 1849, where it hung next to Hunt's *Rienzi*. The picture is based on a passage from Keats' poem *Isabella or The Pot of Basil*:

Fair Isabel, poor simple Isabel!
　Lorenzo, a young palmer in Love's eye!
They could not in the self-same mansion dwell
　Without some stir of heart, some malady;
They could not sit at meals but feel how well
　It soothèd each to be the other by.

Isabella is shown at table with Lorenzo and his family; his brothers, seated on the left, show their malevolence towards Isabella, one by mockingly raising his glass, the other by kicking her dog. Millais used many of his artist friends and relations as models for the picture.

Walter Howell Deverell (1827–1854)
Twelfth Night, Act II, Scene IV

1850
Canvas 102 × 133 cm/40¼ × 52½ ins
Forbes Magazine Collection

Deverell was a close friend of the Brotherhood, though never a member. He shared their enthusiasm for Shakespearian subjects and has here depicted himself as Orsino in the centre, with Elizabeth Siddal as Viola on the left, and Rossetti as the jester. Both the architecture and the perspective are disjointed and there is a curious Arab band playing in the background; however, the picture is an important document in the Pre-Raphaelite story. Deverell died tragically young, and is now chiefly remembered for this picture, and also for having first discovered Elizabeth Siddal, working as a shop-girl near Leicester Square.

it 'cannot fail to establish the fame of the young painter'. The *Art Journal* also had high praise for Hunt's *Rienzi*, asserting that Hunt must be 'a man of genius . . . he is of a surety destined to occupy a foremost place in Art'. Collinson's picture was ignored but all three pictures were sold, and Millais felt confident enough to write to Rossetti that 'the success of the PRB is now *quite certain*'.

This confidence was to be rudely shattered in the following year, 1850. The main reason for this was that the secret of the initials PRB leaked out, probably because of gossip between artists and critics. The art establishment reacted angrily to what it regarded as a presumptuous and provocative secret society, formed by rebellious young art students. Another reason was the publication of *The Germ*, the shortlived magazine of the Brotherhood, of which four issues were published at the beginning of 1850. Brief though its existence was, *The Germ* occupies an important place in the history of the movement. It was a literary and artistic magazine, intended as a mouthpiece for the group's ideas, and Rossetti was the guiding spirit. His early poems were published in it, and all the other members of the Brotherhood, except Millais, contributed poems, articles and etchings to it. Various outsiders were invited to contribute, notably Coventry Patmore, then virtually unknown, Christina Rossetti, Ford Madox Brown, Walter Howell Deverell and William Bell Scott. The magazine was a total failure, and sold very few copies, in spite of being ignominiously

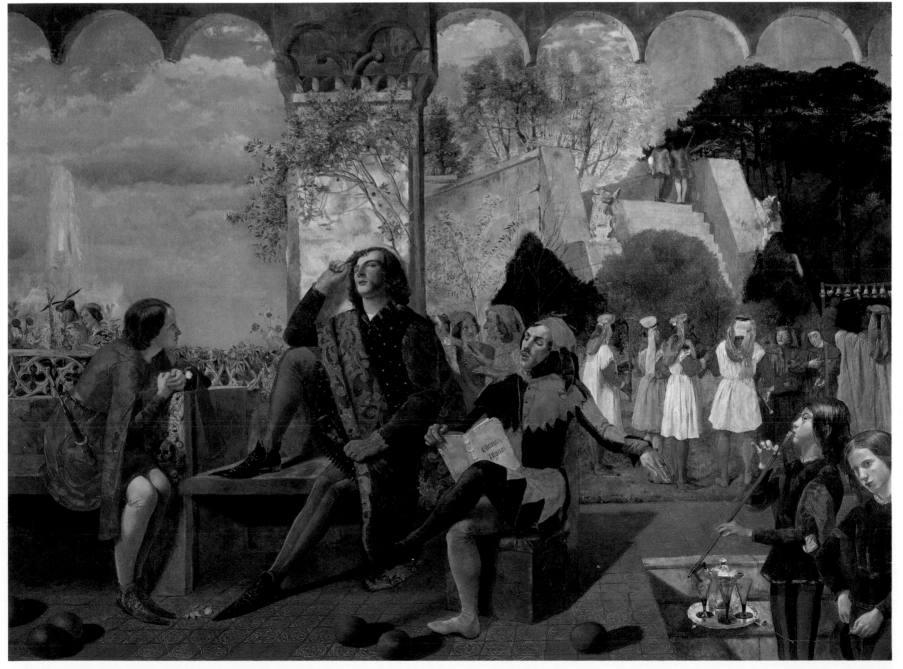

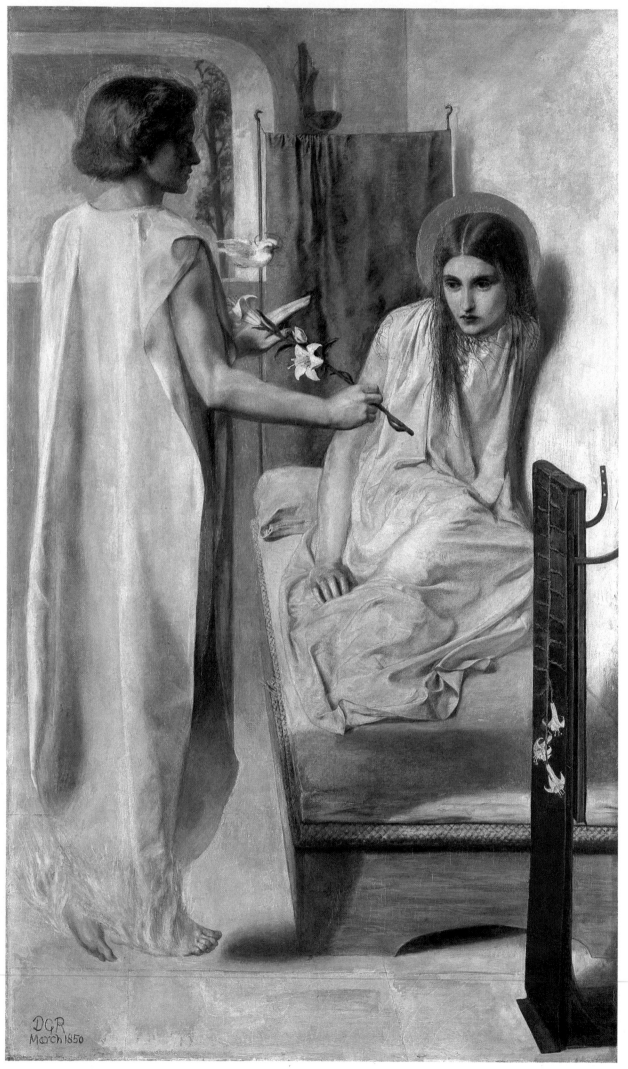

Dante Gabriel Rossetti
Ecce Ancilla Domini

Signed and dated March 1850
Canvas mounted on panel 73 × 42 cm/
$28\frac{5}{8} \times 16\frac{1}{2}$ ins
Tate Gallery, London

Rossetti's second Pre-Raphaelite
picture, exhibited at the Portland
Gallery, where it was bitterly attacked
by the critics. As a result, Rossetti
refused to exhibit again in London. The
model for the Virgin was once again
Rossetti's sister Christina. The crimson
cloth which she had been embroidering
in *The Girlhood of Mary Virgin* now
stands completed in the foreground.
The picture remained unsold, and
Rossetti continued to work on it until
1853 when he wrote, 'this blessed
afternoon this blessed white eye-sore
will be finished'. Eventually it was sold
to a Mr McCracken of Belfast, one of the
first patrons of the Pre-Raphaelites,
described by Rossetti as 'an Irish
maniac'.

Dante Gabriel Rossetti, study for *Ecce
Ancilla Domini*, 1850.

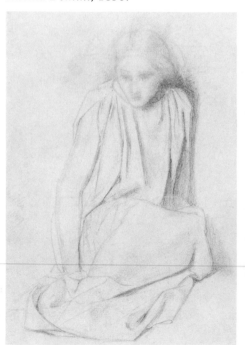

Sir John Everett Millais
Christy in the House of His Parents

Signed and dated 1850
Canvas 86 × 140 cm/34 × 55 ins
Tate Gallery, London

Exhibited at the Royal Academy in 1850 with a quotation from Zachariah xiii, verse 6:

And one shall say unto him, What are these
Wounds in thy hands? Then he shall answer
Those with which I was wounded in the house of my
friends.

This was the picture most violently attacked by the critics, especially Charles Dickens, who delivered a famous diatribe in *Household Words*, describing it as 'mean, repulsive and revolting'. What seemed to anger the critics was that Millais dared to depict the Holy Family as ordinary people, with complete honesty and realism. As a result the picture was derisively referred to as *The Carpenter's Shop*, the title by which it is now generally known.

hawked outside the Royal Academy. It was intended to act as propaganda for the movement, and in that it certainly succeeded. By the spring of 1850, quite a large section of the art world knew about the PRB and *The Germ*, with disastrous results.

The reaction of the critics was to turn on the Brotherhood with venom. Rossetti and Deverell exhibited their pictures, *Ecce Ancilla Domini* (p. 16) and *Twelfth Night* (p. 15), at the Free Exhibition in April, where they met with a hostile reception. Meanwhile the *Illustrated London News* published a gossipy piece about the PRB, describing them sarcastically as 'practitioners of "Early Christian Art" ... who – setting aside the medieval schools of Italy, the Raffaeles, Guidos and Titians, and all such small-beer daubers – devote their energies to the reproduction of saints squeezed out perfectly flat.' Worse was to come at the Royal Academy, where there were contributions from Millais, Hunt, Collinson and another convert to the cause, Charles Allston Collins, brother of the writer Wilkie Collins. Millais' *Christ in the House of His Parents* (below) – also known as *The Carpenter's Shop* – bore the brunt of the attacks. *The Times* thundered: 'Mr. Millais' principal picture is, to speak plainly, revolting. The attempt to associate the Holy Family with the meanest details of a carpenter's shop, with no conceivable omission of misery, of dirt, of even disease, all finished with the same loathsome minuteness, is disgusting.' Even more devastating was the celebrated diatribe by Charles Dickens in *Household Words*. He dismissed the work of the Pre-Raphaelites as 'mean, repulsive and revolting', and went on to single out Millais' *The Carpenter's Shop*. The figure of the young Christ he described as 'a hideous, wry-necked, blubbering, red-headed boy, in a bed gown ...' and his mother as a 'woman so hideous in her ugliness that ... she would stand out from the rest of the company as a Monster, in the vilest cabaret in France, or the lowest gin shop in England.' None of the other Pre-Raphaelites fared much better – Hunt's *A*

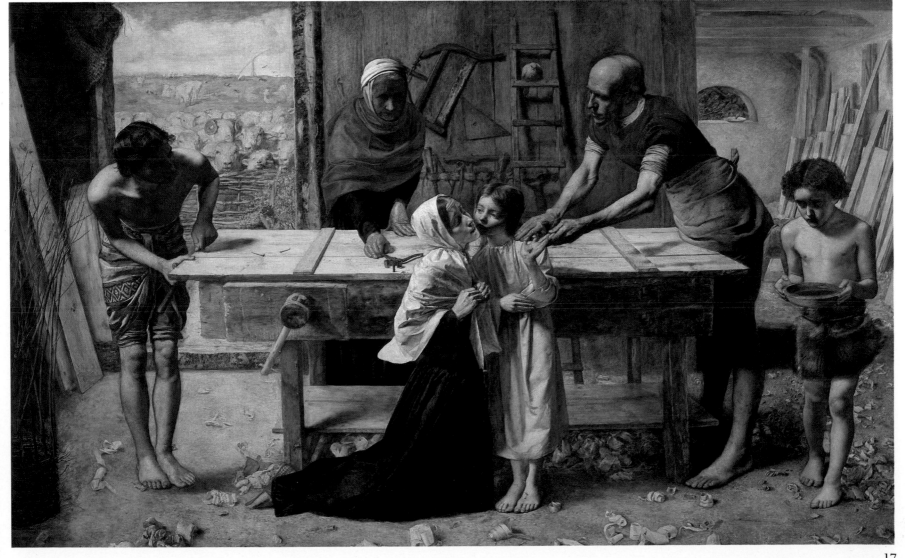

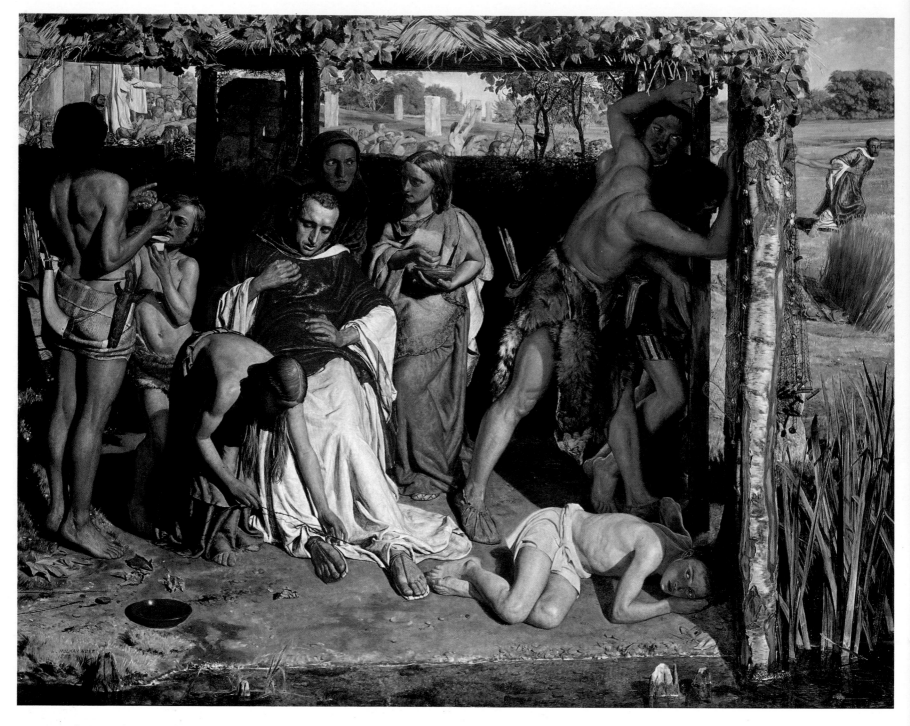

Converted British Family Sheltering a Christian Priest (above), and Collinson's *Answering the Emigrant's Letter* were both attacked. 'Abruptness, singularity, uncouthness are the counters which they play for fame', said the *Athenaeum*. Looking at the pictures now, it is difficult to see why the critics were goaded into such fury. It was partly because they resented the impertinent pretentions of the PRB in forming themselves into a secret society. Also, they suspected the Brotherhood of Roman Catholic tendencies, a justifiable fear, as many of the pictures were religious, but an unfounded one.

These vicious attacks on the Brotherhood came as an unpleasant jolt, and neither Rossetti, Millais nor Hunt sold any of their pictures. Rossetti vowed never to exhibit in public again. Recriminations broke out, with Millais accusing Rossetti of leaking the secret of the PRB. Millais' parents also blamed Rossetti for bringing their brilliant son into disgrace. Hunt was plunged into financial trouble and was able to continue painting only through the kindness of two Academicians sympathetic to the Brotherhood, William Dyce and Augustus Leopold Egg. It was Egg who commissioned Hunt's next picture, *Claudio and Isabella* (p 19). Collinson's reaction was to resign from the Brotherhood. He had originally been invited only because of his engagement to Christina Rossetti, which was later broken off. It is difficult to find

William Holman Hunt (1827–1910)
A Converted British Family Sheltering a Christian Priest from the Persecution of the Druids

Signed and dated 1850
Canvas 111 × 133 cm/$43\frac{3}{4}$ × $52\frac{1}{2}$ ins
Ashmolean Museum, Oxford

The early Christian theme of this picture owes its origin to a Royal Academy Gold Medal competition on the subject of 'An Act of Mercy'. Several of Hunt's friends sat for the figures – William Michael Rossetti for the priest and Elizabeth Siddal for the girl beside him. The landscape and hut were painted on the Lea Marshes, Essex. Hunt wrote later that the vine and corn had been introduced to suggest 'the civilizing influence of the divine religion', and the net over the door to suggest Christianity, and because the Druids held fish as sacred. The picture hung at the Royal Academy next to Millais' *Christ in the House of His Parents*, to which it has obvious affinities.

William Holman Hunt
Claudio and Isabella

Signed and dated 1850
Oil on panel 76 × 43 cm/29⅞ × 16¾ ins
Tate Gallery, London

An illustration to Shakespeare's play
Measure for Measure, Act III, Scene I.
Isabella visits her brother Claudio in prison
and he pleads with her to sacrifice her
honour to save his life. The choice of such a
scene is typical of Hunt's preoccupation
with sin and guilt and his intensely
moralistic approach to art. The prison was
painted in the Lollard's prison at Lambeth
Palace. Although this is one of Hunt's early
Pre-Raphaelite works, dated 1850, it was
not completed and exhibited at the Royal
Academy until 1853.

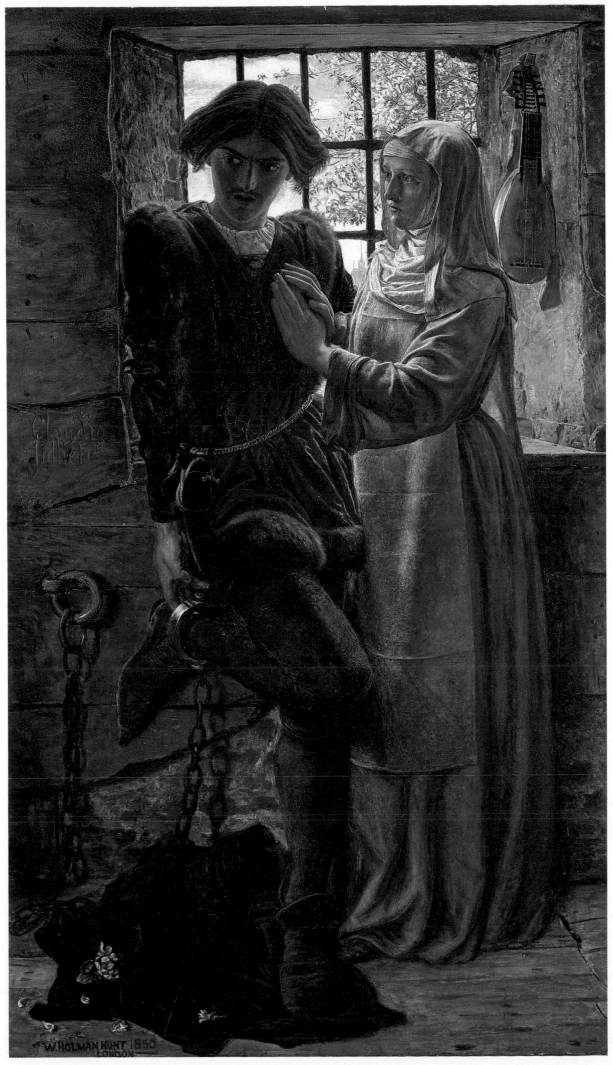

a trace of Pre-Raphaelite influence in his pictures, which are mostly pleasant narrative and cottage scenes, with the sole exception of *The Renunciation of Queen Elizabeth of Hungary* (below). His main contribution to Pre-Raphaelite meetings seems to have been his habit of falling asleep. A melancholy and religious individual, he was converted to Roman Catholicism, and retired to a monastery.

In spite of the bitter personal attacks made on them by the critics, Millais and Hunt refused to be diverted from their chosen path. Rossetti went his own, very individual way, and his art was to be of greater relevance to the later phase of the movement. The leadership of the Brotherhood passed to Hunt and Millais, particularly the latter, the most brilliantly accomplished of the group, and the painter of its most memorable masterpieces. Although the individual styles of Rossetti, Hunt and Millais are very different, their drawings of this period show a remarkable unanimity of style. Executed in pen and ink, they have a spiky, angular intensity, which epitomizes this first, 'gothic' phase of the movement.

Even at this difficult phase, the darkest hour of the PRB, the movement was not without its supporters. Deverell and Collins were converts to the cause, and another important follower was to be Arthur Hughes, who was converted by reading *The Germ*. The Pre-Raphaelites also found a staunch patron in Thomas Combe, the superintendent of the Oxford University Press. Millais and Collins stayed and painted at his house in Oxford during 1850, and the first of his many purchases of Pre-Raphaelite pictures was Hunt's *Druids*, which he bought for £160. Combe was a typical, independent-minded, middle-class Victorian patron, the type that was later to buy most of the Pre-Raphaelites' work.

James Collinson (1825–1881)
The Renunciation of Queen Elizabeth of Hungary

*c*1848–50
Canvas, arched top 120 × 182 cm/47$\frac{3}{8}$ × 71$\frac{1}{2}$ ins
Johannesburg Art Gallery

Queen Elizabeth of Hungary was married to King Louis IV of Thuringia in 1221. After his death in a crusade she was deposed as regent on the grounds that she had wasted the national revenues on charity. She therefore renounced her throne and her rank, and retired to the convent of Kitzingen, where she died. Later she was canonized, and Charles Kingsley told her story in *The Saint's Tragedy* (1848), where Collinson would most probably have read it. Although set in the thirteenth century, Collinson has depicted the scene in an obviously nineteenth-century gothic revival church, with encaustic tiling on the floor.

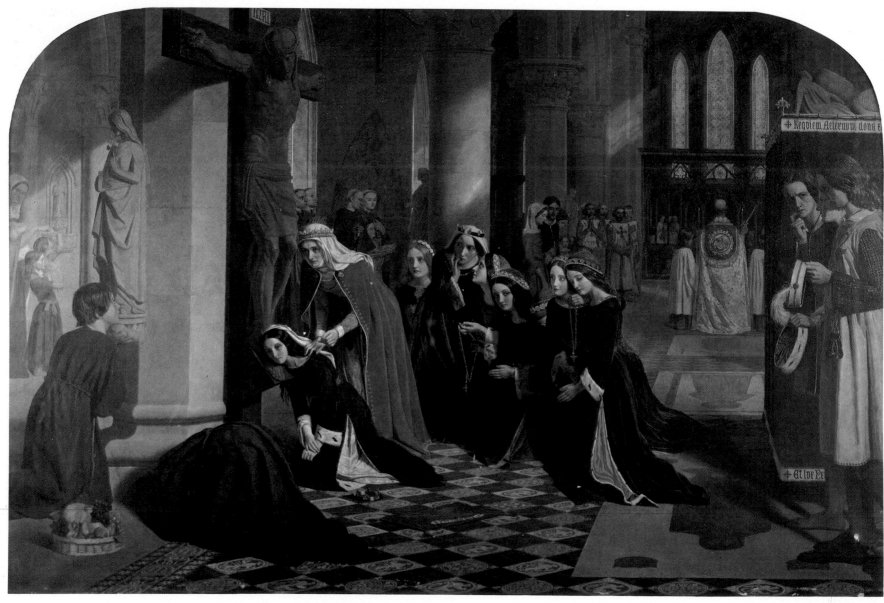

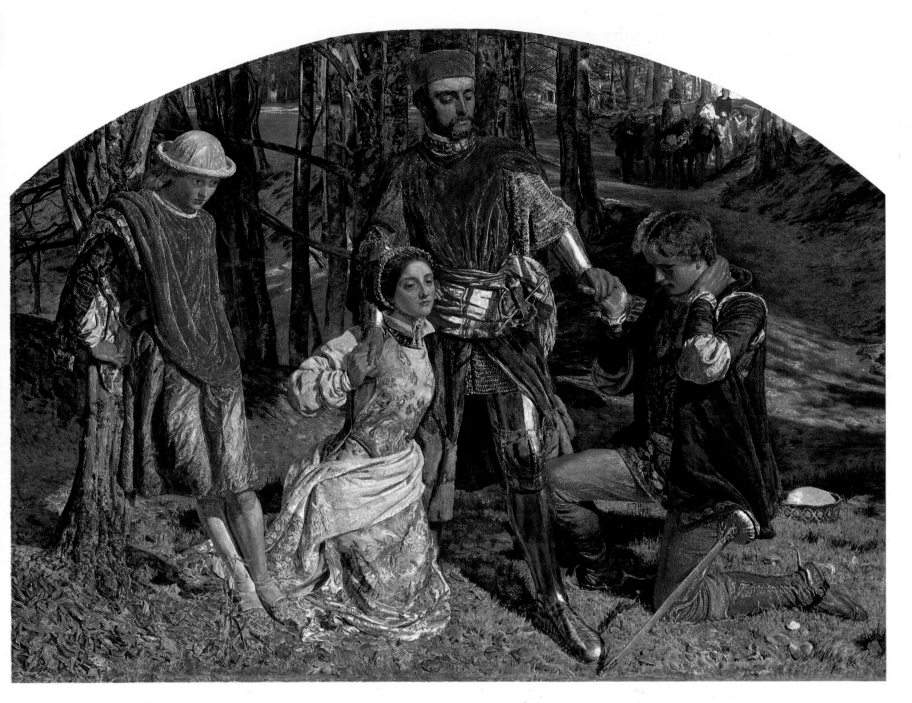

William Holman Hunt
Valentine Rescuing Sylvia from Proteus

Signed and dated 1851, Kent
Canvas 98 × 133 cm/38⅜ × 52½ ins
Birmingham City Museum and Art Gallery

An illustration to Shakespeare's *Two Gentlemen of Verona*, Act V, Scene IV. As with *Claudio and Isabella*, Hunt has chosen a highly equivocal moment, when Valentine arrives at the end of the play to find his friend Proteus attempting to seduce Sylvia, with whom he, Valentine, is in love. Valentine is speaking the lines 'Ruffian, let go that rude, uncivil touch; Thou friend of an ill fashion!' The woods were painted at Knole in Kent, and various friends sat for the figures, including Elizabeth Siddal for Sylvia. The picture was badly hung at the Royal Academy Exhibition in 1851, and was violently attacked, as were all Millais' pictures, Charles Allston Collins's *Convent Thoughts*, and Ford Madox Brown's *Chaucer*.

At the Royal Academy exhibition of 1851, the Pre-Raphaelites were back in force. Millais was the most impressively represented, with three outstanding works, *Mariana* (p. 31), *The Woodman's Daughter* (p. 32) and *The Return of the Dove to the Ark*. Hunt contributed *Valentine Rescuing Sylvia* (above), Madox Brown sent the enormous *Chaucer* (p. 47), and Collins *Convent Thoughts* (p. 23). Once again the press attacked. The abusive, jeering and sarcastic tone of the reviews may sound almost incredible to the modern reader, but it serves to remind us just how vitriolic nineteenth-century criticism could be. *The Times* led the way: 'We cannot censure at present as amply or as strongly as we desire to do, that strange disorder of the mind or the eyes, which continues to rage with unabated absurdity among a class of juvenile artists who style themselves PRB.' This time Hunt and Millais had used the Pre-Raphaelite technique consistently, painting *Valentine Rescuing Sylvia* and *The Woodman's Daughter* entirely in pure colours over a wet white ground. This too was picked on by the reviewer, who condemned their 'absolute contempt for perspective and the known laws of light and shade, and aversion to beauty in every shape, and a singular devotion to the minute accidents of their subjects.'

But help was at hand. Through the influence of the poet Coventry Patmore, John Ruskin was persuaded to come to the aid of the beleaguered Brotherhood. Although only 32 years old, Ruskin was already England's leading art critic, and his intervention was to be of crucial importance in turning the tide for the Pre-

Raphaelites. He wrote two celebrated letters to *The Times*, which he later published in a pamphlet and developed in lectures. He made it clear from the start that he had 'no acquaintance with any of these artists . . . and only very imperfect sympathy with them.' He was also suspicious of their 'Romanist and Tractarian tendencies', but remonstrated with the critics for failing to appreciate 'the finish of drawing and splendour of colour' of these 'admirable though strange pictures'. He also praised their attention to natural detail, particularly the water-lilies in Collins' *Convent Thoughts*, and in the second letter hoped that the Pre-Raphaelites 'may, as they gain experience, lay in our England the foundation of a school of art nobler than the world has seen for three hundred years'. Words like these from England's most influential critic were just what the Brotherhood needed, and Ruskin's letters mark a turning-point in their fortunes. A letter of thanks was written from Millais' house in Gower Street, and on the same day Ruskin and his attractive wife Euphemia (known as Effie) called round to meet Millais. For Ruskin and Millais, it was the beginning of a fruitful, but ultimately tragic friendship.

At first Ruskin was delighted with his new protégé. He saw in Millais the successor to his boyhood idol, Turner, and it is to Ruskin that the credit must go for recognizing and encouraging Millais' genius. Although he was not an easy pupil, Millais was encouraged by Ruskin's support to continue painting in the Pre-Raphaelite style. But however much Ruskin tried to take Millais under his wing, he remained stubbornly independent. He refused to bow to Ruskin's worship of Turner; he also refused to go to Switzerland with him. Instead he stayed in Surrey with Hunt and Collins, working on his pictures for the Academy of 1852. Here the Pre-Raphaelites were again well-represented, Millais by *Ophelia* (p. 33), and Hunt by *The Hireling Shepherd* (p. 41). Ford Madox Brown sent two important works, *Pretty Baa-Lambs* (p. 50) and *Christ Washing Peter's Feet* (p. 48). This time the critics were more polite. The tide was now running in the Pre-Raphaelites' favour. In the autumn of 1851, Hunt's *Valentine Rescuing Sylvia* was awarded the first prize at the annual Liverpool Exhibition. This was the first time a Pre-Raphaelite picture had won any kind of award. Liverpool was to provide them with many of their most important patrons, and also with a whole school of disciples and followers.

Paradoxically, this worldly success coincided with the gradual break-up of the Brotherhood. Collinson had resigned in 1850. No one was elected to fill his place. Deverell and Arthur Hughes were proposed, but the matter lapsed, out of sheer apathy. William Michael Rossetti's journal of the Brotherhood ceased in May 1851. Meetings became less and less frequent. In 1852 Woolner left for Australia. Rossetti, meanwhile, had been going his own way, producing his own personal brand of Pre-Raphaelitism. All attempts to interest him in landscape painting, religious or modern-life subjects failed. He turned instead to literature – Shakespeare, and above all his beloved Dante. Around 1851 he began to produce the small, intense, watercolours on medieval and literary themes that were to be his most valuable contribution to the Pre-Raphaelite movement, and which are still regarded by many as his finest works. Also in 1851 he began his tragic love affair with Elizabeth Siddal, already the heroine of many Pre-Raphaelite pictures. This affair was to end in their marriage, and her suicide, with momentous consequences for Rossetti's career. In the summer of 1853 Ruskin invited Millais to join him and his wife on a trip to Scotland. This ill-fated holiday, at Glenfinlas, was to result in Millais' celebrated portrait of Ruskin (p. 35), but also led to the break-up of the Ruskins' marriage, a scandalous divorce, and Effie's eventual marriage to Millais, after two exceptionally harrowing years for all three of them. Late in 1853, Millais was elected an Associate of the Royal Academy, and in January 1854 Hunt announced his plans to visit the Middle East. These two events effectively marked the end of the Brotherhood, and Rossetti summed up the feelings of all of them when he wrote 'so now the whole Round Table is dissolved'. The Pre-Raphaelite Brotherhood was at an end. But Pre-Raphaelitism was only just beginning.

Charles Allston Collins (1828–1873)
Convent Thoughts

Signed and dated 1851
Canvas, arched top 84 × 59 cm/33⅛ × 23¼ ins
Ashmolean Museum, Oxford

Charles Allston Collins, brother of the novelist Wilkie Collins, was a close friend of Millais during the early Pre-Raphaelite period, although he later gave up painting. *Convent Thoughts*, his most famous work, was exhibited at the Royal Academy in 1851, where it shared in the general denunciation by the critics of all things Pre-Raphaelite. Collins's picture is typical of the early, gothic phase of the movement, and the religious piety of these works led many critics to accuse the painters of being Roman Catholic sympathizers. The mood of this picture is certainly similar to Rossetti's early paintings, but the flowers and the garden reflect Millais' influence.

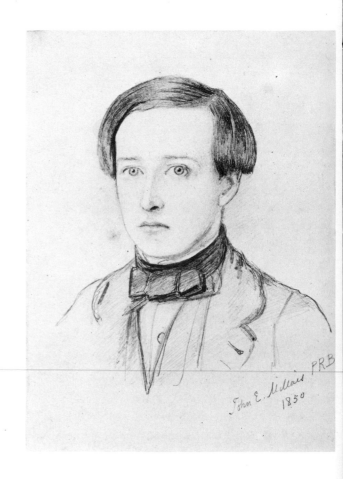

Sir John Everett Millais, portrait of Charles Allston Collins, 1850.

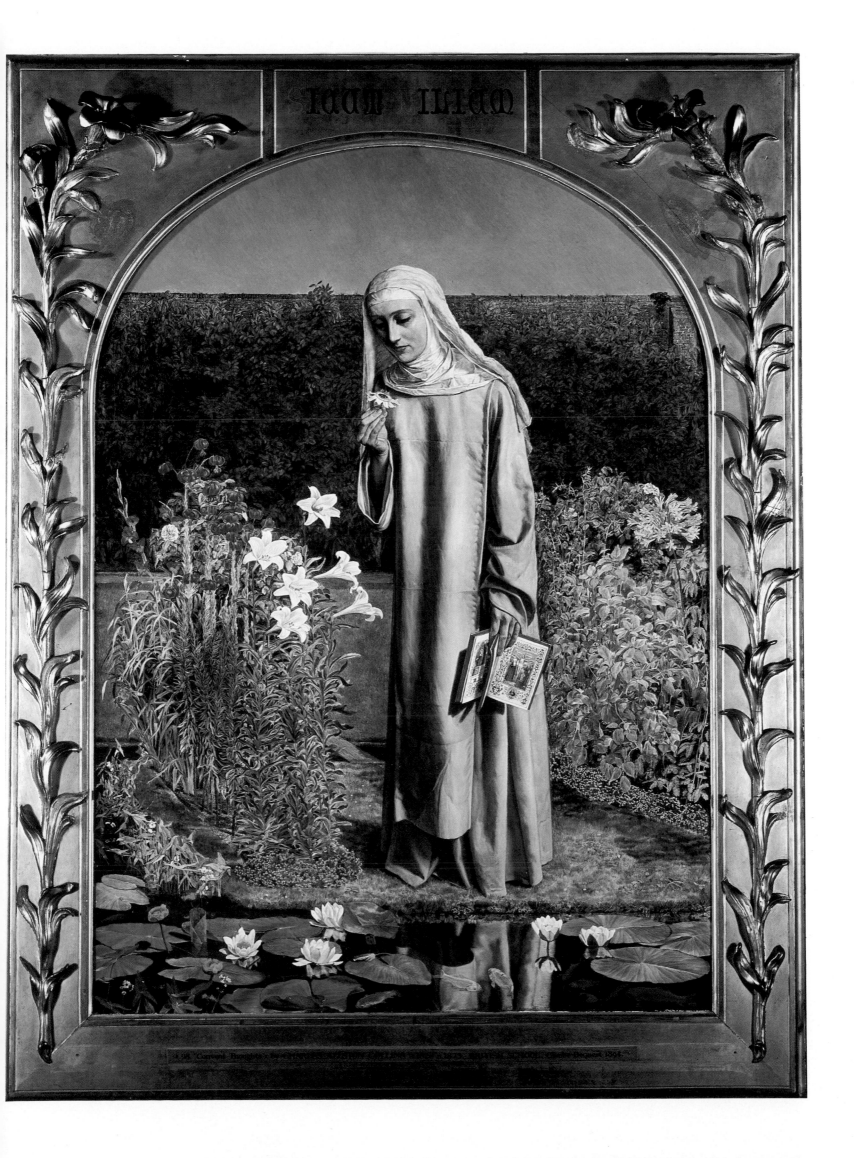

23

Dante Gabriel Rossetti 1828–1882

In any account of the Pre-Raphaelite movement, it is Rossetti who must come first. He was the intellectual force behind the Brotherhood, and by far its most intelligent member. Though he lacked the technical brilliance of Millais, or the patient determination of Hunt, he amply made up for it by the force of his personality, his imaginative and creative ability, and the breadth of his literary knowledge. Rossetti's unconventional character and tragic life fascinated his contemporaries, and have continued to attract the attention of writers and historians ever since. There are more books about Rossetti than about any other Pre-Raphaelite artist. He has even been regarded by some writers as the greatest painter-poet England has ever produced.

Rossetti was born in London, of Italian parentage. His father, Gabriel Rossetti, was a political exile, and Professor of Italian at King's College. All his children – Maria, Dante Gabriel, William Michael and Christina – had artistic or literary ability. Dante Gabriel left school at 13, and entered Sass's Academy, an art school which prepared students for the Academy Schools. After four years, he entered the Royal Academy in 1845 as a probationary student. From the start, Rossetti, was torn between painting and literature. He was lazy, mercurial and impetuous, and found the Academy teaching dull and wearisome. He had very little natural facility as a draughtsman. However, his knowledge of English and European literature was prodigious, and he particularly loved the poetry of his namesake, Dante. He was also one of the earliest admirers of William Blake, and succeeded in buying one of Blake's sketchbooks with ten shillings borrowed from his brother. In 1847, Rossetti wrote admiring letters to two poets, Leigh Hunt and William Bell Scott, asking whether he should be a painter or a poet. Fortunately for posterity, he decided to be both.

Tiring of the Academy teaching methods, Rossetti stopped attending, and wrote to Ford Madox Brown asking if he might be taken on as a pupil. The letter was full of extravagant praise, and the distrustful Madox Brown suspected a hoax. He stormed round to Rossetti's house carrying a cudgel, and was astonished to find that his letter was entirely genuine. Flattered, he agreed to take Rossetti as a pupil. It was the beginning of a friendship that was to last until Rossetti's death. But the master-pupil relationship was short-lived. Brown set Rossetti to paint still-life subjects – jugs and bottles in the studio – and he quickly lost patience. He hankered to tackle more ambitious subjects. Later in the same year, 1848, he visited the Royal Academy Summer Exhibition, where he saw and greatly admired a picture by a fellow-student at the Academy, Holman Hunt's *The Eve of Saint Agnes*. He congratulated Hunt personally, and the two became friends. It was to be an historic friendship. Out of their discussions and exchange of ideas the Pre-Raphaelite Brotherhood was born.

Far left: **Dante Gabriel Rossetti**, self-portrait, 1847.
Left: *Elizabeth Siddal plaiting her hair*, undated.

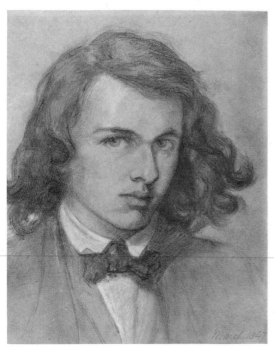
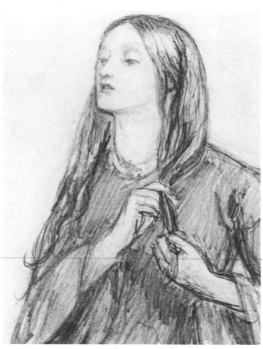

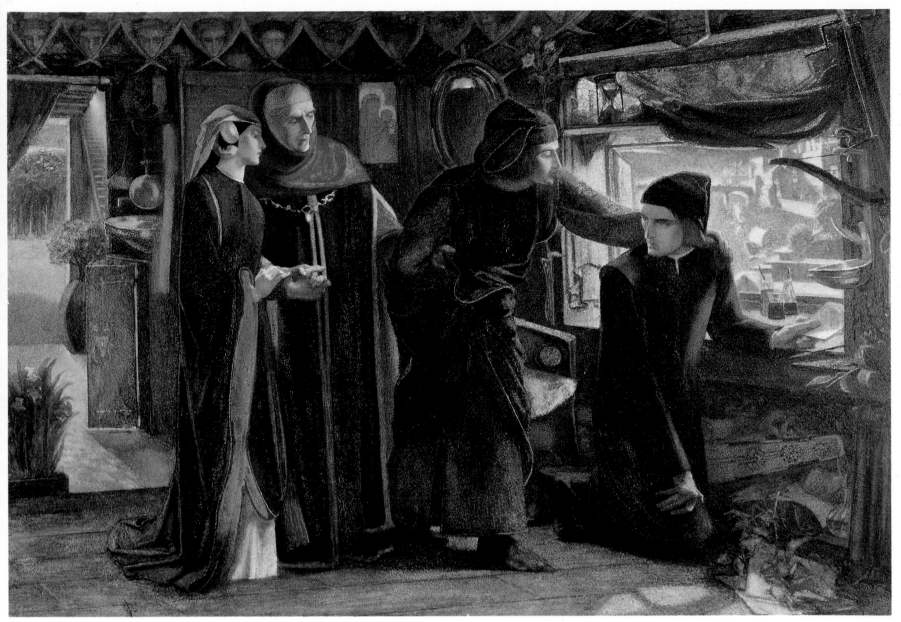

Dante Gabriel Rossetti
The First Anniversary of the Death of Beatrice (Dante drawing an Angel)

Signed and dated 1853
Watercolour 42 × 61 cm/16½ × 24 ins
Ashmolean Museum, Oxford

Dante was Rossetti's favourite poet, and in 1848 he completed his translation of the *Vita Nuova*. This gave him many ideas for pictures, such as *Dante's Dream*, which were to preoccupy him to the end of his life. Another was *Dante drawing an Angel on the Anniversary of the Death of Beatrice*, for which he had already made a pen and ink drawing in 1848. In this more highly finished watercolour, the composition has been reversed, with Dante on the right instead of the left. It depicts a moment during Dante's writing of his autobiography when he is so preoccupied with his thoughts of Beatrice, and with drawing an angel, that he fails to notice the arrival of some friends, who stand watching him.

Rossetti decided to leave Madox Brown, and move into Hunt's studio instead. With the £70 Hunt had received for *The Eve of Saint Agnes*, they moved into a studio in Cleveland Street. Frederick George Stephens later recalled that 'Nothing could be more depressing than the large gaunt chamber where Rossetti executed two memorable paintings, and from which posterity must perforce date the inception of Pre-Raphaelitism . . .' The two pictures were *The Girlhood of Mary Virgin* (p. 8) and *Ecce Ancilla Domini* (p. 16), which were Rossetti's contribution to the opening phase of the movement. Hunt gave him much help and technical advice with both pictures, as Rossetti was still not technically proficient in oils. But it was Rossetti's personality, as much as anything, that brought the Brotherhood into being. Millais was later to quarrel with Rossetti, finding him impossible to deal with, but in the early days he exercized a mesmerizing influence over his colleagues. He was witty and irreverent, bursting with ideas and enthusiasm. Early portraits show him to have been strikingly good-looking, with his dark, Italian looks, long hair and dreamily poetic manner. His character was a strange mixture, reflecting his Anglo-Italian origins. The latin side of his character was moody, temperamental and restless; but he also had a streak of down-to-earth cockney humour, delighting in coarse jokes, nonsense and horseplay. There was an atmosphere of boyish high jinks about the early days of the Pre-Raphaelites. Although half Italian, Rossetti never visited Italy, and shared with Hunt and Millais a pride in all things English. Rossetti, more than any of them, enjoyed the seamier side of Bohemian life in London. He was not religious, nor did he suffer from the moral inhibitions that so plagued most of his contemporaries. He was a most un-Victorian Victorian.

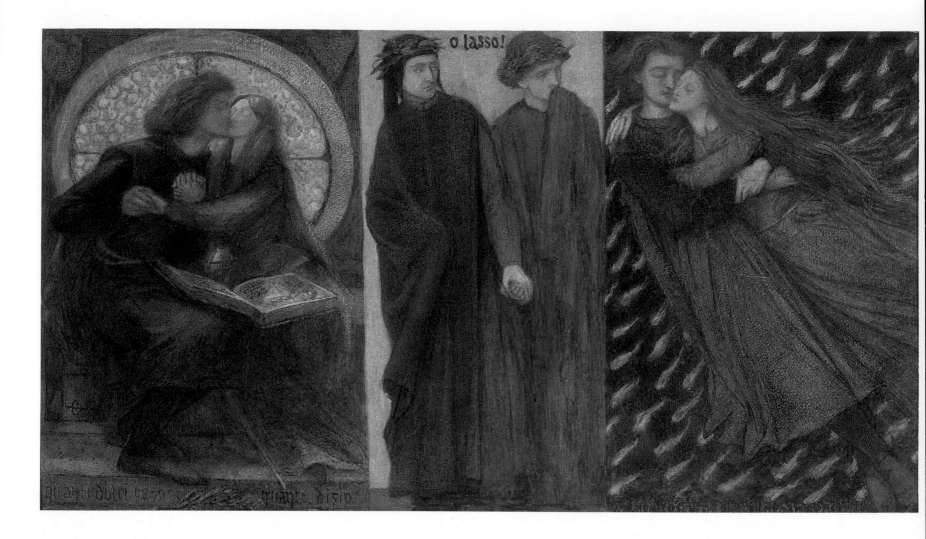

After completing his first two pictures, Rossetti and Hunt went on holiday together, visiting Belgium and Paris. They both greatly admired the early Flemish painters, particularly Van Eyck and Memling, and this was to have some influence in shaping Rossetti's style. On their return, Rossetti and Hunt tried painting landscapes near Sevenoaks in Kent. The weather was appalling and Rossetti quickly gave up. Landscape simply was not his *métier*. He read through the New Testament seeking inspiration for more religious subjects, but could not find one that interested him. He started a modern-life subject, *Found*, but this too proved difficult. He continued to wrestle with it for the next thirty years, and it was still unfinished at his death. Finding, therefore, that he could not compete with his colleagues in the Brotherhood on their own ground, Rossetti began to explore new subjects of his own. Working mainly in watercolour, on a small scale, he began to paint literary and historical subjects, usually set in the medieval period. *The First Anniversary of the Death of Beatrice* (p. 25) was the first of many subjects he was to choose from the poetry of Dante. He also painted scenes from Shakespeare, Keats and Browning – three of his favourite poets. These extraordinary watercolours are among the most remarkable products of the Pre-Raphaelite movement. Small, highly-coloured and two-dimensional, they glow with jewel-like colours, and project an intensely romantic vision of the Middle Ages. What they may lack in technical finish, they make up for in intensity of colour and feeling. For many people, these are the quintessential Pre-Raphaelite pictures, and certainly it was Rossetti's watercolours that so inspired Morris and Burne-Jones, thus influencing the whole direction of the second phase of the movement.

By 1853, therefore, Rossetti was moving in a different direction from his Brotherhood colleagues. There was another reason – his love affair with Elizabeth Siddal. She was the first of the Pre-Raphaelite 'stunners', the phrase they used for beautiful girls. Deverell discovered her working in a milliner's shop off the Strand, and persuaded her to pose as Viola in his *Twelfth Night* (p. 15). She quickly became

Dante Gabriel Rossetti
Paolo and Francesca da Rimini

1855
Watercolour 25 × 44 cm/9¾ × 17½ ins
Tate Gallery, London

An illustration to Dante's *Inferno*, Canto V. Paolo and Francesca are shown kissing in the left panel; Dante and Virgil, in the centre, watch the lovers compassionately as, in the third panel, they float in eternity through the flames of hell, locked in each other's arms. This watercolour was one of several commissioned by Ruskin, by then a friend and admirer of Rossetti. In the tragic story of Paolo and Francesca, Rossetti must have found a reflection of his own love affair with Elizabeth Siddal.

The Wedding of Saint George and the Princess Sabra

Signed with monogram and dated 1857
Watercolour 34 × 34 cm/13½ × 13½ ins
Tate Gallery, London

Medieval romance and medieval literature were the inspiration for many of Rossetti's finest pictures, especially the watercolours painted between 1855 and 1860, regarded by many as his greatest works. Here the Princess Sabra is cutting off a lock of her hair, to give as a favour to Saint George. In a letter, James Smetham described this watercolour as 'one of the grandest things, like a golden dim dream. Love "credulous all gold", gold armour, a sense of secret enclosure in "palace chambers far apart . . ."' It was painted by Rossetti for William Morris.

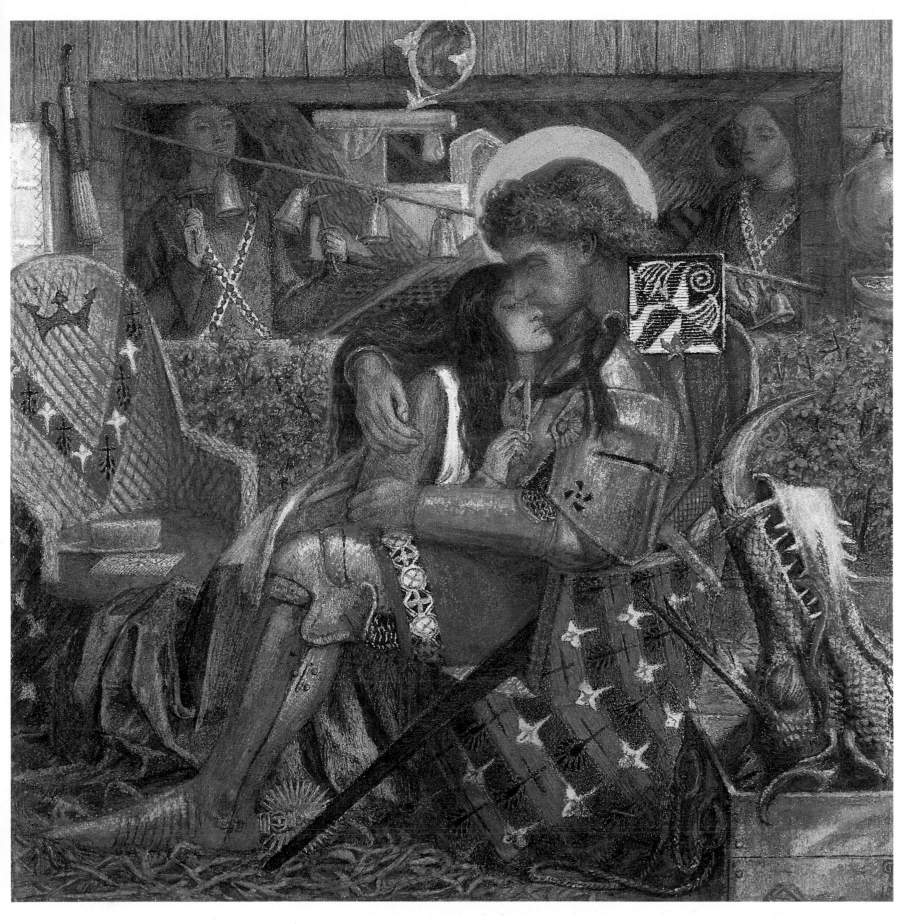

the favourite model of the Brotherhood posing for Hunt's *Valentine Rescuing Sylvia* (p. 21) and also for Millais' *Ophelia* (p. 33). She was a silent, reserved girl, the daughter of lower middle-class parents; she had a pale white skin, beautiful red hair, and a soulful expression. The Pre-Raphaelites were to immortalize her; she is the very image of the Pre-Raphaelite woman. During 1851, Rossetti fell more and more under her spell, and in 1852 they set up house together in Chatham Place, near the Thames at Blackfriars Bridge. As Rossetti's infatuation increased, he became possessive about Lizzie, or 'Guggums', as he called her. Only a few close artist friends were allowed to

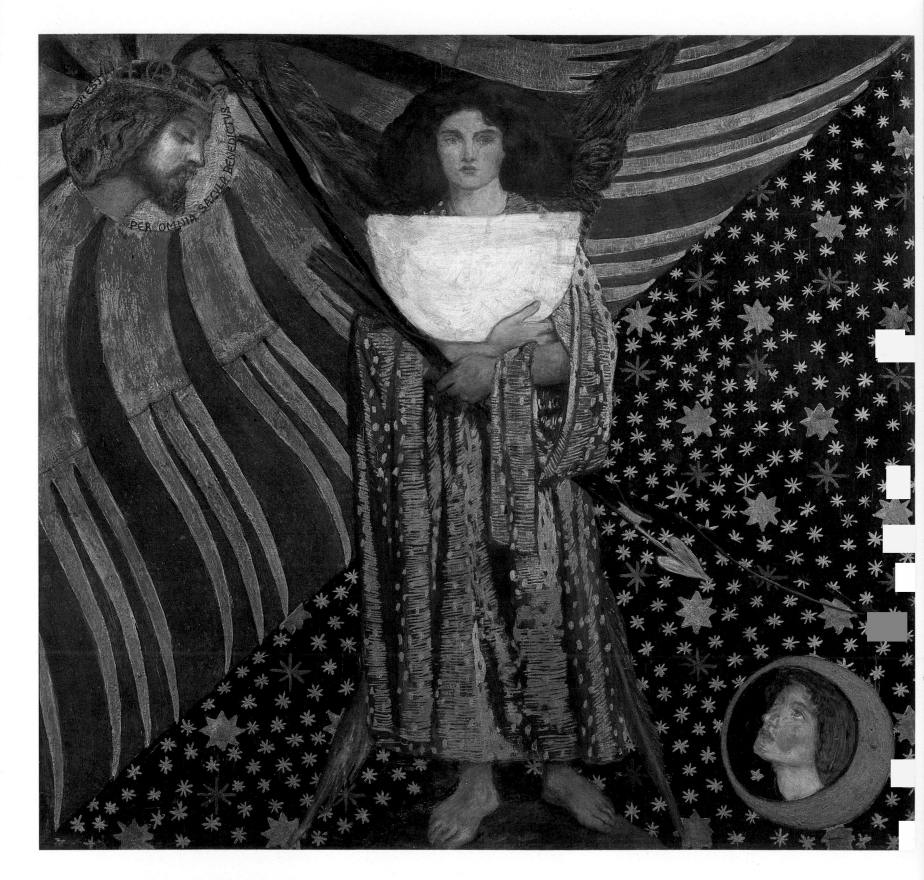

use her as a model, but Rossetti himself drew her constantly. Many of them are his finest drawings, and reflect the claustrophobic intensity of the private world in which he and Lizzie lived. Ford Madox Brown, one of the few visitors to Chatham Place, wrote in 1855 'Rossetti showed me a drawer full of ''Guggums''; God knows how many . . . it is like a monomania with him. Many of them are matchless in beauty . . . and one day will be worth large sums.' It was an accurate prophecy, as these drawings are now among Rossetti's most admired works. Ruskin, who became a close friend of Rossetti in the 1850s, also fell under Lizzie's spell; she was, he wrote, 'beautiful as the reflection of a golden mountain in a crystal lake'. He encouraged her to draw, and write verses, and she produced some creditable drawings and watercolours of medieval subjects in the Rossetti vein.

Dante Gabriel Rossetti

Dantis Amor

1859
Oil on panel 75 × 81 cm/29½ × 32 ins
Tate Gallery, London

Originally painted to decorate a cabinet at the Red House, home of the newly married William and Jane Morris. This was the central panel of a set of three, all illustrating Dante's *Vita Nuova* and the *Divine Comedy*. It depicts an angel as a figure of love, holding a bow and arrow and a sundial. The background represents the sky – on the left, the head of Christ surrounded by golden rays of sun; on the right, the head of Beatrice encircled by the moon, set against a background of golden stars.

How Sir Galahad, Sir Bors, and Sir Percival were fed with the Sanc Grael; but Sir Percival's Sister died by the Way

Signed with monogram and dated 1864
Watercolour 29 × 42 cm/11½ × 16½ ins
Tate Gallery, London

One of Rossetti's finest medieval watercolours. The design is based on one of the murals, *The Attainment of the Sanc Grael*, painted by Rossetti for the library of the Oxford Union in 1857.

In 1856 the first meetings took place between Rossetti and the two young Oxford students who were to become his disciples, Morris and Burne-Jones. This marks the beginning of the second phase of the Pre-Raphaelite movement, and is in its way almost more significant than the formation of the original Brotherhood. Certainly the consequences were to be equally far-reaching. The first tangible result was to be murals for the new library designed by Benjamin Woodward in the Oxford Union Debating Society. Although now virtually invisible, and heavily restored, these murals, like *The Germ*, fill an important niche in the Pre-Raphaelite story. The theme of the murals, chosen by Rossetti, was to be Malory's *Morte d'Arthur*, which had now replaced Dante as the group's favourite reading. Appropriately, the artists involved numbered seven, like the Brotherhood. They were Dante Gabriel Rossetti, Edward Burne-Jones, William Morris, John Hungerford Pollen, Arthur Hughes and two younger students, Valentine Cameron Prinsep and John Roddam Spencer-Stanhope. The whole episode was full of fun and games, and they all had a hilarious time. Different scenes from the *Morte d'Arthur* were chosen, and the intervening spaces filled in by leaves, flowers, and wombats, currently Rossetti's favourite animal. The murals can no longer be seen in their original condition, but Rosssetti produced a number of superb watercolours on Arthurian themes, some of which originated from the Oxford episode.

The murals completed, they all returned to London, Morris and Burne-Jones moving to Rossetti's old rooms in Red Lion Square. This happy bachelor phase came to an end in 1860, by which time all three were married – Morris to Jane Burden, Burne-Jones to Georgiana Macdonald, and Rossetti, at last, to Elizabeth Siddal. Their

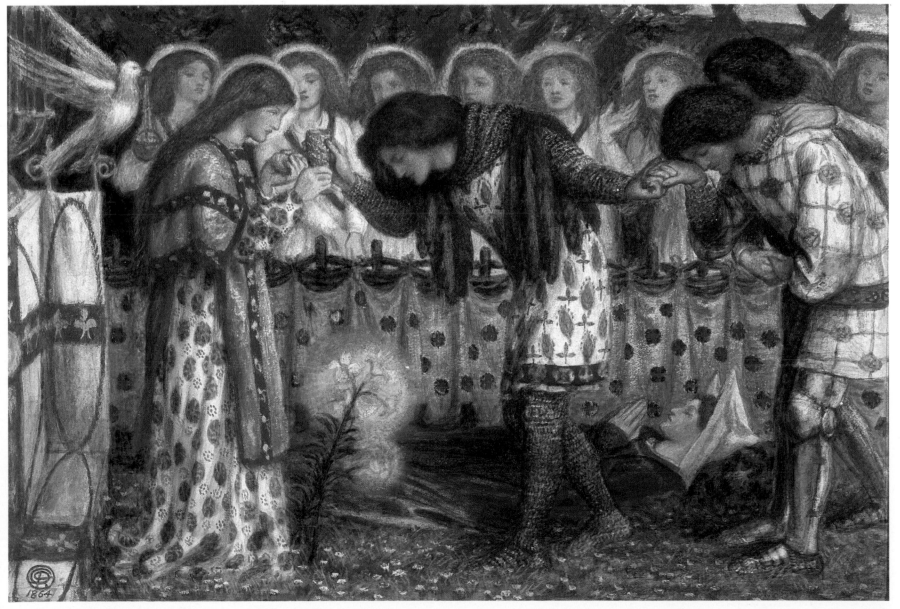

relationship had been growing more difficult all the time, and was complicated by Lizzie's increasingly poor health. Rossetti married her out of loyalty, but the marriage was not a happy one, and only made their problems worse. In 1862, while Rossetti was out dining with Algernon Swinburne, Lizzie took an overdose of laudanum, from which she died. Rossetti was overcome with remorse, convinced that he had caused her death. He put into her coffin the manuscripts of all his early poems, although his disreputable friend Charles Howell later persuaded him to have them dug up again. It was a traumatic turning-point in Rossetti's career. Chatham Place was too haunted by memories for him to remain there, so he moved to a house in Cheyne Walk, Chelsea, which was to remain his home until his death. Still obsessed by Lizzie's memory, he painted *Beata Beatrix* (p. 97) as a memorial to her. This remarkable and moving picture marks a new departure in Rossetti's life and art, which belongs more properly to the second phase of the movement.

John Everett Millais 1829–1896

Millais was the most naturally talented and technically brilliant artist in the Brotherhood. Apart from the years 1850 to 1851, when the critics were savaging all Pre-Raphaelite pictures, his life was one long success story, starting with a silver medal from the Royal Society of Arts when he was only nine, and ending with the Presidency of the Royal Academy in the last year of his life. The youngest son of an old Jersey family, he entered the Royal Academy Schools in 1840, at the age of eleven. He mastered all the academic styles currently in vogue during the 1840s with astonishing ease. His picture *Cymon and Iphigenia* (1848) is a brilliantly precocious essay in the manner of William Etty. It was the Pre-Raphaelite Brotherhood which gave his prodigious talents a much-needed sense of direction, and between 1850 and 1860 he was to paint some of the most brilliant masterpieces of the Pre-Raphaelite movement.

At first it was Holman Hunt who exercized the strongest influence over Millais. There are obvious similarities between Millais' *Christ in the House of His Parents* (p. 17) and Hunt's *Druids* (p. 18) for example. They also shared an enthusiasm for Shakespearean subjects. Millais' early drawings, on the other hand, reflect Rossetti's influence, with their spiky, gothic angularity, and macabre subject matter. *The Disentombment of Queen Matilda* is a typical example. But Millais quickly absorbed these influences, and from then on forged an individual style of his own. With *Mariana* (p. 31) and *Ophelia* (p.33) he combined the romantic, medievalizing spirit of Rossetti with Hunt's meticulous observation. Millais' greater facility enabled him to achieve incredible feats of natural observation, and also to paint faster. *The Woodman's Daughter* (p. 32) was his only contribution to the social realist side of Pre-Raphaelitism. This was not an aspect that appealed much to Millais; his only other

Sir John Everett Millais
Mariana

Signed and dated 1851
Panel 60 × 50 cm/23½ × 19½ ins
The Makins Collection

Exhibited at the Royal Academy in 1851, together with *The Woodman's Daughter* and *The Return of the Dove to the Ark*. Millais gave the picture no title, but exhibited it with some lines from Tennyson's poem *Mariana*:

She only said, 'My life is dreary –
    He cometh not' she said;
She said 'I am aweary, aweary –
    I would that I were dead.'

The stained glass was derived from windows in Merton College Chapel, Oxford, and the garden from Thomas Combe's garden, also in Oxford.

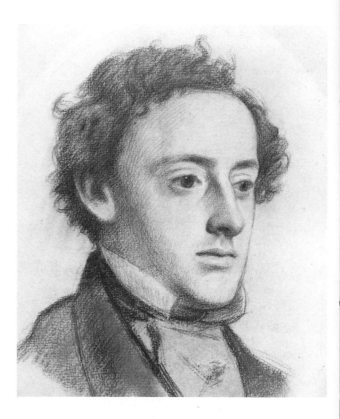

Above: **William Holman Hunt**, portrait of Millais, 1853. Left: **Sir John Everett Millais**, *The Disentombment of Queen Matilda*, 1849.

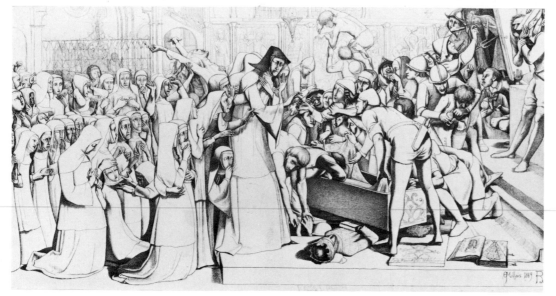

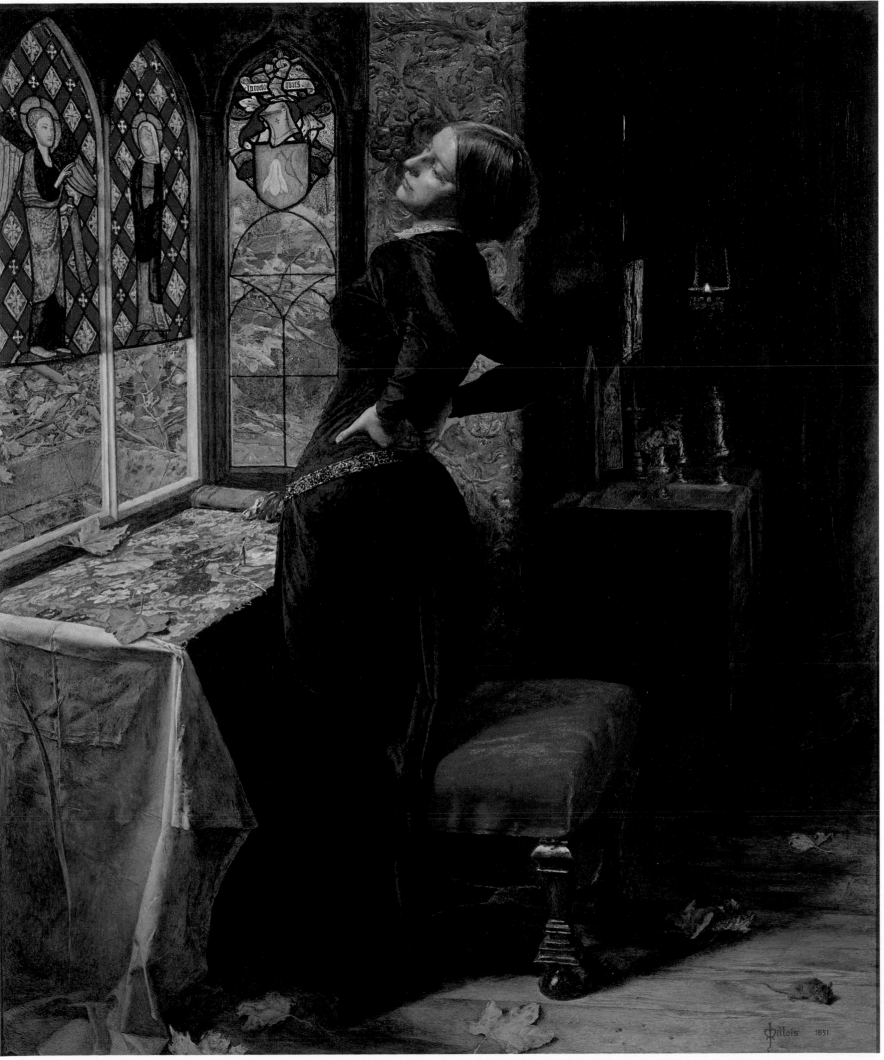

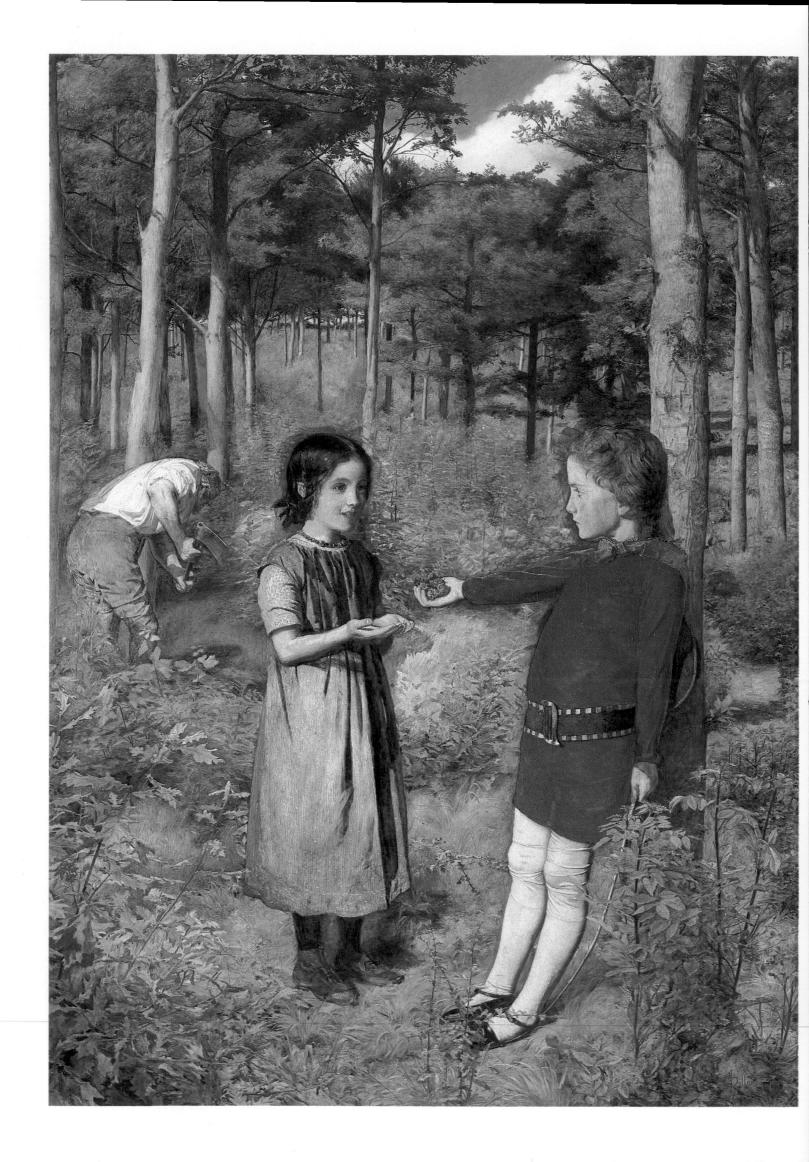

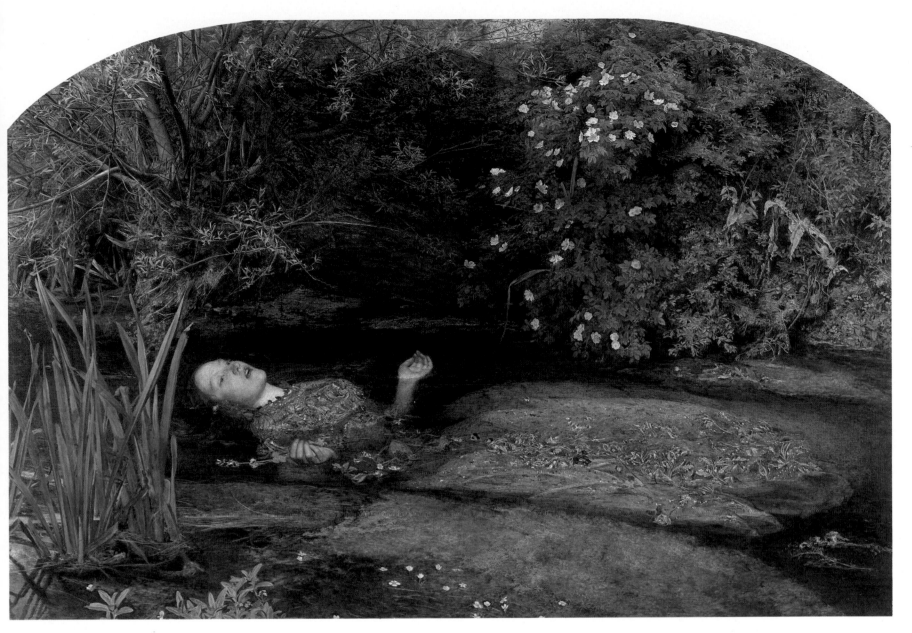

Sir John Everett Millais
The Woodman's Daughter

Signed and dated 1851
Canvas 84 × 65 cm/35 × 25½ ins
Guildhall Art Gallery, London

The title is that of a poem by Coventry Patmore, and
the picture was exhibited at the Royal Academy in
1851 with a quotation from it. The poem describes
how a rich squire's son goes to watch a woodman
and his daughter at work, and befriends the
daughter by giving her fruit. Patmore was a friend
and supporter of the PRB, and it was through his
influence that Ruskin came to the Brotherhood's
defence in 1851. The landscape background was
painted in the woods on Lord Abingdon's estate at
Botley Park, near Oxford. The girl's boots were
borrowed from a cottager on the estate, and Millais
wrote to Mrs Combe, 'If you should see a country
child with a light lilac pinafore on, lay hands on the
same, and send it with the boots.' The strawberries
were specially bought at Covent Garden Market
during March.

Sir John Everett Millais
Ophelia

Signed and dated 1852
Canvas 76 × 102 cm/30 × 40 ins
Tate Gallery, London

One of the outstanding masterpieces of the PRB,
combining a Shakespearian subject with a
Ruskinian intensity of natural observation. The
background was painted in the summer of 1851 on
the River Ewell in Surrey. During the winter of
1851–52, Elizabeth Siddal posed for Ophelia, lying
fully-dressed in a bath kept warm by means of
lamps underneath. Millais purchased an antique
dress for her to pose in, and it took him nearly four
months to complete the figure. According to
William Michael Rossetti, this picture is the best
likeness of Elizabeth Siddal ever painted. The idea
of painting the mad Ophelia drowning was highly
original at the time, although it was to be repeated
by many later Pre-Raphaelite artists.

attempt was *The Rescue* of 1855. His greatest talent lay in combining poetic subject-matter and natural detail. This reached its peak with his two masterpieces of 1856, *The Blind Girl* (p. 36) and *Autumn Leaves* (p. 38).

Portraiture was another side of the Brotherhood's activities that should not be overlooked. They all produced portraits, of themselves, friends and patrons, which in their clarity, honesty and high technical finish bear comparison with Holbein, Dürer and other early Flemish and German artists. Millais' most famous portrait is that of *John Ruskin* (p. 35). Possibly no portrait has ever been painted in such extraordinary circumstances. Ruskin failed to get Millais to come with him to Switzerland, but he did persuade him to join him and his wife on their trip to Scotland in 1853. They stayed at Glenfinlas, near Brig o'Turk, in the Trossachs. Millais began to paint his portrait of Ruskin standing on some rocks beside a stream. The setting reflects Ruskin's passion for geology, botany and all natural phenomena; he was clearly trying to make Millais paint in a more 'Ruskinian' style. Unfortunately, the Scottish trip had another more serious result. The Ruskins' marriage had not been a happy one, and had not been consummated. It is said that Ruskin, accustomed to the smooth blandness of classical sculptures, was shocked by the sight of his wife's pubic hair, and could not bring himself to make love to her. Effie was an attractive and high-spirited girl, and she and the youthful Millais fell in love. After protracted and scandalous divorce proceedings, the Ruskins' marriage was annulled, enabling Millais and Effie to marry in 1855. Most people sided with the young lovers and blamed Ruskin, but inevitably there was a division of opinion and Queen Victoria refused to receive Millais' wife, until he requested it as a favour on his deathbed.

Ruskin behaved generously, and warmly praised Millais' pictures at the Royal Academy Exhibition of 1856. This certainly was a vintage year for Millais, with three outstanding works – *The Blind Girl, Autumn Leaves,* and *Peace Concluded*. The first two are perhaps Millais' most beautiful pictures, combining poetic mood with wonderful natural detail, keeping the narrative element to the minimum. Ruskin compared *Autumn Leaves* to Giorgione's work, and there certainly is enough poetry and mystery about it to make the comparison apt. The following year, Millais' main work was *A Dream of the Past – Sir Isumbras at the Ford* (p. 39), and this time Ruskin changed his tune. He attacked the picture vehemently, denouncing it as 'not merely a fall – it is a catastrophe'. For once, Ruskin was unfair. Although the picture has weaknesses – the horse is too large, and the composition awkward – the mood and colouring are delightful, and it deserves to be ranked with Millais' other late Pre-

Sir John Everett Millais
Portrait of John Ruskin

Signed and dated 1854
Canvas 79 × 68 cm/31 × 26¾ ins
Private collection

Ruskin, the great champion of the Pre-Raphaelites, commissioned this now famous portrait from Millais in 1853. It was begun in the summer of that year in the Trossachs, where Millais, Ruskin and his wife Effie were spending their ill-fated holiday together. Ruskin was keen that Millais should paint rocks and water, and a spot was selected at Brig o'Turk, by the river at Glenfinlas. Ruskin wrote to his father, 'Millais has fixed on a place, a lovely piece of worn rock, with foaming water and weeds and moss, and a whole overhanging bank of dark crag . . . I am sure the foam of the torrent will be something quite new in art.'

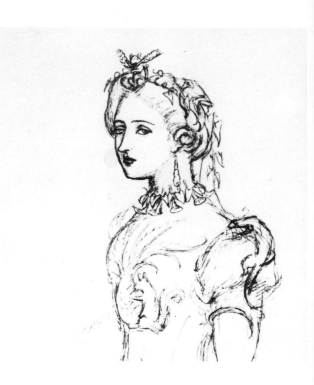

Above: **Sir John Everett Millais,** study of Effie for *Natural Ornament* (detail), 1853. Left: *The Vale of Rest,* 1859.

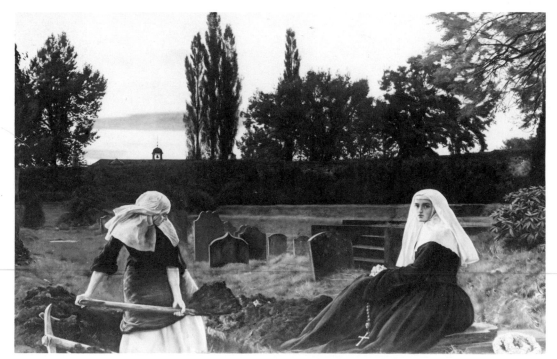

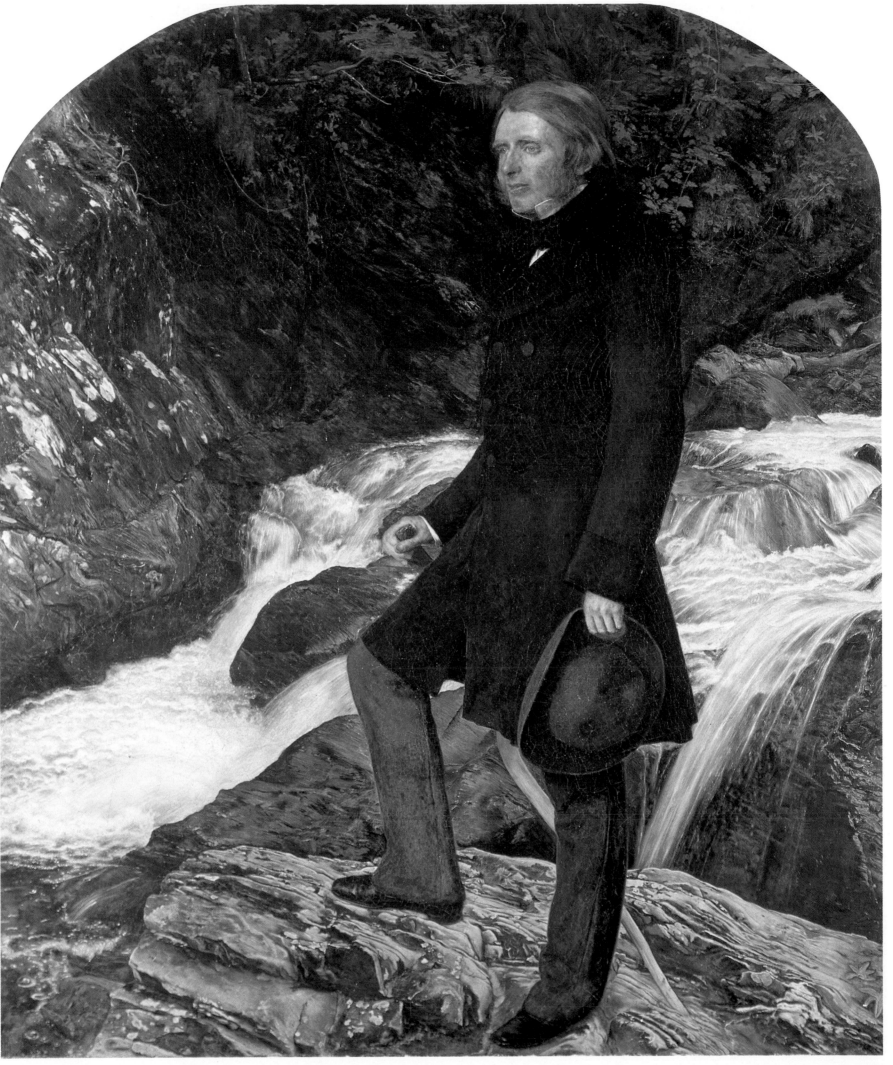

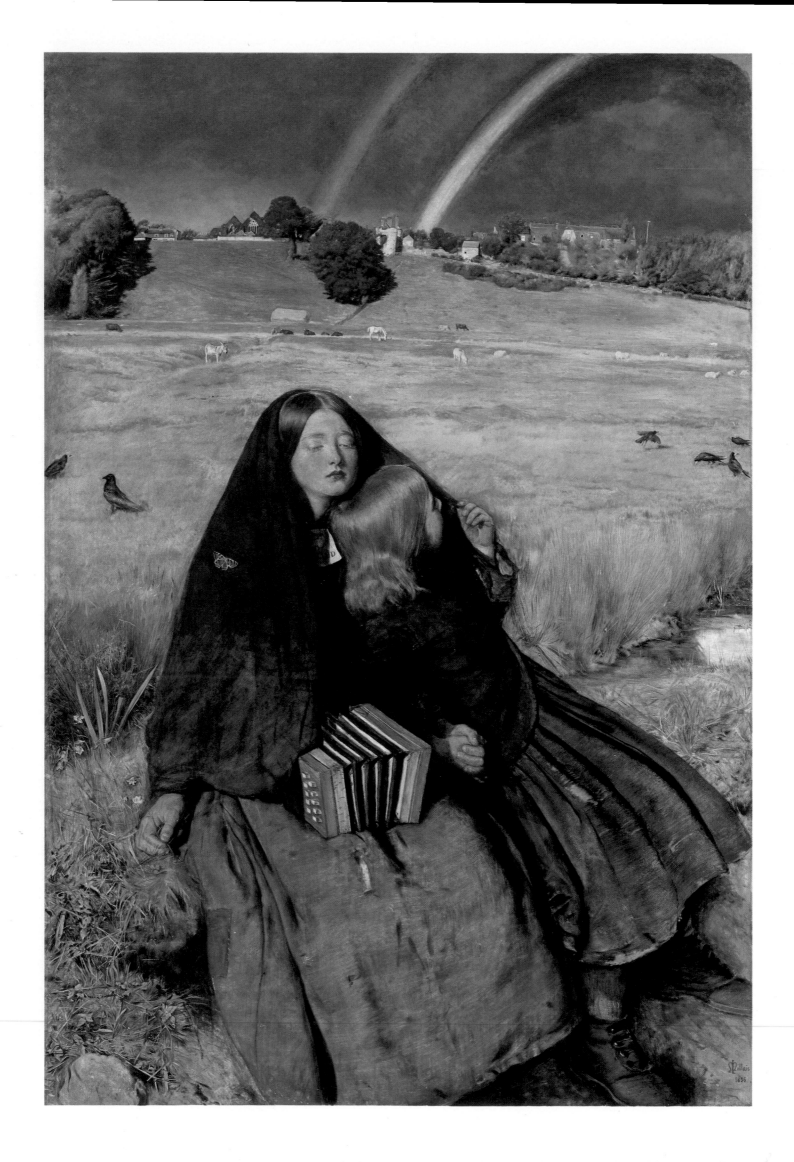

Sir John Everett Millais
The Blind Girl

Signed and dated 1856
Canvas 81 × 62 cm/32 × 24½ ins
Birmingham City Museum and Art Gallery

A blind beggar girl and her companion rest by a roadside, waiting for a passing shower to clear. The background is a view of Winchelsea from the east; the two girls, Matilda and Isabella, were local girls from Perth, where Millais often stayed with Effie's parents. Technically, it is perhaps the most brilliant of all Millais' Pre-Raphaelite works, especially the landscape with the rainbow and thunder-clouds. Rossetti described it as 'one of the most touching and perfect things I know', and Ruskin praised the intensely luminous brilliance of colour, 'The freshly wet grass is all radiant through and through with the new sunshine; the weeds at the girl's side as bright as a Byzantine enamel, and inlaid with blue veronica . . .'

Raphaelite works. The technique is rather looser than his earlier works, and already shows him beginning to move away from strict Pre-Raphaelite ideas.

Millais' marriage must have contributed to this change. The couple soon began to raise a large family, and there was a need to produce more pictures, faster. The Pre-Raphaelite technique was too laborious and he wrote that he could no longer afford to spend a day painting an area 'no larger than a five shilling piece'. His last truly Pre-Raphaelite picture was *The Vale of Rest* (1859), which depicts nuns digging a grave in a convent cemetery. The prevailing mood of this beautiful picture is similar to *Autumn Leaves*; the theme common to both is melancholy, a concern that looks forward to Symbolism and Art Nouveau. Already in such pictures as *The Order of Release* and *The Black Brunswicker*, Millais had deliberately begun to choose more popular and appealing subjects. Eventually, he was to give up the Pre-Raphaelite style altogether, painting in a broader, looser manner that harks back to Reynolds and Gainsborough, both artists whom he was later to admire and emulate.

The remainder of Millais' career belongs to Victorian art history, and not to the story of Pre-Raphaelitism. He was the only member of the Brotherhood to abandon its principles completely, and as a result he was financially more successful and more popular than any of them. His historical pictures, portraits and sentimental pictures of children were enormously popular, and at the height of his fame he could earn over £30,000 a year, a colossal sum in those days. He lived in grand style, and was the first English artist to be made a baronet. He was also a great sportsman, passionately fond of fishing and stalking, and photographs of him, with tweeds, deerstalker and smoking a pipe, show him looking more like a Victorian squire than an artist. He was certainly not an intellectual; his son wrote that 'probably no artist in England ever read less on art than did Millais.' But few English artists had such abundant talents. Until recently, it has been fashionable to denounce Millais' later works as inferior to his Pre-Raphaelite period. This viewpoint is no longer tenable. His later work is certainly uneven, but in its different way, just as worthy of consideration, and just as successful. Some of his portraits, in particular those such as *Hearts are Trumps*, or his portrait of Gladstone, are among the finest of the late Victorian period. Millais' abandonment of Pre-Raphaelitism was a great loss to the movement, but to regard the rest of his career as irrelevant would be a grossly one-sided viewpoint. Millais was one of the most brilliant artists of the Victorian age, and Ruskin was more just when he wrote: '. . . whether he is good one year, or bad, he is always the most powerful of them all.'

Right: **Sir John Everett Millais**, *The Order of Release*, 1853. Far right: *The Black Brunswicker*, 1860.

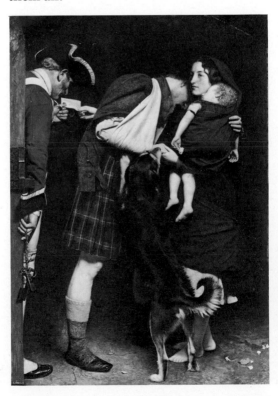

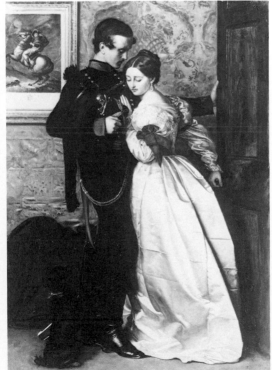

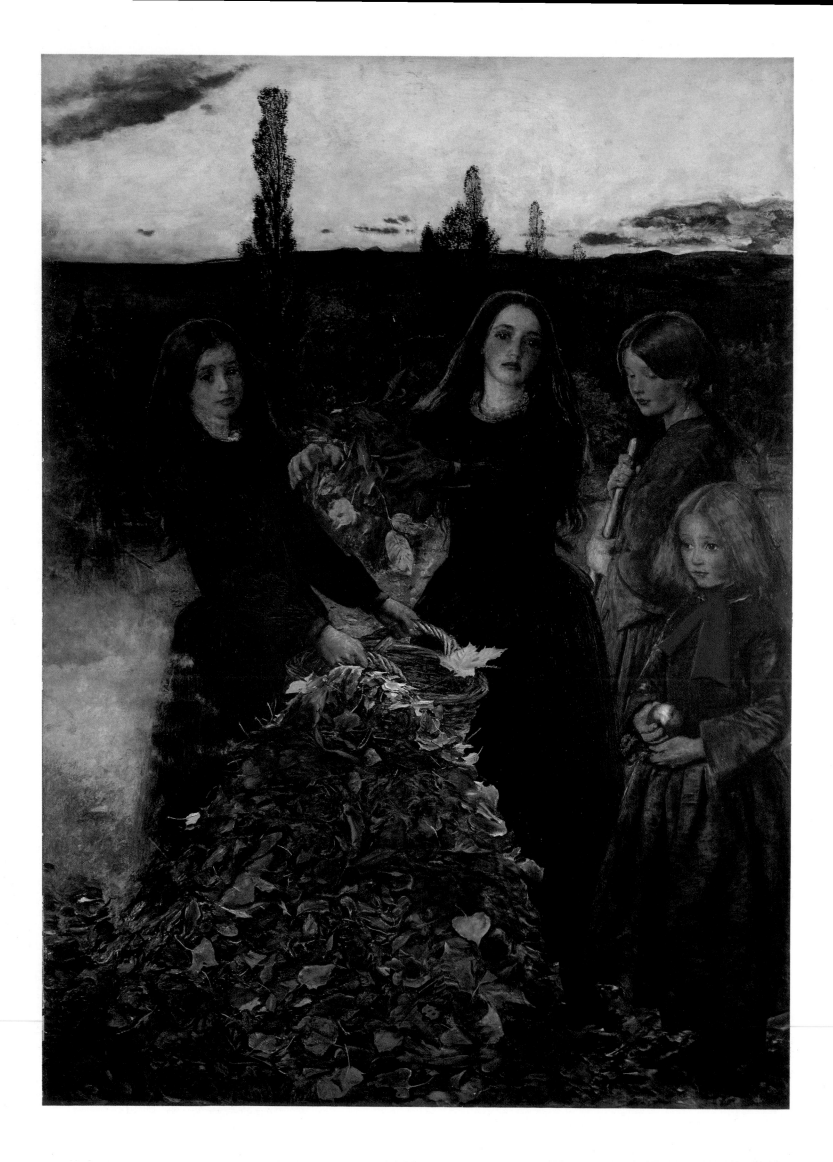

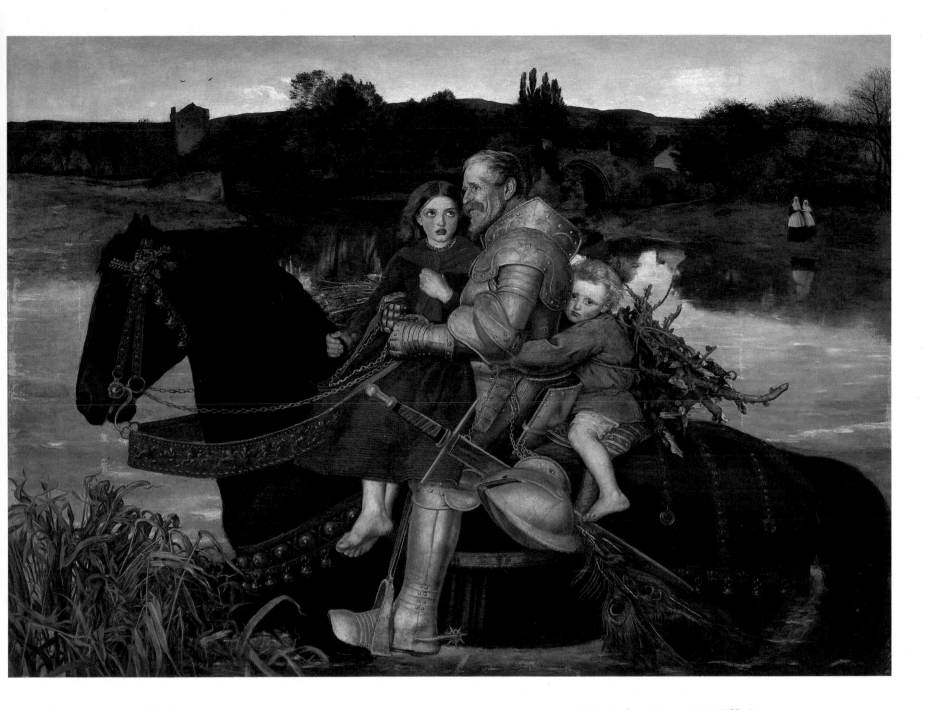

Sir John Everett Millais
Autumn Leaves

Signed and dated 1856
Canvas 104 × 74 cm/41 × 29⅛ ins
Manchester City Art Gallery

Painted in the garden of Annat Lodge, Perth, where
Millais lived for a time after his marriage. The
models were two of Effie's sisters, Sophie and Alice,
and two local girls, Matilda and Isabella, who also
modelled for *The Blind Girl*. The horizon is a view of
the hills above Perth, looking towards Ben Vorlich.
It is the most hauntingly beautiful of all Millais' Pre-
Raphaelite pictures, and is regarded by many critics
as his masterpiece. Ruskin wrote that it was 'by
much the most poetical work the artist has yet
conceived; and also, as far as I know, the first
instance of a perfectly painted twilight'. Holman
Hunt recalled a remark made to him by Millais
about 1851, which must have been the genesis of the
picture, 'Is there any sensation more delicious than
that awakened by the odour of burning leaves? To
me nothing brings back sweeter memories of the
days that are gone . . .'

Sir John Everett Millais
A Dream of the Past – Sir Isumbras at the Ford

Signed and dated 1857
Canvas 124 × 170 cm/49 × 67 ins
Lady Lever Art Gallery, Port Sunlight

Exhibited at the Royal Academy in 1857 with a
quotation from a pseudo-medieval romance by Tom
Taylor (*Metrical Romance of Sir Ysumbras*). The
background was painted at the Bridge of Earn in
Perthshire and the model for the knight was a
Colonel Campbell. The little boy was Millais' son,
Everett. The picture was widely attacked by the
critics, including Ruskin, who declared it was 'not
merely a fall – it is a catastrophe'. It was also
caricatured in a print by Frederick Sandys, showing
Hunt, Millais and Rossetti riding a donkey.
However the composition is striking, if somewhat
awkward, and the background has the same haunting
beauty as *Autumn Leaves* and *The Vale of Rest*.
The technique is looser than that of his earlier
works and the sentimental nature of the subject
foreshadows Millais' change of style.

William Holman Hunt 1827–1910

Holman Hunt is still the least known and appreciated of the Brotherhood, although he was the only one to remain faithful to its principles. Hunt lacked the natural facility of Millais, or the attractive personality of Rossetti, but his immense determination and forceful character were of crucial importance in the early days of the Brotherhood. His resolution was what kept the Brotherhood together in difficult times, and he was frequently referred to as its President. Although there have been several books and exhibitions devoted to his work, his character still remains elusive and misunderstood, and his paintings neglected.

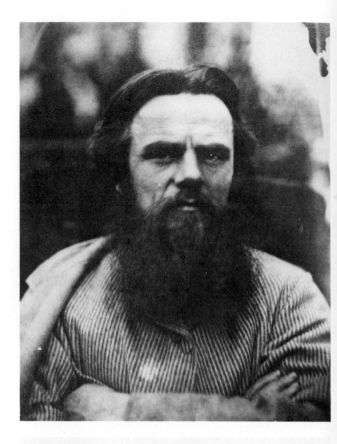

Life for Hunt was always a struggle, partly because of poverty, partly because of constant agonizing over his work. His origins were humble, and he received little support or encouragement from his family. He started work as a clerk at the age of twelve, and at first was able to paint only in his spare time. After two unsuccessful attempts, he was accepted as a probationer at the Royal Academy Schools in 1844. Here Hunt met Millais, the infant prodigy of the Schools, and in 1848 Hunt introduced Rossetti to Millais, thus bringing about the formation of the Brotherhood. It was also Hunt who introduced the Brotherhood to the writings of Ruskin.

Hunt's sincerity, honesty and determination were the driving force behind the Brotherhood. His refusal to accept compromise or defeat earned him lifelong respect and admiration from his colleagues. For Hunt the painstaking technique of the Pre-Raphaelite style meant months of incessant labour to finish one picture. He believed that great art could only be the result of hard work, and all his life he struggled to finish his pictures, sometimes taking five or even ten years to complete them. In 1863 he wrote, 'I am so weary of work! . . . I *can't* get anything finished. I work and work until I feel my brain as dry as an old bit of cork, but completion slips away from me.' More than either Millais or Rossetti, Hunt represents the serious, moralizing side of the Pre-Raphaelite movement. He was a religious man, and believed that art must be 'a handmaid in the cause of justice and truth'. With his mane of red hair and bushy beard, he looked like an Old Testament prophet, but he was also a cheerful, irreverent companion in his early days, 'with a laugh which answers one's own like a grotto full of echoes', as Rossetti described him. The moralizing, Ruskinian spirit pervades all his work, and he alone of the Pre-Raphaelites devoted himself to major religious pictures, calculated to appeal to the widest possible audience. Although he eventually strayed beyond the confines of strict Pre-Raphaelite ideas, he remained faithful to its basic ideals, and he can therefore, with justification, be classified as the only true Pre-Raphaelite, in the narrowest sense of the term.

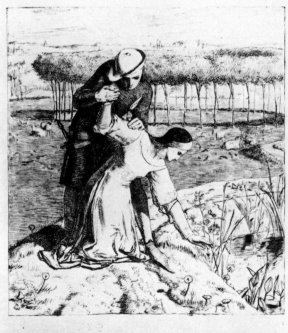

Hunt's first Pre-Raphaelite picture was *Rienzi*. The picture was painted out of doors, in full sunlight, and all the details were studied from nature. The choice of dramatic subjects from literature was typical of Hunt. Like Rossetti, he had a wide knowledge and love of English literature, and it was he who introduced Millais to the poetry of Keats and Tennyson. These two poets, and Shakespeare, were to remain an inspiration to Hunt for the rest of his life. His next picture, *Druids* (p. 18), was the first of his many pictures on religious themes, and already shows his method of using symbolic objects to suggest the moral and allegorical message. This was a technique that Hunt used with increasing elaboration throughout his life. *Claudio and Isabella* (p. 19) and *Valentine Rescuing Sylvia* (p. 21) were his first Shakespearean scenes painted on Pre-Raphaelite principles. Both are more complex than might at first appear, as Hunt has deliberately selected highly charged emotional moments from each play, full of moral and sexual undertones. Hunt's preoccupations with sin and guilt, retribution and redemption, are reflected in many of his pictures, and provide us with some clues to his own complex character. Like Rossetti, Hunt fell victim to a *femme fatale*, the beautiful red-haired model Annie Miller. With typical evangelical and high-minded zeal, Hunt tried to reform her, and even to marry her, but both ended in conspicuous failure. Hunt remained a bachelor until 1865, when he married Fanny Waugh. After her premature death, he married Fanny's sister, Edith, in 1875.

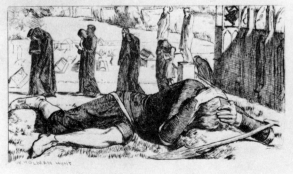

Above: Photograph of William Holman Hunt by Julia Margaret Cameron, 1864. Below: **William Holman Hunt**, frontispiece to *The Germ*, 1850.

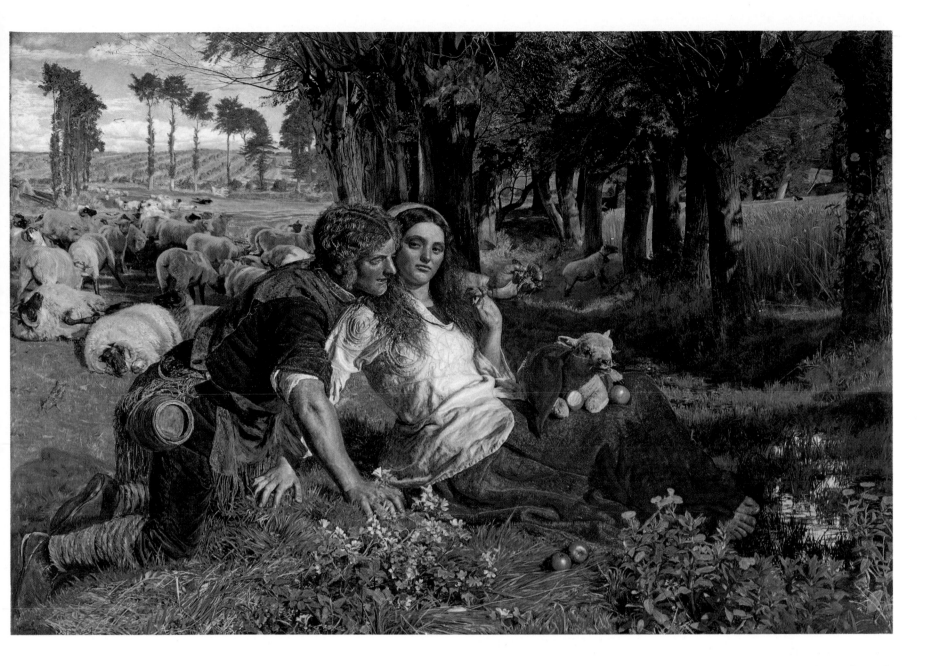

William Holman Hunt
The Hireling Shepherd

Signed and dated Ewell 1851
Canvas 77 × 110 cm/30⅛ × 43⅛ ins
Manchester City Art Gallery

Exhibited at the Royal Academy in 1852, with a quotation from the Fool in *King Lear*:

Sleepest or wakest thou, jolly shepherd;
   Thy sheep be in the corn;
And for one blast of thy minikin mouth,
   Thy sheep shall take no harm.

This is the finest of Hunt's early works, and probably the best known. The model for the girl was Emma Watkins, a farm girl who worked on an estate at Ewell in Surrey, and the landscape was also painted near Ewell where Hunt's uncle owned a farm. Although the picture might appear to be a simple scene of rustic flirtation in a breath-takingly beautiful landscape, Hunt's intention was to point a more serious moral. The shepherd is symbolic of the church neglecting its flock, while in the background the sheep are straying into the corn, and a lamb on the girl's lap is eating green apples.

This was still forbidden under English law, and so the marriage took place abroad. This taint of illegality was to hang like a cloud over Hunt, and eventually became an obsession for his widow. Some may find the atmosphere of religious fervour and moral repression that surrounds Hunt's life and work both morbid and gloomy, but, unlike Rossetti, Hunt was a typical man of his age and class.

Hunt's next major Pre-Raphaelite picture was *The Hireling Shepherd* (above), another elaborate moral fable, but also a brilliant piece of painting. Hunt was a superb colourist, and continued to explore problems of light and colour throughout his career. It was said that he could see the moons of Jupiter with the naked eye, and his pictures have a penetrating, almost surrealistic clarity of detail that exceeds anything produced by the other Pre-Raphaelites. *The Hireling Shepherd* also provided the inspiration for many other Pre-Raphaelite landscape painters. Hunt could have been a brilliant landscape painter had he wished, but this talent always played a subordinate role in his art. In 1853 Hunt painted his last pictures before the Brotherhood dissolved, *The Awakening Conscience* (p. 42) and *The Light of The World* (p. 43), intended as secular and religious versions of the same theme. In both pictures Hunt uses his own particular method of backing up the visual image with elaborate symbolic detail. In *The Awakening Conscience*, for example, almost every object in the room has significance, the furniture with its 'fatal newness', as Ruskin described it in a letter to *The Times*, the books '. . . marked with no happy wearing of beloved leaves; the torn and dying bird upon the floor; the gilded tapestry, with the fowls of the air feeding on the ripened corn', the picture of the woman taken in adultery, and

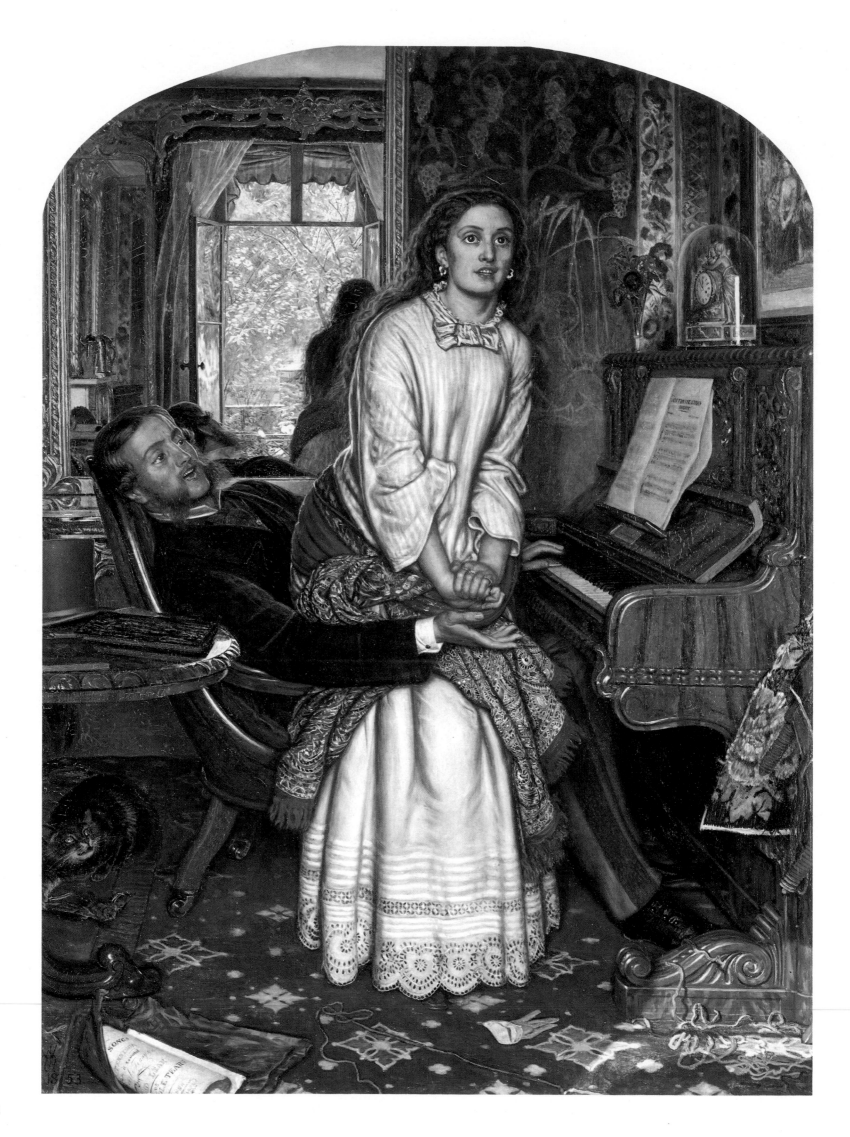

William Holman Hunt

The Awakening Conscience

Signed and dated 1853
Canvas, arched top, 74 × 55 cm/29¼ × 21⅝ ins
Tate Gallery, London

The first Victorian picture to grapple with the thorny problem of prostitution. A kept woman, sitting at the piano with her lover, is suddenly stricken by remorse, and starts up, while the man goes on playing the piano, ignorant of what has happened. Hunt attempted to treat the subject with the utmost seriousness, inscribing one religious quotation on the frame, and two more in the Royal Academy catalogue, but this did not prevent the critics from attacking it. The *Athenaeum* critic wrote that it was 'drawn from a very dark and repulsive side of domestic life . . .' but Ruskin once again came to the rescue, writing a long explanation and defence of the picture in *The Times*.

The Light of the World

Signed with monogram and dated 1853
Canvas, arched top 125 × 60 cm/49⅜ × 23½ ins
Wardens and Fellows of Keble College, Oxford

Probably the most famous of all Victorian religious images, exhibited at the Royal Academy in 1854 together with *The Awakening Conscience*. It illustrates a passage from *Revelations*: 'Behold, I stand at the door, and knock; if any man hear my voice, and open the door, I will come in to him, and will sup with him, and he with me.' Hunt began the picture at Worcester Park Farm in the winter of 1851, working in an orchard at night. Millais recorded that Hunt was 'cheerfully working by a lantern from some contorted apple tree trunks, washed with the phosphor light of a perfect moon . . .' The picture was not finished until 1853, when it was sold to Thomas Combe of Oxford, whose wife later presented it to Keble College. Much later in life, Hunt painted a second, much larger version, which now hangs in St Paul's Cathedral.

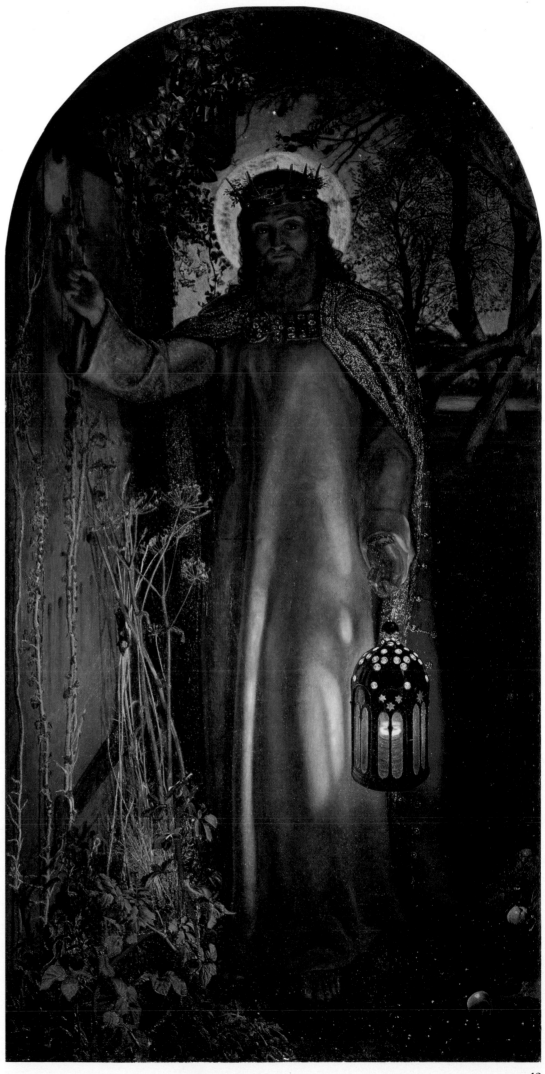

even the music on the piano and on the floor. The frame is carved with bells and marigolds, symbols of warning, and inscribed with religious quotations. As if this were not enough, when Hunt exhibited the picture at the Royal Academy it was accompanied by two further biblical quotations. *The Light of The World* is an allegory of man's failure to heed the teachings of Jesus. The door is symbolically overgrown with ivy, brambles and weeds; the hinges and handle are rusty. The picture was enormously popular and endlessly reproduced in books and prints, but this has not weakened its power as a key Victorian religious image. Both this and *The Awakening Conscience* are remarkable, and highly individual pictures. There has been nothing quite like them in English art, either before or since. Their high technical finish and complex symbolism make them comparable only with early German or Flemish religious pictures. But although Hunt admired Van Dyck, Tintoretto and many other Italian artists, his own art was ruggedly insular and individual.

Early in 1854, Hunt left for the Holy Land, an event which effectively marked the end of the Brotherhood. He made this decision because he wanted to paint biblical subjects on the spot, in the very places where they had originally happened. This was typical of Hunt's thoroughness, and also typical of the rational, scientific spirit of the age. David Wilkie and David Roberts had preceded Hunt to the Middle East, but they were topographers rather than serious religious artists. The result was one of the most original and eccentric of all Hunt's works, *The Scapegoat* (below). Even lovers of Victorian painting are still divided over this picture, which arouses admiration and dislike in equal measure. To lavish such time and labour on such an unpromising subject may seem to have been misguided, but it is an extraordinarily powerful

William Holman Hunt
The Scapegoat

Signed with monogram and dated Oosdoom, Dead Sea, 1854
Canvas 86 × 138 cm/33¾ × 54½ ins
Lady Lever Art Gallery, Port Sunlight

Painted on Hunt's first trip to the Middle East in 1854. The subject represents the Talmudic tradition of driving a sacrificial white goat out into the wilderness on the Day of Atonement. A filet of red wool was bound to the goat's horns, in the belief that it would turn white if the propitiation was accepted. Hunt worked for days at Oosdoom on the shores of the Dead Sea, painting the background, and later brought a goat back to England, together with a quantity of Dead Sea mud and stones, to complete the picture in his studio. The picture was received respectfully, but with puzzlement, at the Royal Academy in 1855. Ford Madox Brown, in his diary, was more just: 'Hunt's *Scapegoat* requires to be seen to be believed in. Only then, can it be understood how, by the might of genius, out of an old goat, and some saline encrustations, can be made one of the most tragic and impressive works in the annals of art.'

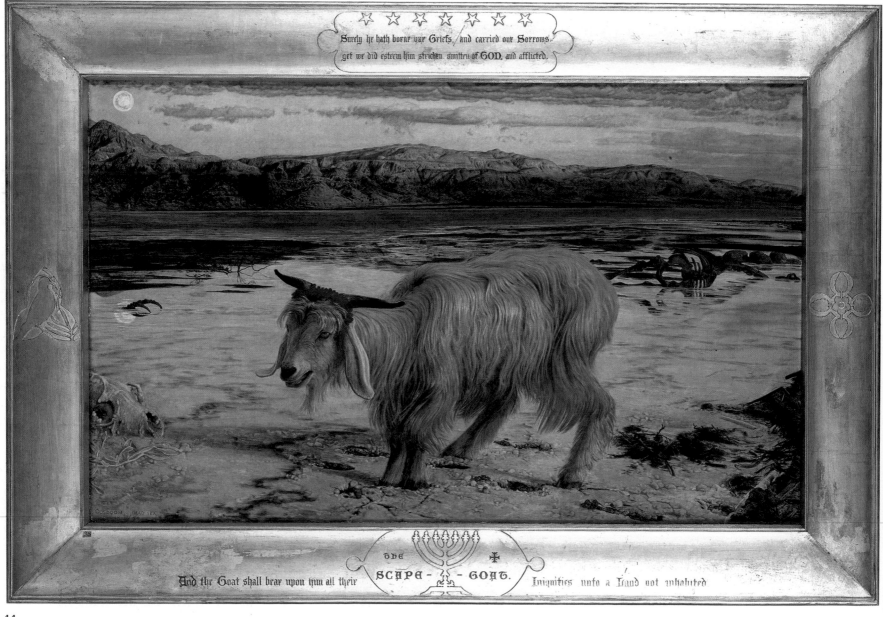

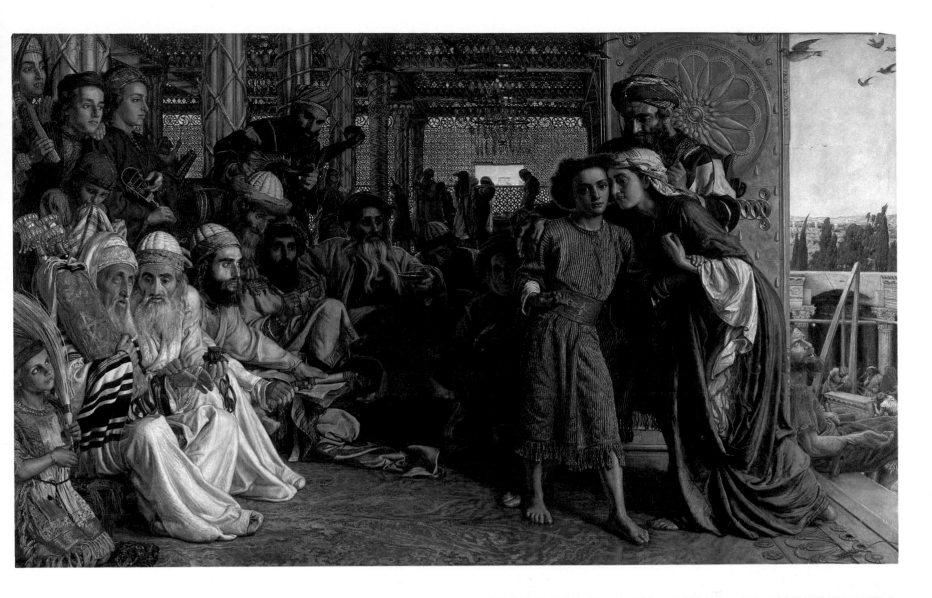

William Holman Hunt
The Finding of the Saviour in the Temple

1854–60
Canvas 86 × 141 cm/33¾ × 55½ ins
Birmingham City Museum and Art Gallery

This was the first major biblical picture to emerge from Hunt's trip to the Middle East. He began it in the Holy Land in 1854–55, but it was another five years before it was completed. Hunt consulted Dickens about the price, and it was eventually sold to the dealer, Ernest Gambart, for the enormous sum of £5,500. The picture was a tremendous public success, and the *Manchester Guardian* wrote that 'No picture of such extraordinary elaboration has been seen in our day . . .'

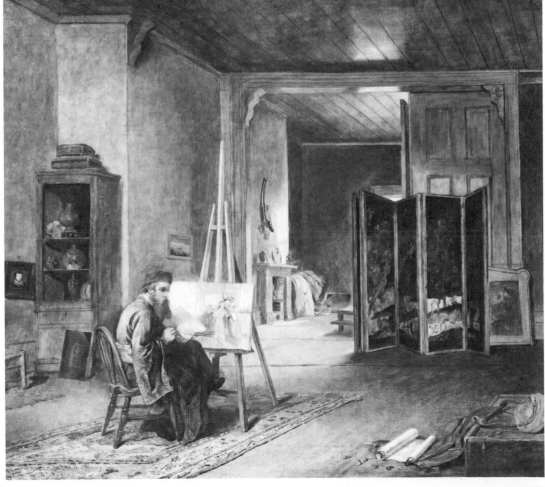

John Ballantyne, William Holman Hunt in his studio at work on a version of *The Finding of the Saviour in the Temple*.

image, set in one of the most macabre and eerie landscapes in English art.

Hunt's next religious picture was *The Finding of the Saviour in The Temple* (p. 45). This was begun in 1854 on his first trip to the Middle East, but not completed until after 1860, after yet another visit to the Holy Land. Hunt had endless troubles finding models, and, although he wanted to finish it on the spot, it had to be completed from English models in his studio. Hunt became fascinated by Jewish customs and history, as is reflected in every detail of this elaborate, highly-wrought picture. His herculean labours were in the end rewarded; the eminent dealer, Ernest Gambart, bought the picture for the unheard-of sum of £5,500. Hunt's years of financial difficulties were at last over; in the future he was to sell his pictures for even higher sums. But after 1860, his work really belongs to the second phase of the movement.

Followers and associates of the Pre-Raphaelite Brotherhood
Ford Madox Brown 1821–1893

Madox Brown was never a member of the Brotherhood, although clearly he was the one artist who should have been. He belonged to a slightly older generation than the Pre-Raphaelites, and his candidature was opposed by Hunt, mainly on the grounds that his paintings were too academic and conventional, but also because he may have resented Brown's influence over Rossetti. In any case, Brown was a lonely and independent character, and may well have refused to join. As it was, his own paintings exercised considerable influence over the Pre-Raphaelites in the early days of the Brotherhood. In return, they also influenced him, and he painted several key pictures in the 1850s and '60s which made a very important contribution to the iconography of the Pre-Raphaelite movement. Brown was undoubtedly the most important Pre-Raphaelite painter outside the Brotherhood.

Brown's upbringing and training were cosmopolitan. He was born in Calais, the son of a ship's purser, and all his art studies took place on the Continent. He studied in Belgium and at the Antwerp academy under Baron Wappers. In 1844 he came to England with his wife, and daughter Lucy – later to marry William Michael Rossetti. He still continued to visit the Continent, and in particular Italy, where he met and was impressed by the Nazarenes. Like the Pre-Raphaelites, the Nazarenes sought to rejuvenate German art by returning to the spirit of the 'early Christian' painters, and Brown's works form a direct link between the two schools. His first two English pictures, *Wycliffe Reading his Translation of The Bible to John of Gaunt* and *Chaucer at the Court of King Edward III* (p. 47) clearly anticipate many characteristics of the Pre-Raphaelites. The detail, the carefully studied costumes, the elaborate composition, the blend of historicism and nationalism, the idealizing of the Middle Ages – all these elements can be found in the works of Rossetti, Hunt and Millais.

Brown kept diaries for most of his life, and we therefore know a great deal more about his artistic thought and struggles than those of the other Pre-Raphaelites. They record almost continual hardship, and also endless technical problems, as Brown tried to come to terms with the Pre-Raphaelite style. One of his first Pre-Raphaelite pictures was *The Pretty Baa-Lambs* (p. 50), first exhibited in 1852, which he painted out-of-doors, in full sunlight. It is an uncompromisingly truthful picture, and shows how determined Brown could be when he turned to the Pre-Raphaelite style. He was the only one of the leading Pre-Raphaelites to concentrate on pure landscape painting, and this aspect of his work will be treated in the chapter on Pre-Raphaelite landscape. In the same year at the Royal Academy, Brown exhibited his first religious picture in the Pre-Raphaelite style, *Christ Washing Peter's Feet* (p. 48). Here also one can see the effect of Pre-Raphaelite ideas on Brown's style. As in Millais' *The Carpenter's Shop* (p. 17), Brown has chosen to show Christ and his disciples as ordinary people. Christ is deliberately portrayed in a humble, unflattering way, and the treatment of the figures is bold and realistic. Brown continued to paint religious and historical pictures in this style, blending Pre-Raphaelite realism with his own highly individual academic mannerism.

Ford Madox Brown
Chaucer at the Court of King Edward III

1845–51

Canvas, arched top 372 × 296 cm/146½ × 116½ ins
Art Gallery of New South Wales, Sydney

Madox Brown's first major picture, begun in Rome in 1845, and finally exhibited at the Royal Academy in 1851; its full title was *Geoffrey Chaucer reading 'The Legend of Custance' to Edward III and his Court at the Palace of Sheen, on the anniversary of the Black Prince's forty-fifth birthday*. The idea for the picture came from Mackintosh's *History of England*, from which Madox Brown conceived 'a vision of Chaucer reading his poems to knights and ladies fair, to king and court, amid air and sunshine'. It was originally planned as a triptych, but only the central panel was completed. A smaller version is owned by the Tate Gallery.

Dante Gabriel Rossetti, portrait of Ford Madox Brown, 1852.

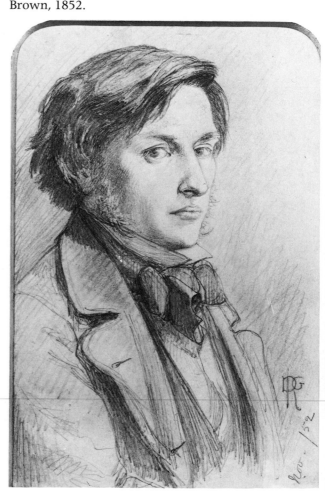

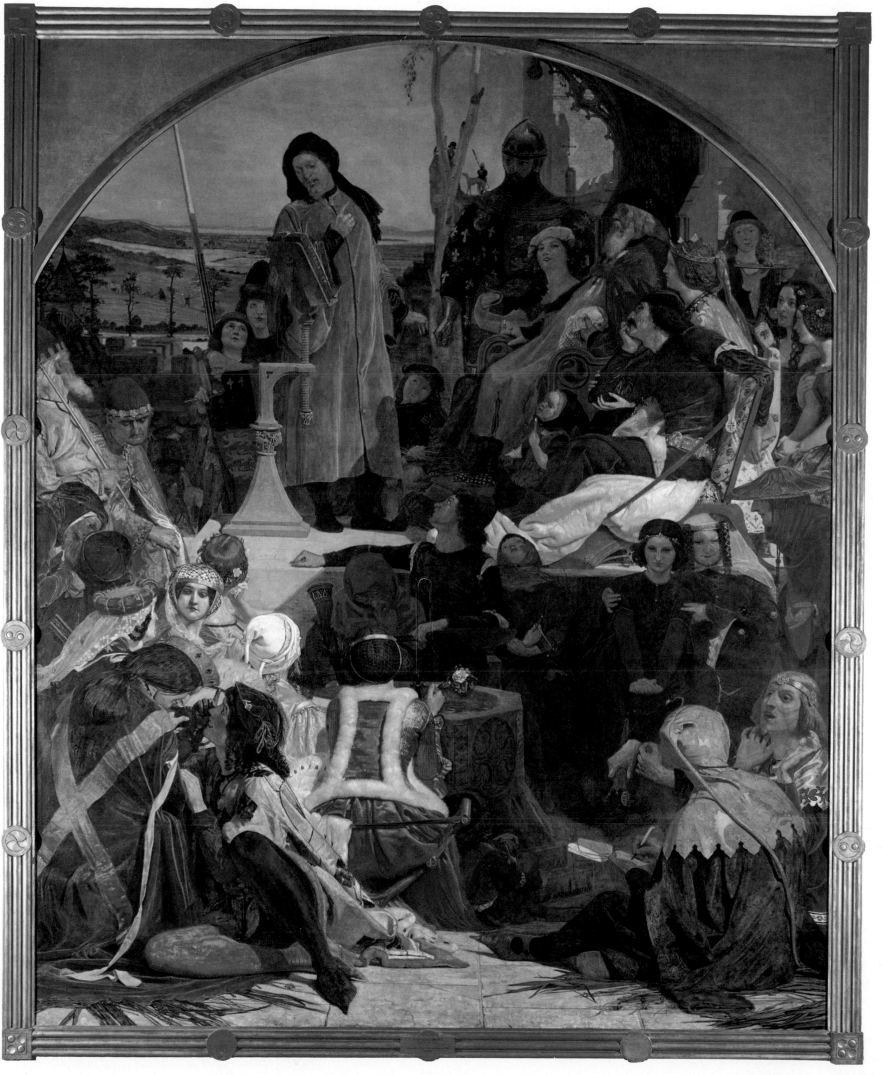

47

There was one other area of the Pre-Raphaelite movement where Brown was to make an important contribution – social realism – with two key pictures, *The Last of England* (p. 11) and *Work* (p. 49). Brown's fame rests largely on these two works, which are among the best-known of all Victorian pictures. Brown wrote of *The Last of England* that 'the picture is, in the strictest sense, historical. It treats of the great Emigration movement which attained its culminating point in 1865 ... I have, in order to present the parting scene in its fullest tragic development, singled out a couple from the middle classes, high enough through education and refinement to appreciate all that they are now giving up ... The husband broods bitterly over blighted hopes and severance from all that he has been striving for ...' Brown himself was bitter about his own lack of recognition, and continued financial difficulties. So much so that he had thought of emigrating himself. Brown also described how the picture was painted: 'To insure that peculiar look of *light all round* which objects have on a dull day at sea, it was painted for the most part in the open air on dull days,

Ford Madox Brown
Christ Washing Peter's Feet

1851–56
Canvas 117 × 133 cm/46 × 52½ ins
Tate Gallery, London

This picture was first exhibited at the Royal Academy in 1852, but extensively repainted between 1854 and 1856, when it was exhibited at the Liverpool Academy, and won the £50 prize. In the earlier version, the figure of Christ was naked, but Brown added clothes during the repainting. The low viewpoint and curious facial types are typical of Brown's eccentric and highly individual style. As usual, many of the Pre-Raphaelites modelled for the figures, including Holman Hunt and all three Rossettis.

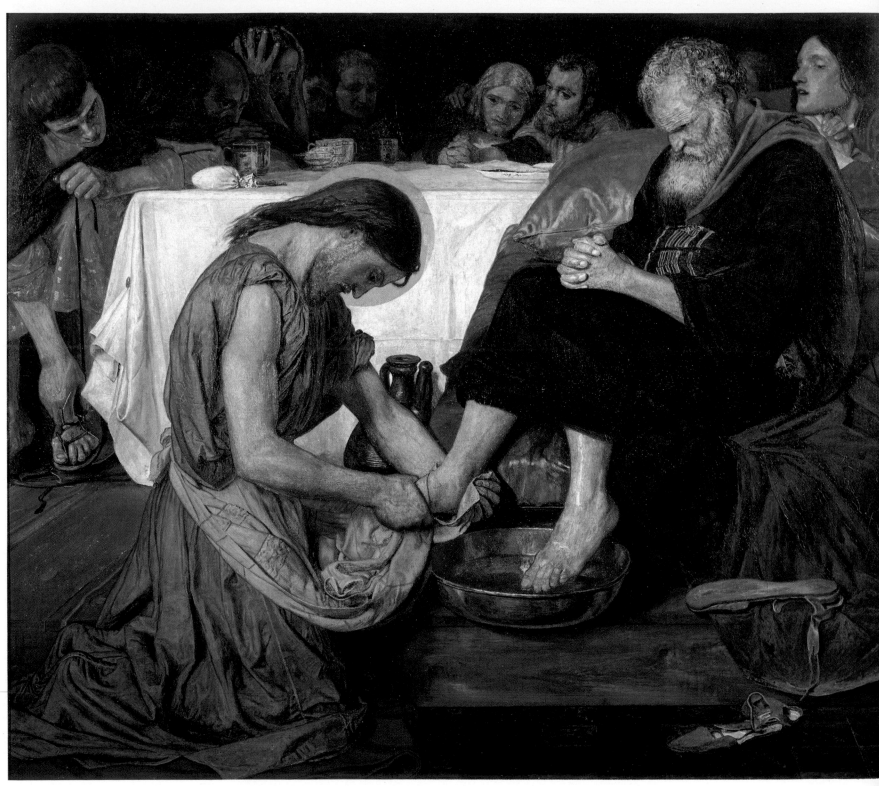

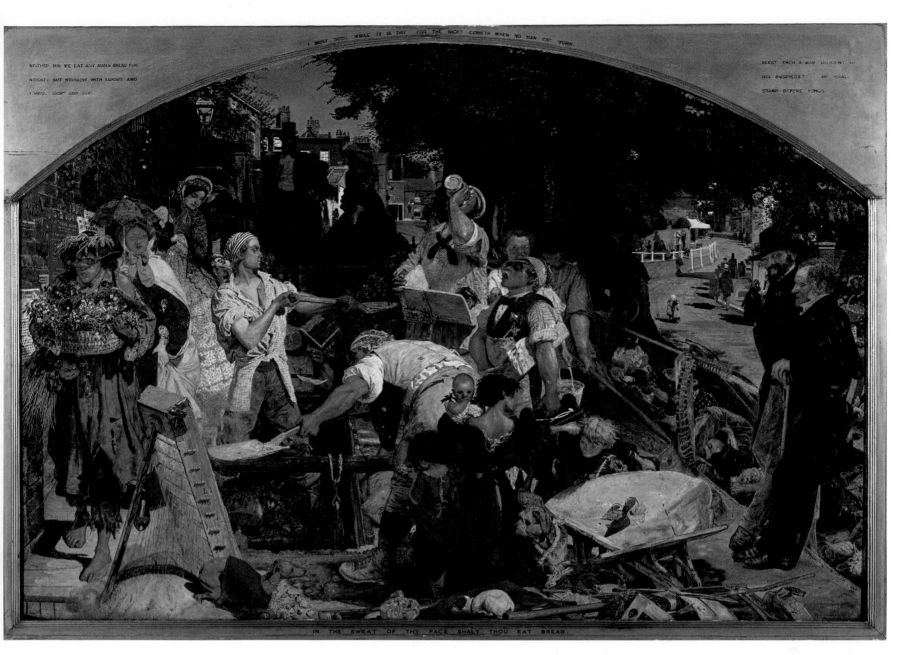

Ford Madox Brown
Work

Signed and dated 1852–65
Canvas 135 × 196 cm/53 × 77⅛ ins
Manchester City Art Gallery

Madox Brown worked for over twelve years, from 1852 to 1865, to produce *Work*, one of the mastcrpicccs of thc Prc-Raphaelite movement. It is one of the most intensely symbolic of all Victorian narrative pictures, intended as a homily in praise of the virtues of work of all kinds. The composition is crowded with figures symbolizing different classes of Victorian society, forms of work, and moralistic contrasts between labour and idleness. The picture was painted in Heath Street, Hampstead, near the artist's home, and the original inspiration was 'the British excavator, or navvy', a group of whom are at the centre of the composition.

and, when the flesh was being painted, on cold days. Absolutely without regard to the art of any period or country, I have tried to render this scene as it would appear.' The last sentence reflects the fearlessly honest search for reality so typical of Madox Brown, and of all the Pre-Raphaelites, especially Holman Hunt. *The Last of England* is a moving portrayal of those forced to leave their homeland by economic hardship, and has deservedly become one of the best-loved of all English paintings.

Brown was a great devotee of the writings of Thomas Carlyle, the most influential early Victorian writer on social problems, and especially admired his book *Past and Present*. What he has attempted in his picture, *Work*, is a kind of pictorial representation of Carlyle's social philosophy. Firstly, manual labour is represented by the group of labourers in the centre, 'as the outward and visible type of work'. Excavations were actually going on in Hampstead at this time, and Brown admired 'the British excavator, or navvy . . . in the full swing of his activity', thinking him just as fit a subject for painting 'as the fisherman of the Adriatic, the peasant of the Campagna, or the Neapolitan Lazzarone'. He thought their costume 'manly and picturesque' and he has posed them in deliberately heroic attitudes. Next to them is a carpenter, with bow tie and fancy waistcoat, and a copy of *The Times* under his arm. He represents the skilled craftsman, a cut above the labourer. In the background are a lady and gentleman on horseback, representing the leisured classes. Brown wrote that the man (modelled by the painter Robert Braithwaite Martineau) is meant to be 'very rich, probably a colonel in the army, with a seat in Parliament, and fifteen thousand a year and a pack of hounds'. The most difficult class to represent was the

49

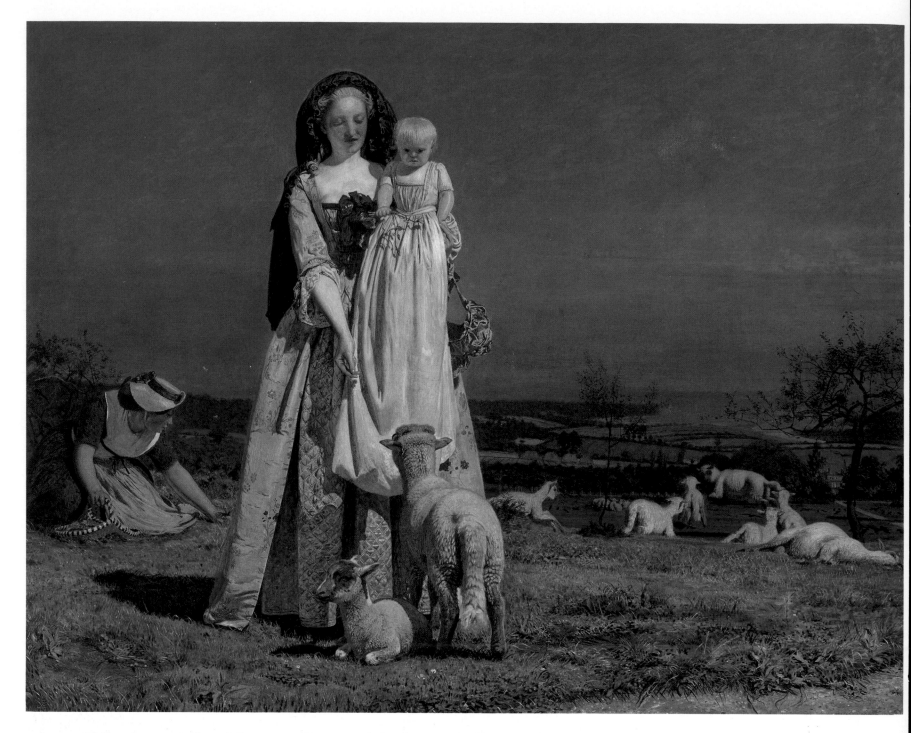

urban middle class – industrialists, merchants and bankers – and Brown has overcome this by including two smartly dressed middle-class ladies on the left. The younger one, with a parasol, was modelled from the artist's wife, and her 'only business in life is to dress and look beautiful for our benefit'. The other is engaged in distributing Temperance tracts, a favourite pastime of high-minded Victorian ladies. On the extreme left is a barefoot girl selling flowers; in the road on the right are orange-sellers and sandwich-board men, all of them representing that vast tribe of street traders so assiduously catalogued by Henry Mayhew in his historic book *London Labour and the London Poor*. Brown wrote that he intended these figures to typify 'town pluck and energy', in contrast to 'country thews and sinews'. Below the rail to the right are sleeping tramps, symbols of idleness, and in the foreground is a group of motherless children in the care of their elder sister. Leaning against the rail on the right are the intellectuals, or brain-workers; Carlyle, in the hat, and John Frederick Maurice, Christian Socialist and founder of the Working Men's Colleges. Almost every detail in the picture makes a moral point, including the terrier dog eyeing the pampered whippet, even down to the posters on the wall, which advertize a Boys' Home, a Working Men's College, a reward for information, and a fragment enigmatically inscribed 'Money! Money! Money!' The frame bears suitable biblical

Ford Madox Brown
The Pretty Baa-Lambs

Signed and dated 1851–59
Canvas 60 × 75 cm/$23\frac{1}{2}$ × $29\frac{1}{2}$ ins
Birmingham City Museum and Art Gallery

Brown's first important landscape in the Pre-Raphaelite style. It was painted at Stockwell, in south London, where the artist was then living, and exhibited at the Royal Academy in 1852. Brown wrote in his diary that the picture 'was painted almost entirely in sunlight which twice gave me a fever while painting . . . The lambs and sheep used to be brought every morning from Clapham Common in a truck; one of them ate up all the flowers one morning in the garden, and they used to behave very ill.' His wife and daughter modelled for the figures.

texts relating to work. The methods are basically those explored by Hunt in *The Awakening Conscience* (p. 42), but here applied to a very different purpose, and carried to far greater lengths. It is indeed the most intensely didactic, moralistic and allegorical of all Victorian narrative pictures. There is as much in it as the Ghent Altarpiece by Van Eyck, and indeed the way each figure is represented with his attributes has an obvious parallel in religious painting. As a work of art, the composition is too crowded for comfort, and it contains too many details and ideas. But it is nonetheless a major Pre-Raphaelite picture, and one of the most outstanding social realist pictures in English art.

Those who wish to emphasize the political and social intentions of the Pre-Raphaelites usually cite *The Last of England* and *Work* to support their argument. Both are to some degree protest pictures, but in both cases Brown has subordinated political aims to artistic ones. In neither picture do we feel that the artist is denouncing the capitalist system; he is simply trying to represent it on canvas. The radicalism of Madox Brown is artistic, not political. *Work* is a glorification of the virtues of work, something which every Englishman believed was the root cause of England's greatness. It is a picture more liable to excite patriotism than a desire for social revolution.

Brown's later career is peripheral to the Pre-Raphaelite story, although he lived until 1893. He taught at the Working Men's College, and he was also involved in design work for Morris and Company. He painted one or two other Pre-Raphaelite pictures in the 1850s, such as *'Take Your Son, Sir!'* and *Stages of Cruelty*. Both of these curious pictures reflect the taste for the grotesque, even macabre, that is never very far below the surface in Brown's art. The first shows a woman holding up her illegitimate baby to her seducer, and the second is an incomprehensible Hogarthian oddity. In time, Brown attained a reasonable level of financial security, and his house in Fitzroy Square became a noted rendezvous for artists and writers, subsequently recalled by his grandson and biographer, Ford Madox Ford. The later part of his career was mainly taken up with work on his twelve murals in Manchester Town Hall, which illustrate the history of the city. Considering their scale, these works are disappointingly mannered and uninspiring. The combination of a heroic style and local history is not a successful one, and Brown has allowed the eccentric and grotesque tendencies in his style too free a rein. However, Madox Brown retains his place as a seminal figure in the Pre-Raphaelite movement, and an artist of great power and originality.

Right: **Ford Madox Brown,** *Stages of Cruelty,* 1856–90. Far right: *'Take Your Son, Sir!'* (unfinished), 1852–92.

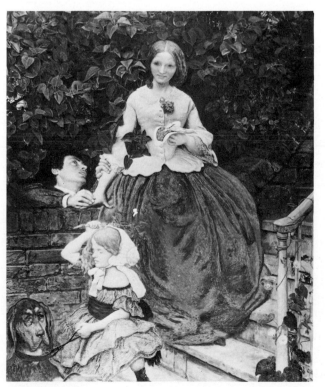

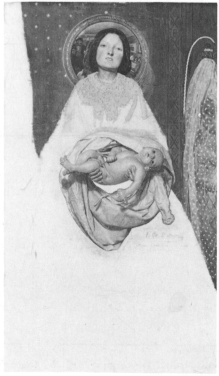

Arthur Hughes 1832–1915

Next to Madox Brown, Arthur Hughes was the most important Pre-Raphaelite follower outside the Brotherhood. Like Brown, he painted some of the best-loved and most familiar masterpieces of the entire movement. Hughes was a modest man, of a shy and retiring nature, and very little is known of his life or his opinions about art. He was a follower by nature, content to imitate and develop the ideas of others – in particular those of Millais – which he did with a subtle and delicate individuality. Between 1852 and 1863 he painted a succession of Pre-Raphaelite masterpieces, which can stand comparison with anything produced by the Brotherhood. An exhibition of his work was held in London in 1971, and since then a number of important pictures have appeared on the art market. This has had the effect of restoring Hughes to his rightful place as a major figure in the Pre-Raphaelite movement.

Hughes was born in London, and in 1846 he entered the School of Design at Somerset House, where he studied under Alfred Stevens. In 1847 he moved to the Royal Academy Schools, where he won a silver medal in 1849 for drawing from the antique. 1850 was a crucial turning-point in his career. He saw a copy of *The Germ* and was so impressed by it that he sought the acquaintance of Rossetti, Hunt and Madox Brown. From then on he was a convert to Pre-Raphaelitism. His first work in the new style was *Ophelia* (below), exhibited at the Royal Academy Exhibition of 1852. By coincidence, Millais' *Ophelia* (p. 33) was exhibited in the same year, but Hughes did not meet Millais until varnishing day before the Academy opened. It was on Millais that Hughes was to model his own style, and many of his pictures are variations on Millais' themes. His next major work was *The Eve of Saint Agnes* (p. 53), a subject painted not by Millais, but by Hunt in 1848. The style of the picture is a throwback to historical pictures of the 1840s, but the details and colouring are pure Pre-Raphaelite, especially the moonlight effects and the stained glass.

In 1856, Hughes exhibited at the Royal Academy what has now become one of his

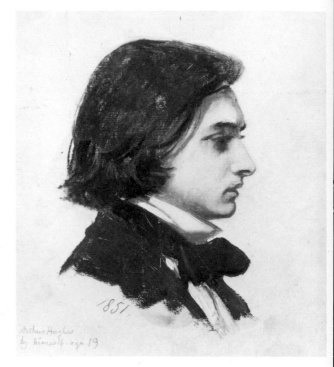

Arthur Hughes, self-portrait, 1851.

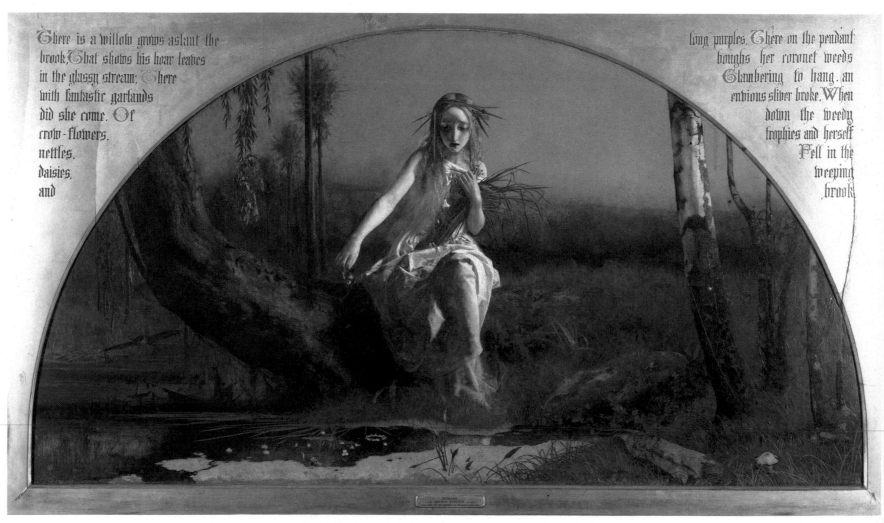

There is a willow grows aslant the brook, That shows his hoar leaves in the glassy stream; There with fantastic garlands did she come. Of crow-flowers, nettles, daisies, and long purples. There on the pendant boughs her coronet weeds Clambering to hang, an envious sliver broke. When down the weedy trophies and herself Fell in the weeping brook.

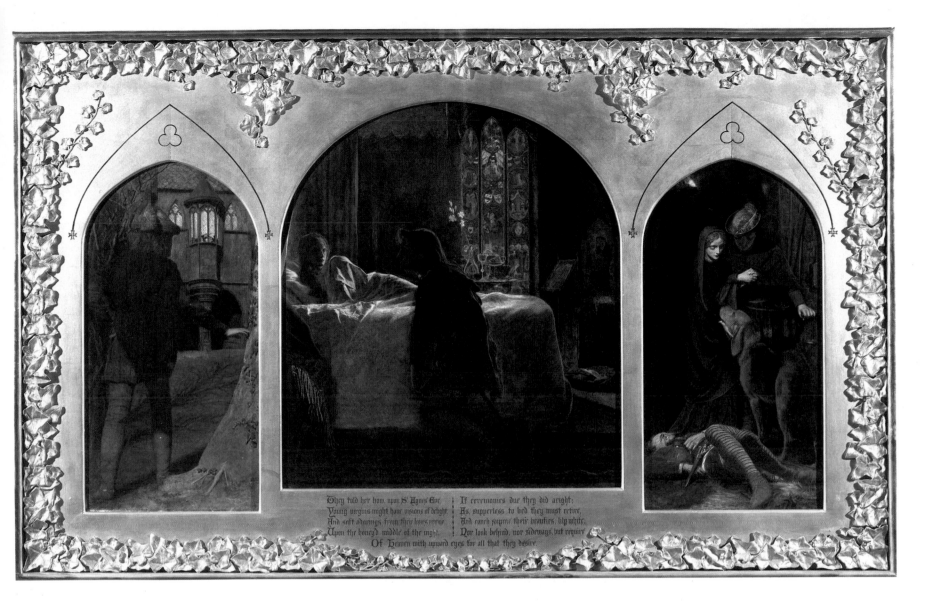

The three panels below the central image read:

They told her how, upon St Agnes' Eve, | If ceremonies due they did aright;
Young virgins might have visions of delight, | As, supperless to bed they must retire,
And soft adorings from their loves receive | And couch supine their beauties, lily white;
Upon the honey'd middle of the night, | Nor look behind, nor sideways, but require
Of Heaven with upward eyes for all that they desire.

Arthur Hughes (1832–1915)
The Eve of Saint Agnes

1856
Canvas, triptych, centre 64 × 57 cm/25½ × 22¼ ins,
sides 59 × 30 cm/23¼ × 11¾ ins
Tate Gallery, London

Keats was a great source of inspiration to all the Pre-Raphaelites, and to Hunt in particular. Hunt painted *The Eve of Saint Agnes* in 1848 which undoubtedly provided the inspiration for Hughes' equally fine version, exhibited at the Royal Academy in 1856. The three scenes depict Porphyro's approach to the castle, his awakening of Madeline in her bedchamber, and the lovers escaping, tiptoeing past the drunken porter. The three panels are combined in a magnificent frame, almost certainly designed by Hughes himself.

(Opposite)
Ophelia

Signed, 1852
Canvas, arched top 69 × 124 cm/27 × 48¾ ins
Manchester City Art Gallery

Doomed love is once again the theme of Hughes' version of *Ophelia*, an unusually powerful and haunting picture. Hughes has depicted Ophelia sitting beside the stream, rather than drowning in it. The yellow slime on the water, and the bat hovering above it make the landscape especially haunting and eerie.

best-known and best-loved pictures, *April Love* (p. 54). Ruskin wrote of *April Love* that it was 'Exquisite in every way; lovely in colour, most subtle the quivering expression of the lips, and sweetness of the tender face, shaken like a leaf by winds upon its dew, and hesitating back into peace.' The detail and colouring are as brilliant as any Millais, and romantic love was a theme perfectly suited to Hughes' talents. Whereas many Pre-Raphaelite pictures on the theme of love are tragic, passionate and guilt-ridden, the mood of Hughes' pictures is always sad, wistful and tender. Also characteristic of Hughes was his method of using the landscape setting to heighten and intensify the emotional situation of the figures. This was a technique which Hughes employed in practically all his pictures, and nowhere is it more telling than in *April Love*. It appears also in *The Long Engagement*, another well-known Hughes picture, which captures with tender pathos the plight of those unfortunate, dutiful Victorian lovers condemned by their parents to lengthy engagements.

Hughes himself had to wait five years before marrying Miss Tryphena Foord in 1855. They had met in 1850, and the marriage was to be a very happy one which produced five children. In 1857, Hughes was one of the artists who joined Rossetti, Burne-Jones and Morris in painting the Oxford murals. This experience had the effect of increasing the influence of Rossetti on Hughes' own paintings. He began to paint romantic Arthurian subjects, such as *The Brave Geraint* (p. 57) and *The Knight of the Sun* (p. 55), in which the mood and colouring are softer and more mysterious. His later religious works, such as *The Nativity* and *The Annunciation* (p. 56), have a mystical, Symbolist feeling which owes much to the influence of Rossetti, and through him, of Blake.

In 1858 Hughes and his family moved out of the centre of London to the suburbs, thus severing himself from direct contact with his colleagues, and from

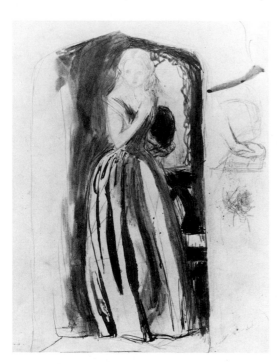

Arthur Hughes, study for *April Love*, undated.

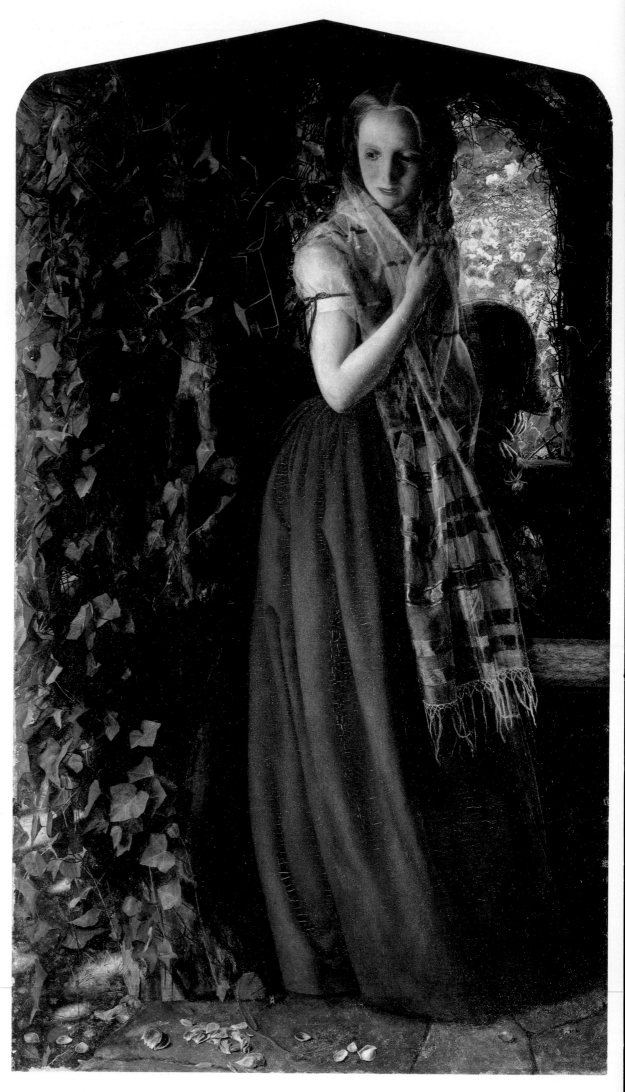

developments in the Pre-Raphaelite movement. In the end this was to have a debilitating effect on Hughes' art, but for a few years he continued to paint Pre-Raphaelite pictures of the highest quality.

During the 1860s Hughes also began to paint narrative pictures of Victorian life, which often included children. In these pictures he combines Pre-Raphaelite detail and colouring with themes that are typical of the mainstream of Victorian narrative

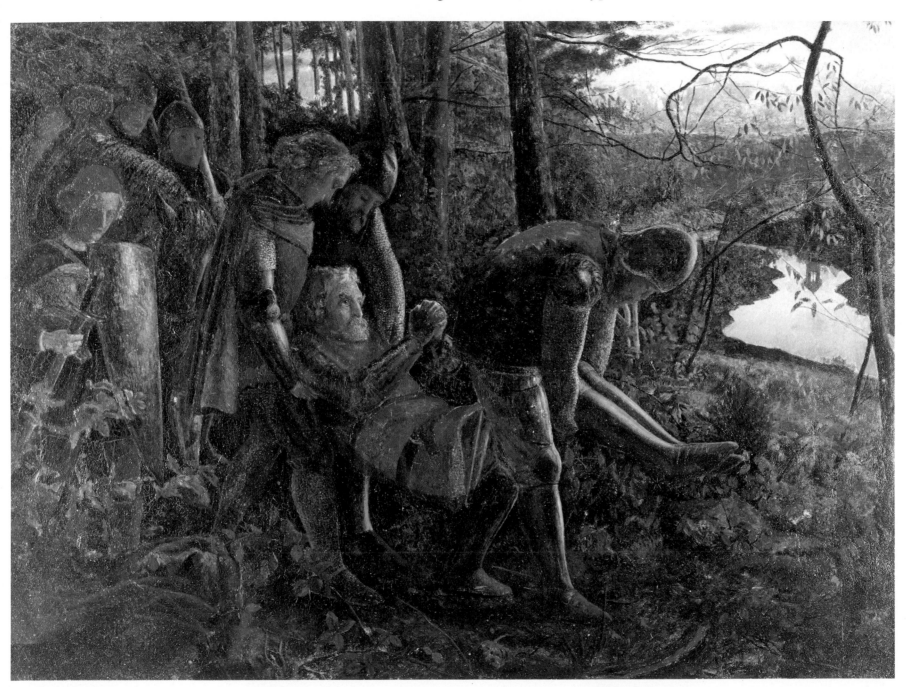

Arthur Hughes
April Love

Signed, 1855–56
Canvas, arched top 89 × 50 cm/35 × 19½ ins
Tate Gallery, London

Exhibited at the Royal Academy of 1856 with a quotation from Tennyson's *The Miller's Daughter*:

Love is hurt with jar and fret,
Love is made a vague regret,
Eyes with idle tears are set,
Idle habit links us yet;
What is love? For we forget.
Ah no, no.

Arthur Hughes
The Knight of the Sun

Signed
Oil on panel 28 × 39 cm/11 × 15½ ins
Private Collection

A sketch for a larger picture, commissioned by the Leeds collector, Thomas Plint, which later entered the collection of William Graham. It depicts a dying knight in armour, who is being carried out to look at the sun and sky. The landscape is beautifully painted, and the whole composition is one of Hughes' finest and most romantic conceptions. Although very little known, it deserves to be grouped with Hughes' best work.

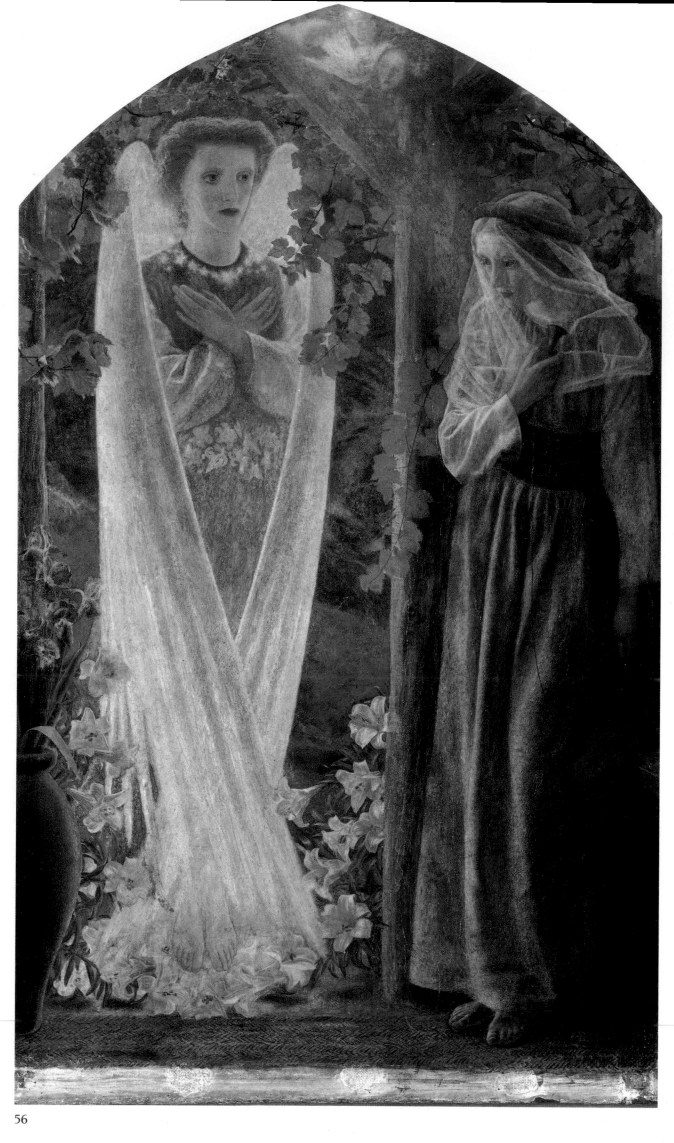

Arthur Hughes
The Annunciation

Signed, 1858
Canvas 57 × 34 cm/$22\frac{3}{8}$ × $13\frac{1}{4}$ ins
Birmingham City Museum and Art Gallery

Hughes worked with Rossetti on the Oxford murals, and the influence of Rossetti, and through him of Blake, is clearly visible in this picture. Hughes painted a number of religious subjects, notable for their intense, visionary quality, very similar to some of Rossetti's best work. But the bright, pure colours, and the detailed accessories are more reminiscent of Millais or Hunt.

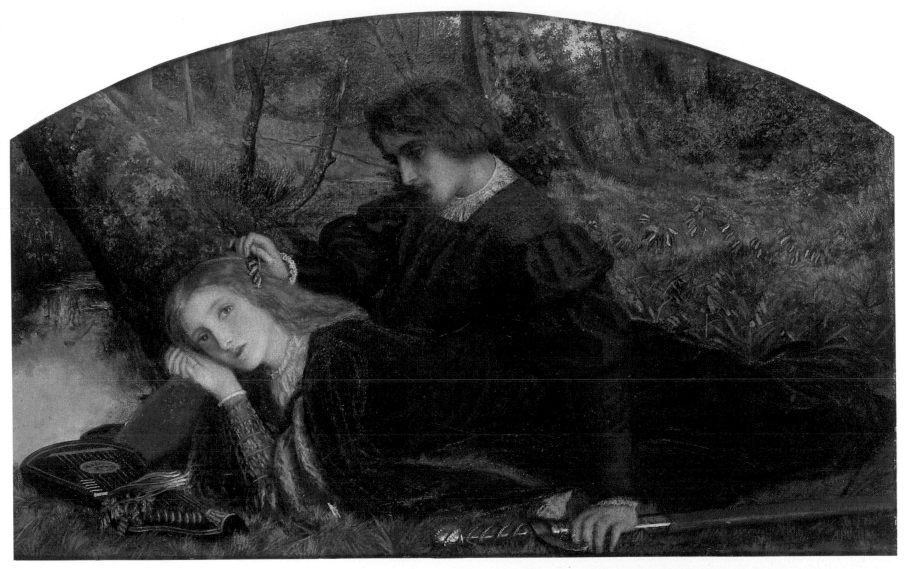

Arthur Hughes
The Brave Geraint (Geraint and Enid)

*c*1860
Canvas, arched top 23 × 36 cm/9 × 14 ins
Lady Anne Tennant

Another of Hughes' tender love scenes, here of
lovers from the Arthurian legends. Rossetti and
Burne-Jones were by now painting scenes from the
Morte d'Arthur, but Hughes' delicate and
sentimental treatment of the theme is quite different
from theirs, and closer to Millais' historical pictures,
such as *The Huguenot* or *The Black Brunswicker*. The
idea of doomed lovers was a constant theme in the
Pre-Raphaelite movement.

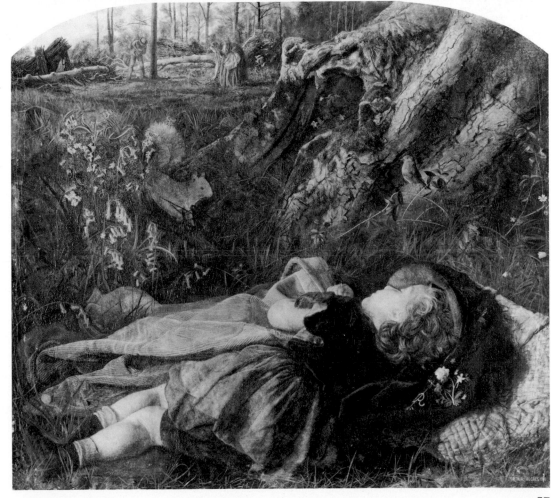

Arthur Hughes, *The Woodman's Child*, 1860.

57

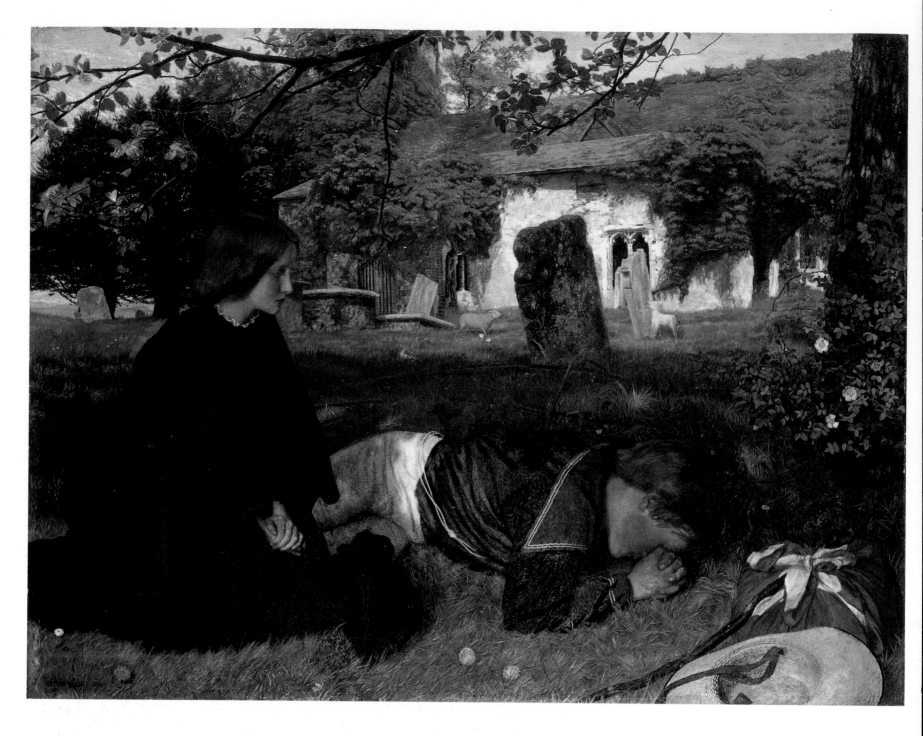

art. The most famous of them is *Home from the Sea* (above), but he painted many others, such as *The Woodman's Child* (1860) and *Home from Work* (1861). Reverence for country life, and the love of parents for their children are the themes that permeate these paintings, and this type of picture was to be frequently imitated during the 1860s.

After 1870 Hughes continued to paint in the same style, but something of the poetry and intensity of his earlier work was lacking. He made a few designs for Morris and Company, and he was also a fine book illustrator. He painted some delightful family portraits, particularly those of the family of James Leathart, the eminent Newcastle collector and patron. Hughes also turned to landscape painting, particularly coastal scenes, which sometimes show a brilliance of colour reminiscent of his pictures of the 1850s and '60s. The technique, however, is broader; Hughes, like Millais, abandoned the meticulous Pre-Raphaelite finish of his earlier period. Although some of his later work is less powerful, it is certainly a mistake to dismiss all Hughes' work after 1870, as some writers have done. He is an artist of rare poetic and imaginative ability, and if his late works are sometimes only an echo of Pre-Raphaelitism, it must be to his credit that he, like Holman Hunt, remained faithful to its principles.

Arthur Hughes
Home from the Sea

Signed and dated 1863
Oil on panel 51 × 65 cm/20 × 25¾ ins
Ashmolean Museum, Oxford

A sailor boy has come back from the sea to find that his mother has died. With his sister he is sorrowing at her grave. The picture was begun in 1856, in the old churchyard at Chingford in Essex. At first the picture contained only the figure of the boy, and was entitled *A Mother's Grave*; later the sister was added, and the title was changed.

Other Pre-Raphaelite followers of the 1850s

As the Pre-Raphaelite movement gathered strength, so the numbers of its followers and imitators increased. In 1855 a number of Pre-Raphaelite pictures were shown at the *Exposition Universelle* in Paris, where they were enthusiastically received. By 1856, Ruskin was able to write in his annual *Academy Notes*, 'animosity has changed into emulation, astonishment into sympathy, and ... a true and consistent school of art is at last established in the Royal Academy of England.' During the 1850s a great number of artists, particularly young ones, were attracted to the Pre-Raphaelite banner. For some, the influence was only temporary, resulting in one or two Pre-Raphaelite pictures; for others, it lasted longer. All of them followed different aspects of the movement, developing those themes and ideas which most appealed to them.

During the period of the Brotherhood, the main associates were Ford Madox Brown, Arthur Hughes, Charles Allston Collins, and Walter Howell Deverell. Two older Academicians who gave friendly help and support to the movement were Augustus Leopold Egg and William Dyce. Egg was mainly a painter of costume pieces on literary or historical themes, but he sympathized with the Brotherhood, and commissioned *Claudio and Isabella* (p. 19) from Holman Hunt in 1850. Egg's own work began to show Pre-Raphaelite influence in its detail and colouring, and his series, *Past and Present*, is a set of three moralistic modern-life scenes on the theme of marital infidelity, which clearly reflect the influence of Hunt's *Awakening Conscience* (p. 42). Pre-Raphaelite influence was even greater in the case of William Dyce, who, as a young man, visited Rome and was strongly influenced by the Nazarenes. In 1850 it was Dyce who took Ruskin's arm at the Royal Academy, and made him look again at Millais' *The Carpenter's Shop* (p. 17). But his own works were later criticized by Ruskin for their Italianate style, and lack of natural detail. Dyce took this to heart, and in 1857 produced *Titian's First Essay in Colour* (p. 60), one of his outstanding Pre-Raphaelite works. This certainly proved that Dyce could paint in Ruskinian style, and the clarity of detail is almost as penetrating as that of Holman Hunt. Dyce

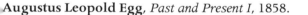

Augustus Leopold Egg, *Past and Present I*, 1858.

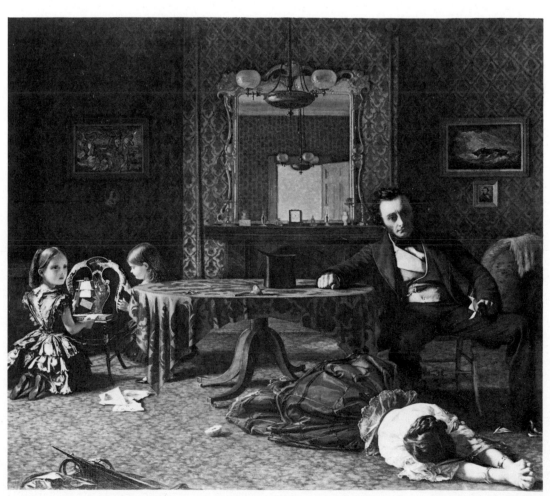

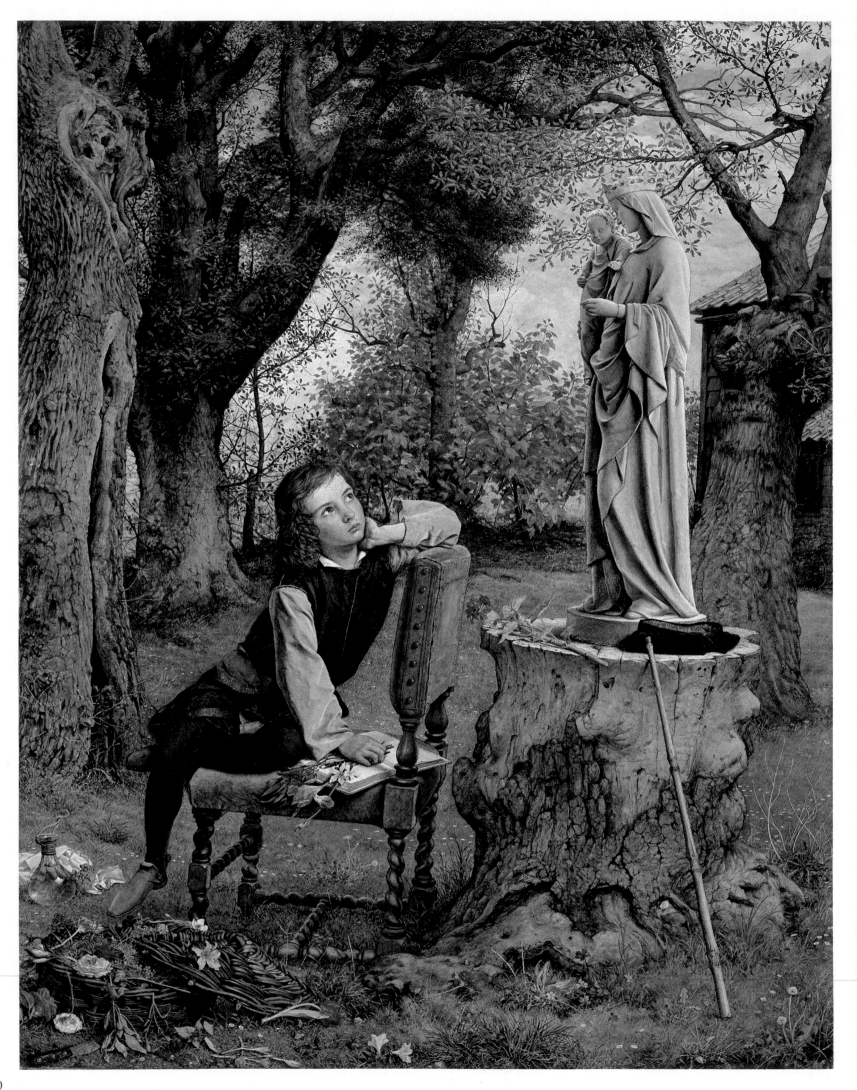

William Dyce (1806–1864)
Titian's First Essay in Colour

1856–57
Canvas 91 × 70 cm/36 × 27¾ ins
Aberdeen Art Gallery

Dyce came from the generation of artists before the Pre-Raphaelites, but he was influenced by their ideas and techniques during the 1850s. He was also a friend and admirer of Ruskin, and his landscapes are among the most outstanding of all Pre-Raphaelite works of this type. In this picture of the young Titian colouring a drawing of a Madonna with the juice of flowers, the details are painted with astonishing accuracy.

William Dyce, George Herbert at Bemerton, 1861.

followed this up with *George Herbert at Bemerton* (1861), but his greatest contribution was to landscape painting, which will be dealt with later.

A similar example of Pre-Raphaelite realism applied to a historical subject is *The Wounded Cavalier* (p. 62) by William Shakespeare Burton. This astonishing feat of naturalistic detail is Burton's only known Pre-Raphaelite work. He later turned to religious work, of an intense, rather Symbolist type. Another obscure figure is John S. Clifton, whose picture, *Love* (p. 63), also follows the romantic, historical style of the Pre-Raphaelites. Both are typical pictures inspired by the Pre-Raphaelites in the mid-1850s, and more examples of this kind may well come to light.

Pre-Raphaelite influence was equally brief in the case of Henry Wallis. Unlike the other Pre-Raphaelites, Wallis studied in Paris as well as London, but there is little evidence of Continental training in his first and most famous picture, *The Death of Chatterton* (p. 68). This haunting and memorable image of the dead poet has rightly become one of the most popular of all Pre-Raphaelite pictures, and it created a sensation at the Royal Academy Exhibition of 1856. Wallis may perhaps have intended it as a criticism of society's treatment of artists, because his next picture of note, *The Stonebreaker* (p. 64), was to be one of the most intensely socialistic pictures of the nineteenth century. Ruskin described it as 'the picture of the year'. Wallis painted one or two other pictures in Pre-Raphaelite style, but this phase of his career

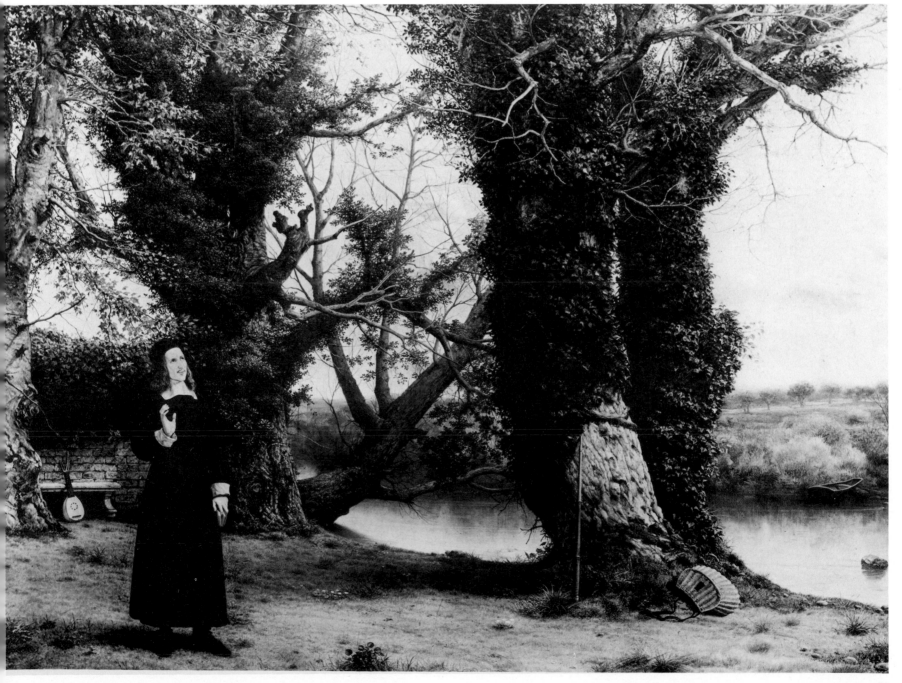

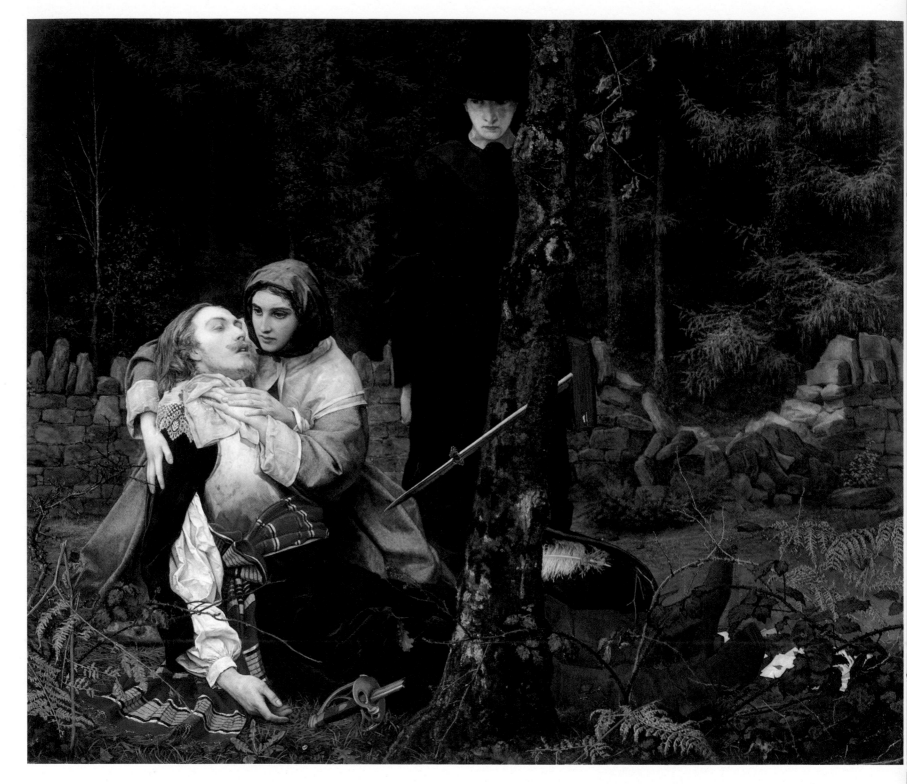

William Shakespeare Burton (1824–1916)
The Wounded Cavalier

Exhibited at the Royal Academy, 1856
Canvas 89 × 104 cm/35 × 41 ins
Guildhall Art Gallery, London

This picture caused a sensation at the Royal
Academy in 1856. It depicts a wounded cavalier,
whose despatches have been stolen, being
succoured by a Puritan girl, whose jealous lover,
carrying a large Bible, looks on with disapproval.
The foreground details are painted with astonishing
precision, and the artist is said to have dug a hole for
himself and his easel, so that he could be closer to
the ferns and daisies that he was painting. Because
the picture lacked a label, it was nearly rejected by
the Academy, but the painter Charles West Cope
withdrew one of his own pictures to make way for it.

John S. Clifton (fl. 1852–1869)
Love

Signed and indistinctly dated 185–
Canvas 107 × 84 cm/42 × 33 ins
Private Collection

Clifton was one of the many artists during the 1850s
to be converted to the Pre-Raphaelite style. His
romantic, medievalizing style is closest to Ford
Madox Brown, although the colours show the
influence of Millais and Arthur Hughes. The picture
was exhibited with the title 'Love' and a long poem
by Samuel Taylor Coleridge. Clifton is very little
known, and exhibited only a few pictures during
the 1850s, after which, like many minor Pre-
Raphaelites, he disappeared from the artistic scene.

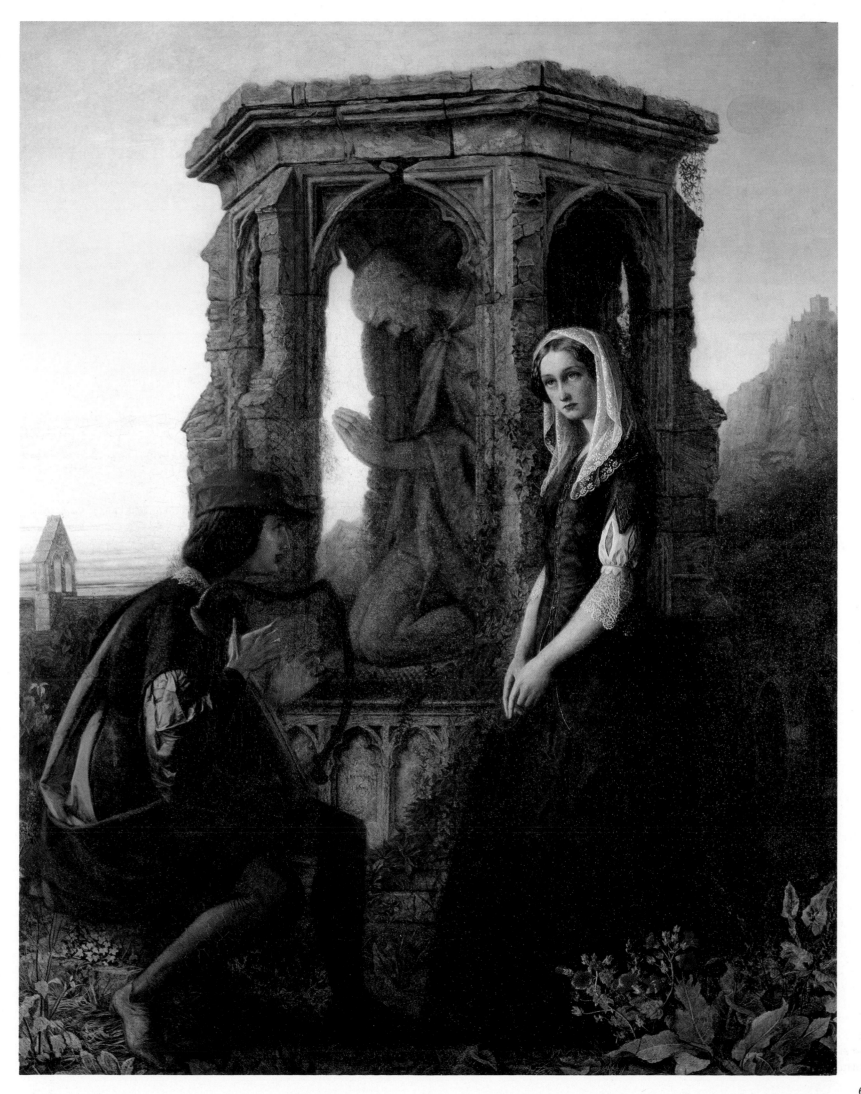

came to an abrupt close in 1858, when he eloped with the wife of the novelist and poet, George Meredith. Thereafter Wallis spent much of his time travelling and living abroad, and he never returned to painting seriously again. He did, however, paint watercolours on his travels, and became a member of the Old Watercolour Society in 1880, but his later works are not at all Pre-Raphaelite in character. Wallis was a man of private means, and devoted himself to the study of ceramics, in which he became a great expert. He is perhaps the most extreme example of an artist who, inspired by the Pre-Raphaelite style, produced a small number of fine pictures, then, having lost interest, passed on to other things. This was a familiar pattern in the 1850s, and applied to many other artists.

In the case of John Brett, however, his conversion to the Pre-Raphaelite style was to be long-lasting and fruitful. Brett was the son of an army officer and entered the Royal Academy Schools at the late age of 23. At first he painted portraits, but in 1856 he met the landscape painter John William Inchbold in Switzerland. In Brett's own words, 'I there and then saw that I had never painted in my life, but only fooled and slopped, and thence forward attempted in a reasonable way to paint all I could see.'

Henry Wallis (1830–1916)
The Stonebreaker

Signed and dated 1857
Oil on panel 64 × 79 cm/25¾ × 31 ins
Birmingham City Museum and Art Gallery

Stonebreaking was regarded in the nineteenth century as the most degrading form of physical labour, usually done by convicts or inmates of workhouses. Wallis's picture, exhibited at the Royal Academy in 1858 without a title, but with a long quotation from Carlyle's *Sartor Resartus* beginning 'Hardly entreated, brother! . . .' is one of the most gloomy social realist pictures of the Pre-Raphaelite movement. In a landscape of haunting and melancholy beauty, the stonebreaker lies dead on a heap of stones, almost seeming to blend into the earth itself, and a stoat warily approaches his foot.

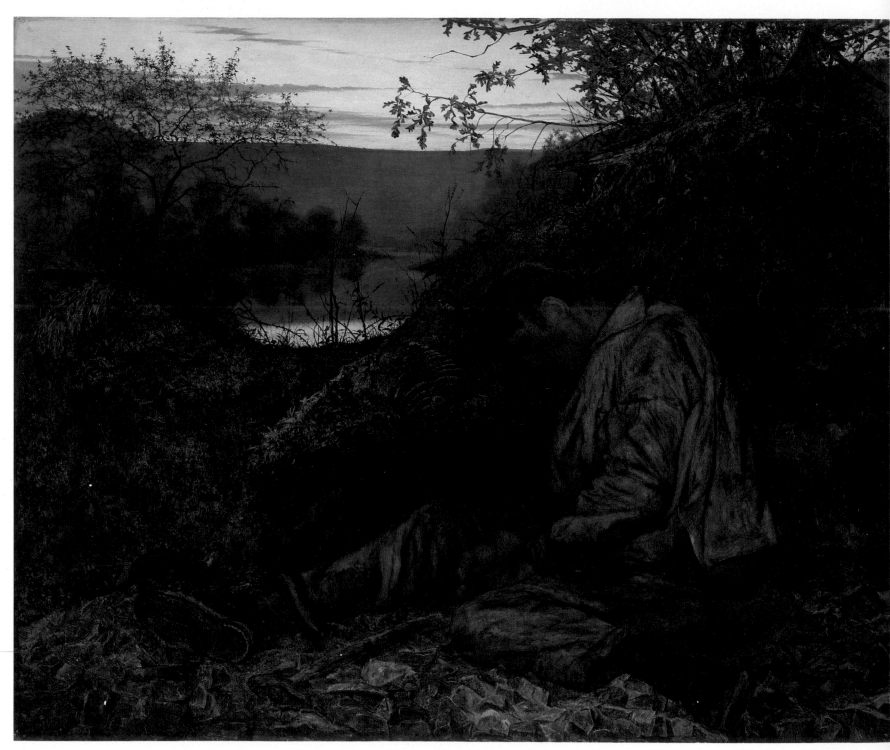

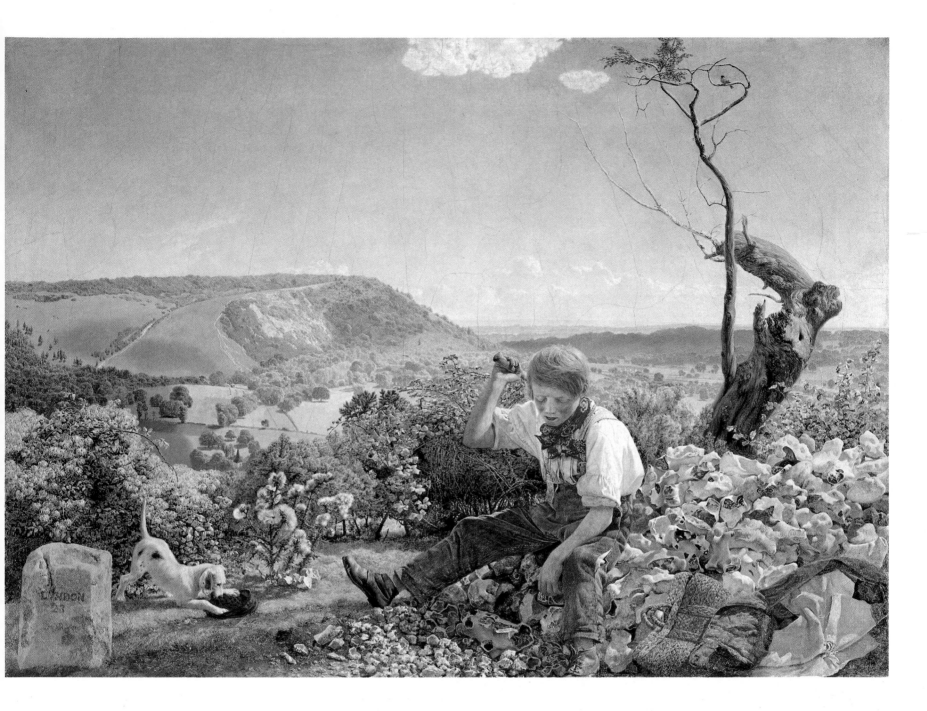

John Brett (1830–1902)
The Stonebreaker

Signed and dated 1857–58
Canvas 50 × 68 cm/19½ × 26⅞ ins
Walker Art Gallery, Liverpool

Exhibited at the Royal Academy in 1858, and praised by Ruskin as 'simply the most perfect piece of painting with respect to touch in the Academy this year'. Brett's stonebreaker is a cheerful and healthy boy, with a dog, sitting amid a landscape of quite striking detail and beauty. It was painted at Box Hill, Surrey, and the milestone reads '23 miles to London'. The contrast between this and Henry Wallis's *Stonebreaker,* exhibited at the Royal Academy in the same year, could hardly be greater. Ruskin also exhorted Brett to paint the chestnut groves of the Val d'Aosta, and the artist dutifully left for Italy a month later.

The first fruits of his conversion to Pre-Raphaelite landscape were *The Glacier at Rosenlaui,* an intensely Ruskinian study of rocks and snow. His next picture of importance was *The Stonebreaker* (above), which, by a curious coincidence, was exhibited at the Royal Academy in 1858, the same year as Wallis's *Stonebreaker.* Brett's picture has an idyllic air of rustic innocence, far removed from the tragic gloom of Wallis's version. The social message, if any was intended, is completely overshadowed by the beauty of the landscape. Ruskin praised both pictures lavishly, and proceeded to take Brett under his wing. Like Ruskin, Brett had scientific interests, and his minute painting of rocks and flowers must have recommended him to Ruskin as a suitable pupil. The relationship was to prove a difficult and not entirely successful one, but provides an interesting example of Ruskin's influence over a young artist.

During the later 1850s, there were many older Academy artists, like Egg and Dyce, who flirted briefly with Pre-Raphaelite ideas. Although he hotly denied it, William Powell Frith was certainly influenced by the Pre-Raphaelites in turning to modern-life subjects, and his technique becomes noticeably Pre-Raphaelite in the 1850s. Another artist in this category was William Maw Egley, mainly a painter of literary and historical subjects. From 1855 to about 1862, he turned to modern-life subjects, in particular the well-known *Omnibus Life in London.* In 1857 he painted *The Talking Oak* (p. 67), a romantic Tennysonian subject very much in the manner of Millais and

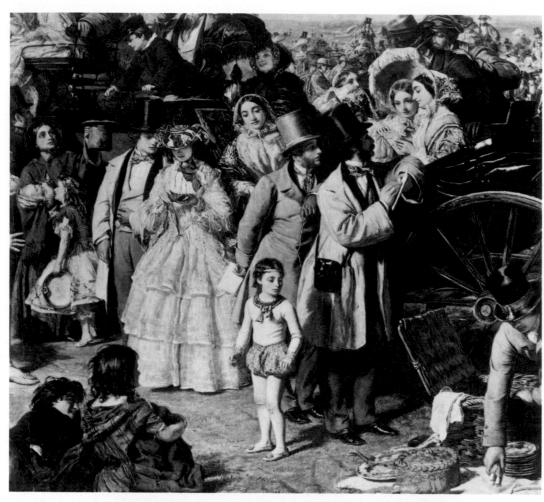

Above: **William Powell Frith**, *Derby Day* (detail), 1858. Below: **William Maw Egley**, *Omnibus Life in London*, 1852.

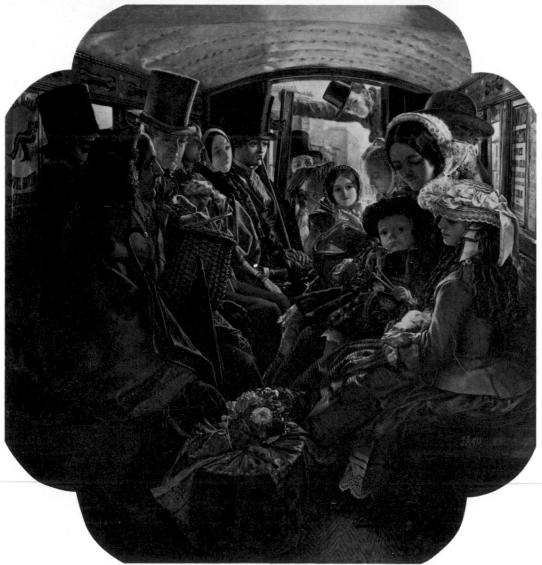

William Maw Egley (1826–1916)
The Talking Oak

Signed and dated 1857
Canvas 74 × 61 cm/29 × 24 ins
Detroit Institute of Arts

Exhibited at the British Institution in 1857 with a quotation from Tennyson:

But tell me, did she read the name
I carved with many vows?

Although Egley flirted only briefly with Pre-Raphaelite subjects and ideas, the intense detail and meticulously high finish of all his pictures reflect the influence of Pre-Raphaelite technique.

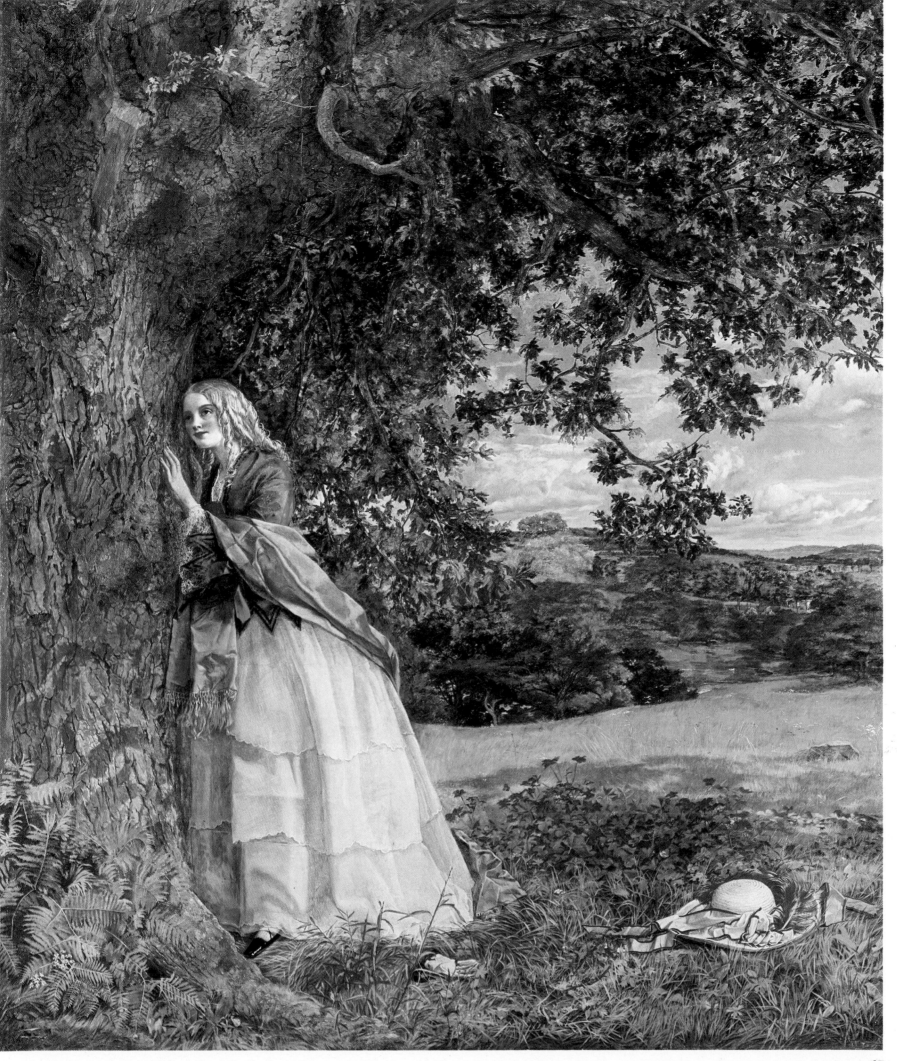

Arthur Hughes. Henry Alexander Bowler also chose a subject from Tennyson with his well-known *The Doubt: 'Can these dry bones live?'* (p. 69). Bowler was primarily an art teacher, and did not have much time for painting. *The Doubt* is his only important picture, but he did paint landscapes in the 1850s and 60s which also show Pre-Raphaelite influence. Michael Frederick Halliday was an amateur artist, who shared a studio for a time with Holman Hunt. His only well-known work is *The Measure for the Wedding Ring* (p. 70), a romantic tryst picture which shows affinities with both

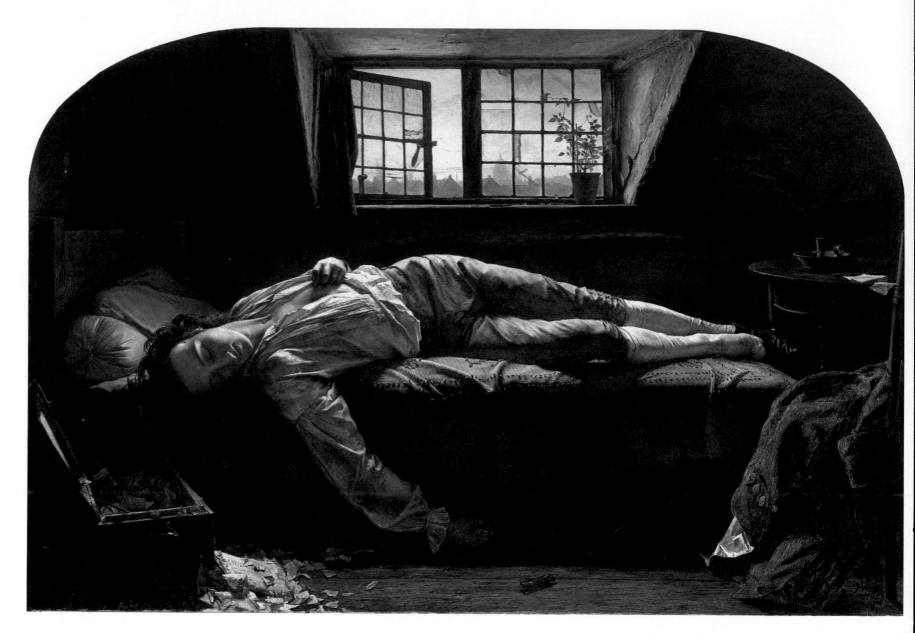

Henry Wallis
The Death of Chatterton

Signed and dated 1856
Canvas, arched top 60×91 cm/$23\frac{3}{4} \times 35\frac{3}{4}$ ins
Tate Gallery, London

Exhibited at the Royal Academy in 1856 with a quotation from Marlowe:

Cut is the branch that might have grown full straight
And burned is Apollo's laurel bough.

Chatterton was an eighteenth-century boy poet who committed suicide, and Wallis painted the picture in the actual attic in Gray's Inn where the poet died. The model for the figure was the novelist George Meredith, then aged about twenty-eight. Two years later Wallis eloped with Meredith's wife, a daughter of the novelist Thomas Love Peacock.

Henry Alexander Bowler (1824–1903)
The Doubt: 'Can these dry bones live?'

Exhibited 1855
Canvas 61×51 cm/24×20 ins
Tate Gallery, London

Exhibited at the Royal Academy in 1855, and intended as an illustration to Tennyson's poem, *In Memoriam*, the theme of which is religious faith assailed by doubt. The artist's answer to the rhetorical title is provided by the inscription *Resurgam* on the grave slab, on which lies a germinating chestnut. The Victorians were fond of pictures of girls in churchyards, but this is the only one which attempts to realize on canvas the religious doubts that lurked beneath the surface of mid-Victorian complacency. Bowler was mainly an art teacher, and this is his only well-known picture.

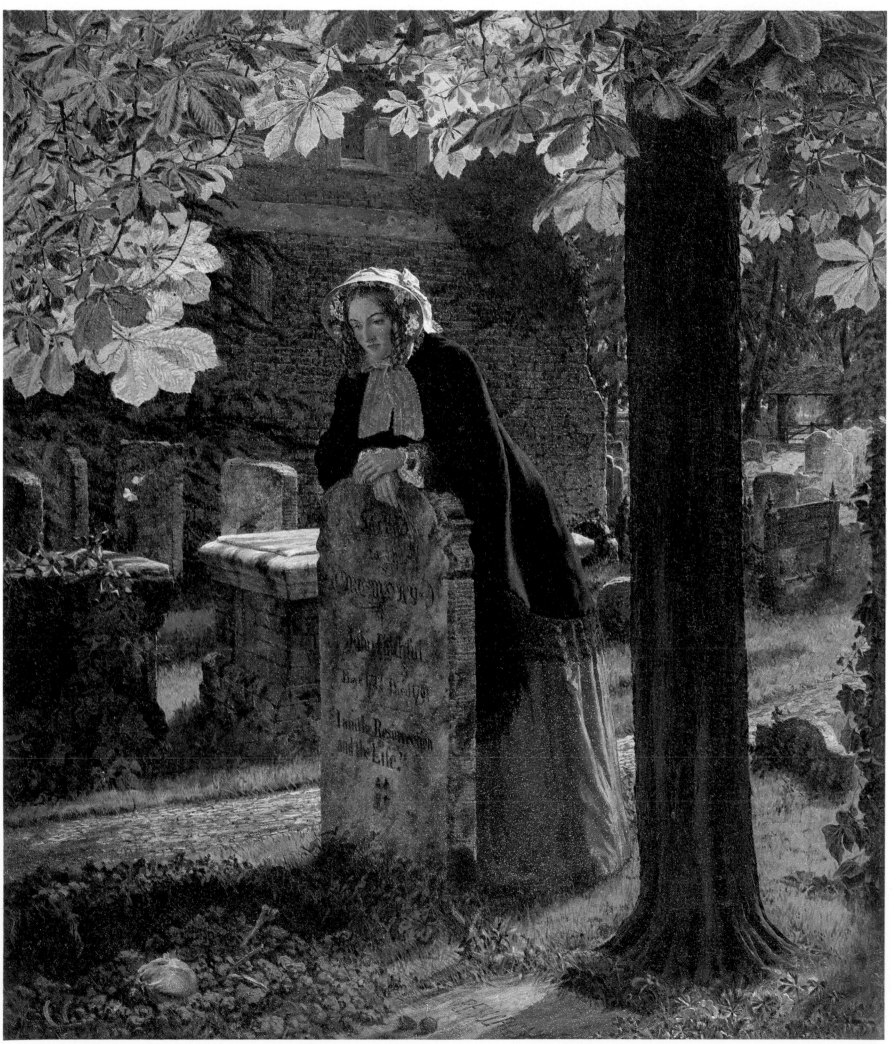

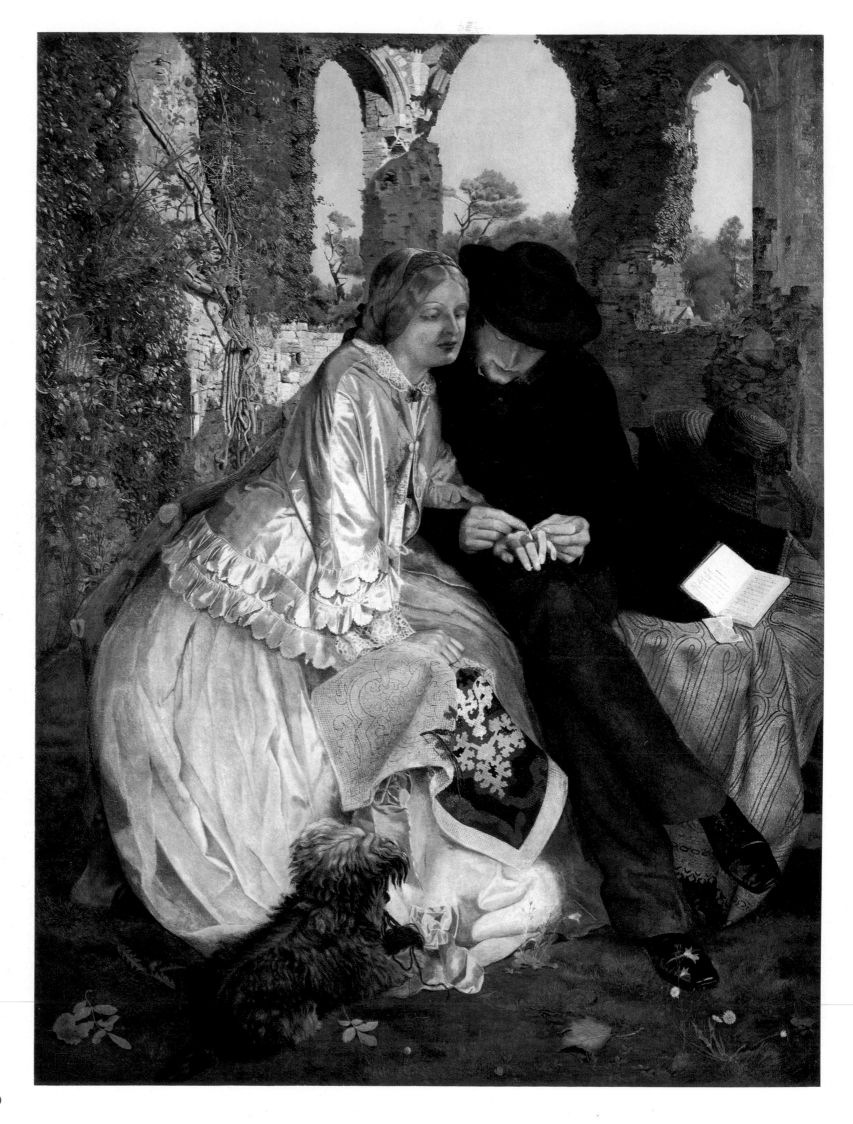

Michael Frederick Halliday (1822–1869)
The Measure for the Wedding Ring

Signed and dated 1855
Canvas 90 × 68 cm/35½ × 26¾ ins
Private Collection

Exhibited at the Royal Academy in 1856. Halliday was a close friend of Holman Hunt, and for a time they shared a studio. This is Halliday's best-known picture, and Millais is known to have helped him paint the landscape background. The mood of the picture is similar to some of Arthur Hughes's tryst subjects, such as *April Love*, which was painted in the same year.

Robert Braithwaite Martineau, *Kit's Writing Lesson*, 1852.

Hughes and Madox Brown. Another friend and pupil of Hunt was Robert Braithwaite Martineau, now best known for his *The Last Day in the Old Home* (p. 72). This is one of the most intensely novelistic of all Victorian pictures, and combines the narrative methods of Frith with the moralistic approach of Holman Hunt. Martineau painted a number of interesting Pre-Raphaelite pictures, such as *Kit's Writing Lesson*, and for a time shared a studio with Hunt and Halliday. Unfortunately he died in 1869 at the age of only 43, thus ending a promising career.

Richard Redgrave was another older Academician sympathetic to the Brotherhood. He is significant as the pioneer of social subjects in the 1840s, and his pictures of governesses and seamstresses are the precursors of the modern-life subjects of the Pre-Raphaelites, in particular Hunt's *Awakening Conscience*. Like Dyce and Bowler, Redgrave was heavily involved in art teaching and administration, and did not have much time for painting. In the 1850s he continued to paint occasional subjects, combining them with an interest in Pre-Raphaelite landscape. An outstanding example of his work at this period is *The Emigrant's Last Sight of Home* (p. 74), a beautiful picture on the theme of emigration, which deserves to be as well-known as Brown's *Last of England* (p. 11). Redgrave continued to paint landscapes and country scenes, but none so fine as this.

The Pre-Raphaelites also made important converts in the provinces. Liverpool was the most important centre of activity, but in Newcastle there was William Bell Scott who was master of the Government School of Design there. Scott was also a poet, and

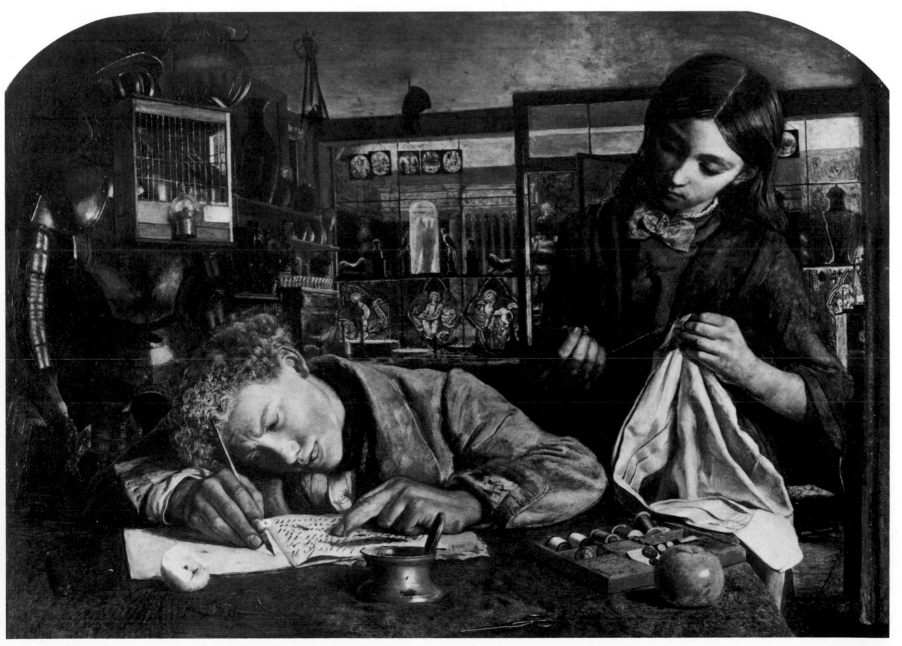

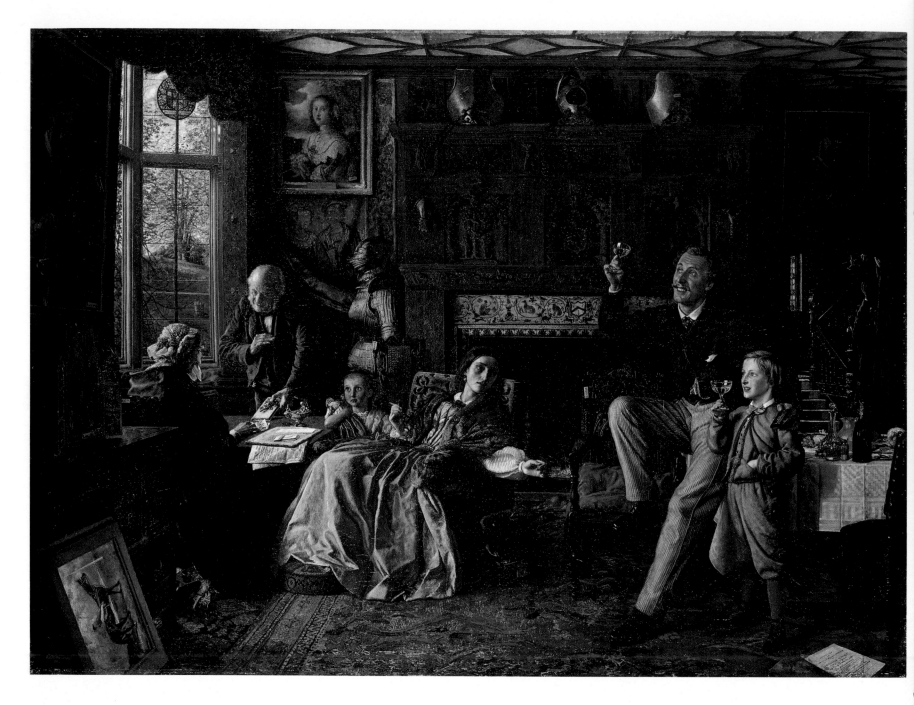

Robert Braithwaite Martineau
(1826–1869)
The Last Day in the Old Home

Signed and dated 1861
Canvas 108 × 145 cm/42½ × 57 ins
Tate Gallery, London

Martineau was a close friend of Holman Hunt, and
shared his interest in modern-life pictures with a
moral message. This moral tale shows a feckless
young aristocrat, who has gambled away everything
on the horses, now drinking his last glass of
champagne in the ancestral home. It is one of the
outstanding examples of the Victorian narrative
picture that can be read like a book, as well as
looked at. Every object in the room has significance
– the picture of horses, the auctioneer's lot numbers,
the sale catalogue on the floor, the newspaper open
at the word 'Apartments', the old mother paying the
family retainer, who in turn gives her the keys – the
observer becomes a detective assembling clues,
solving the problem of who everyone is and what is
happening.

William Bell Scott (1811–1890)
Iron and Coal

*c*1855–60
Canvas 188 × 188 cm/74 × 74 ins
Wallington Hall, Northumberland (National Trust)

This is the last of a series of eight pictures painted
by Scott for Sir Walter Trevelyan to decorate the
inner courtyard of Wallington Hall, Northumberland.
It depicts the busy industrial life of Victorian
Tyneside. The central figures are ironworkers,
wielding hammers. Beside them is a working
drawing of a locomotive, and in the foreground are
the air-pump of a marine engine, an anchor, and the
shell and barrel of an Armstrong gun, on which the
girl is sitting, holding a school-book and her father's
lunch. Behind is a pit-boy, with a whip and Davy
lamp, looking out over the bustling quayside of
Newcastle. In the background, full of masts and
smoke and telegraph wires, a train steams across
Stephenson's High Level Bridge. It is one of the few
Victorian pictures which attempts to glorify the
Industrial Revolution.

Rossetti wrote him an admiring letter in 1847. Later he contributed poems to *The Germ*. As a result of his isolation in Newcastle, Scott never became closely involved with the Brotherhood, but he was always an important peripheral figure, and his own paintings conform to Pre-Raphaelite ideas. His best-known picture is *Iron and Coal* (below) at Wallington in Northumberland. This is one of the most interesting and unusual of all Victorian modern-life pictures, and also one of the few to follow the example of Brown's *Work*. Scott was a prolific painter, watercolourist and illustrator. He produced many other pictures of a rather idiosyncratic type, and also

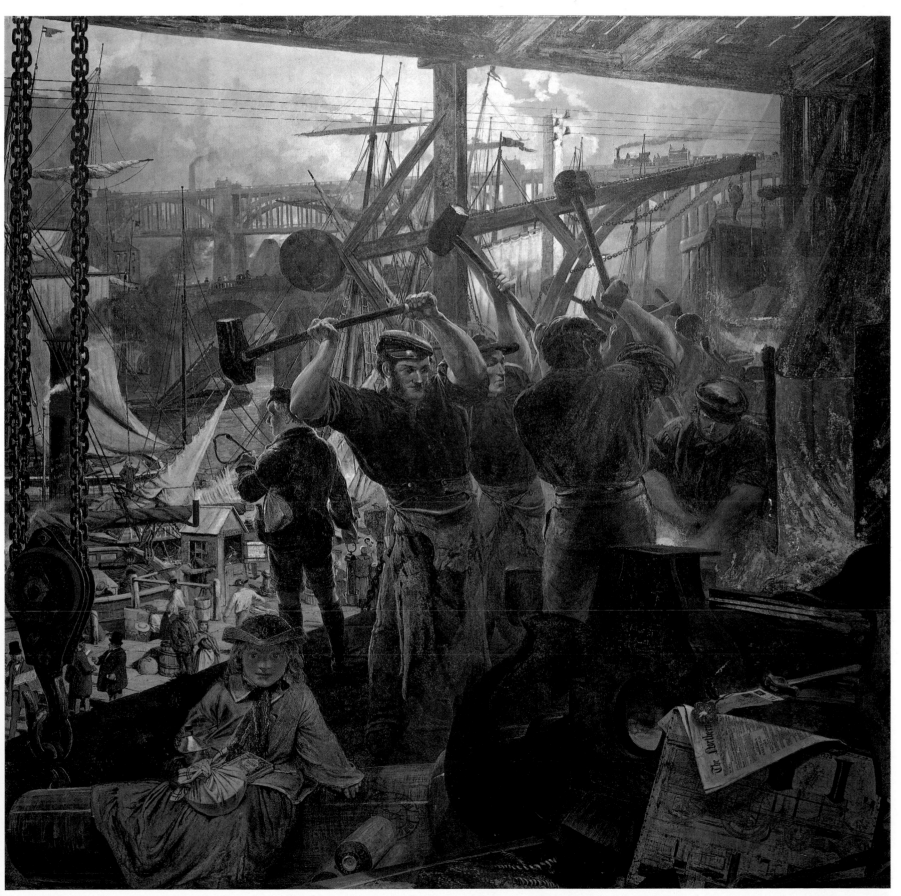

painted some fine landscapes. The Pre-Raphaelite technique did not come easily to him and he never completely mastered it. He was a cantankerous and difficult man, and his *Autobiographical Notes*, published in 1892, are full of recriminations against other, more successful, artists. It was Scott, however, who advised and encouraged the Newcastle collector, James Leathart, to buy many of the Pre-Raphaelites' finest works, thus establishing one of the major Pre-Raphaelite collections.

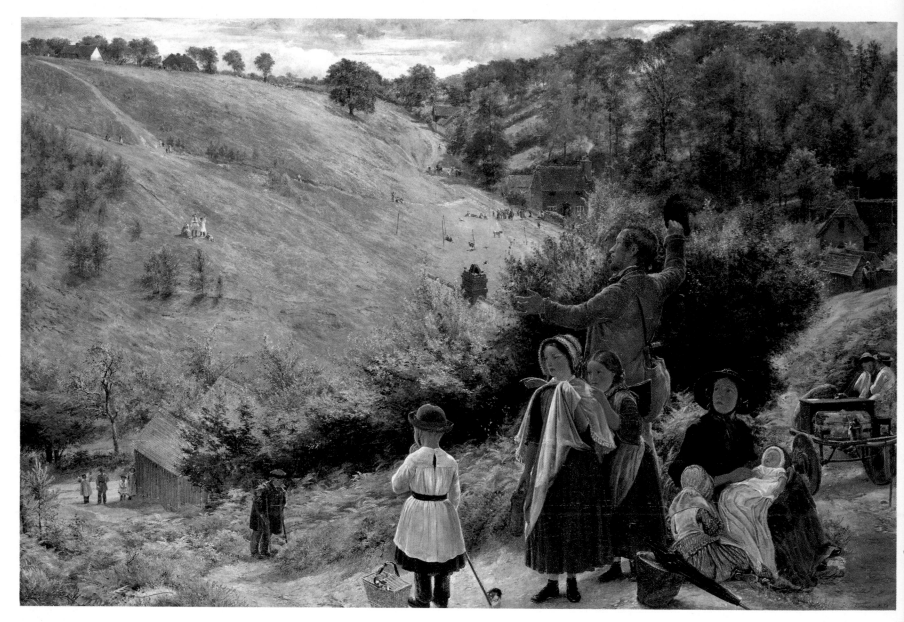

Richard Redgrave (1804–1888)
The Emigrant's Last Sight of Home

Signed and dated 1858
Canvas 69 × 99 cm/27 × 39 ins
Tate Gallery, London

Painted at Leith Hill, near Abinger in Surrey, where Redgrave had a house, and exhibited at the Royal Academy in 1859. Ruskin commented on the beauty of the landscape, which is painted in brilliant Pre-Raphaelite colours. Unlike Redgrave's social pictures of the 1840, such as *The Governess*, the mood of this picture is dominated by the landscape rather than the unhappy family of emigrants who are being forced to leave it.

Sir Joseph Noel Paton (1821–1901)
The Bluidie Tryst

Signed with monogram and dated 1855
Canvas 73 × 65 cm/28¾ × 25⅝ ins
Glasgow Museum and Art Gallery

This story comes from a Scottish poem about a lover who was murdered by the nine brothers of a girl whom he had dishonoured:

They shot him dead at the Nine-Stone Rig,
Beside the Headless Cross,
And they left him lying in his blood,
Upon the moor and moss.
They dug his grave but a bare foot deep,
By the edge of the Nine-Stone Burn,
And they covered him o'er with the heather flower,
The moss and the lady fern.

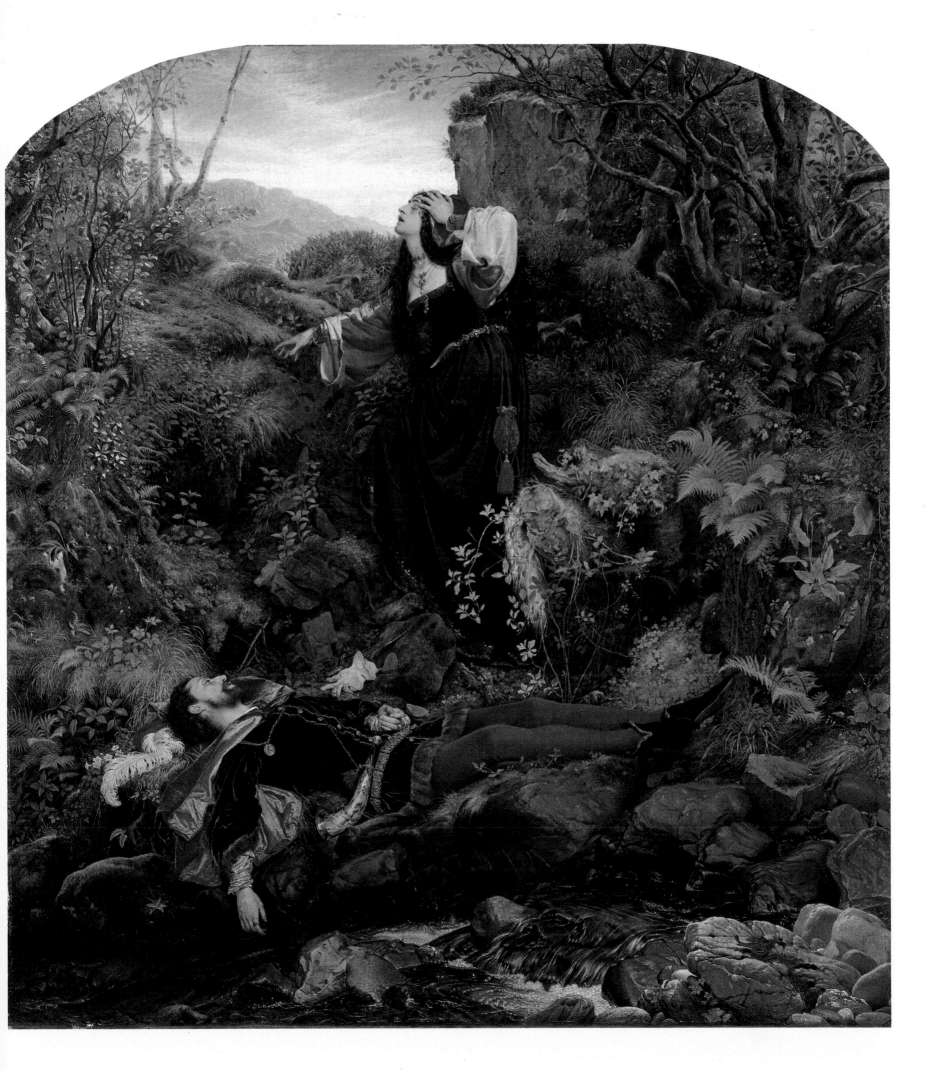

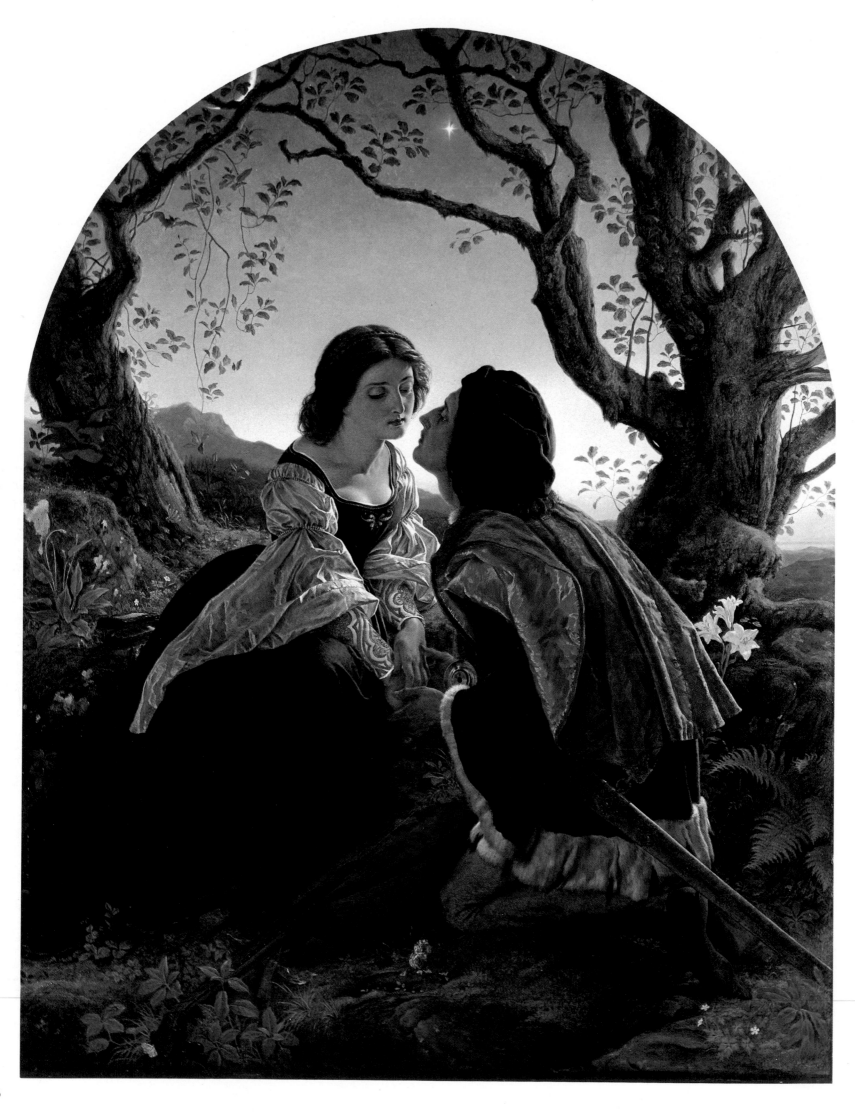

Sir Joseph Noel Paton

Hesperus

Signed and dated 1857
Millboard 91 × 69 cm/36 × 27 ins
Glasgow Museum and Art Gallery

A highly romantic picture of Arthurian lovers. Hesperus was a knight called 'Evening Star' by Tennyson, but in the *Morte d'Arthur* he is 'The Green Knight of Sir Pertolope', one of the four brothers who guarded the passages of the Castle Perilous. Paton's interest in Arthurian subjects at this early date shows that he must have been in close touch with the Pre-Raphaelites; around 1857 Rossetti was also beginning to paint subjects from the *Morte d'Arthur*.

In Scotland the most notable Pre-Raphaelite follower was Sir Joseph Noel Paton. Paton studied at the Royal Academy Schools, where he became friendly with Millais, and through him absorbed the aims and ideas of the Brotherhood. He then returned to Scotland, where he was to have a distinguished career as member of the Royal Scottish Academy and 'Queen's Limner for Scotland', which earned him a knighthood. During the 1850s he was fully sympathetic to Pre-Raphaelite ideas, and as a result produced some outstanding pictures, such as *The Bluidie Tryst* (p. 75) and *Hesperus* (p. 76). Both pictures are highly romantic in theme, and show that Paton had completely mastered Pre-Raphaelite techniques. He was a highly accomplished and educated man, and the range of his pictures is accordingly wide. In addition to romantic historical subjects, he was a noted painter of fairies and also occasional modern-life subjects. Later he devoted himself increasingly to religious paintings in a more monumental style which earned him even greater popularity and acclaim than his Pre-Raphaelite works. However, he still remains one of the most interesting and distinguished figures on the fringe of the Pre-Raphaelite movement.

Liverpool was by far the biggest source of patrons and followers for the Pre-Raphaelites. After Hunt's *Valentine Rescuing Sylvia* (p. 21) won the £50 prize at the Liverpool Academy in 1851, Pre-Raphaelite pictures carried off the same prize four times between 1852 and 1858. This naturally encouraged the Pre-Raphaelites to send

Right: **William Lindsay Windus**, *Too Late*, 1858.

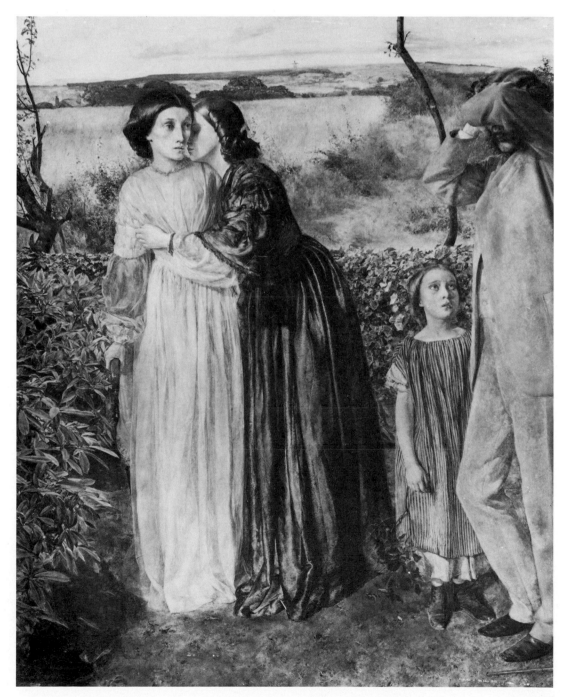

their best pictures there, and notable local collections were formed by such men as John Miller and George Rae of Birkenhead. A whole school of Pre-Raphaelite followers sprang up, of whom the most interesting was William Lindsay Windus. In 1856, his first Pre-Raphaelite picture, *Burd Helen* (p. 79), was greatly admired by Ruskin and Rossetti. Unfortunately his next important work, *Too Late*, was attacked by Ruskin and other critics as too morbid and obscure. This, combined with the death of his wife, was too much for the sensitive Windus, who destroyed most of his previous work and hardly painted again. Other notable Liverpool artists include James Campbell, John Lee and William Huggins, all of whom were influenced in different ways by Pre-Raphaelite ideas and techniques. Another almost forgotten artist was Thomas Wade, who lived in Preston, Lancashire. His *Carting turf from the moss* demonstrates the use of Pre-Raphaelite techniques and ideas, particularly those of Madox Brown. Liverpool was also a great centre for Pre-Raphaelite landscape painters, in particular William Davis.

Pre-Raphaelite influence was also considerable in America, although there it was more of a literary affair than an artistic one. The Exhibition of British Art in New York in 1857 contained many Pre-Raphaelite pictures, and some fine collections were formed in the United States, notably those of Charles Eliot Norton at Harvard, and Samuel Bancroft at Wilmington, Delaware. Bancroft's interest in Pre-Raphaelite pictures was first awakened when he saw a collection in a friend's house in Manchester. Maria Spartali, a famous beauty and also a pupil of Rossetti, married the American journalist William J. Stillman, and her work had some influence on American collectors, whose patronage of English art became increasingly important during the later Victorian period.

William Lindsay Windus (1822–1907)
Burd Helen

Signed with initials, dated 1856
Canvas 84 × 67 cm/33¼ × 26¼ ins
Walker Art Gallery, Liverpool

Exhibited at the Royal Academy in 1856, where it was lavishly praised by both Rossetti and Ruskin. It illustrates a story from an old Scottish ballad, of a girl who ran all day beside the horse of her faithless lover, and, when they reached the river Clyde, swam across rather than lose him. Windus was one of the best of the Liverpool artists to be influenced by the Pre-Raphaelites. Unfortunately his next picture, *Too Late*, was violently attacked by Ruskin, and the neurotic Windus was so distressed that he virtually gave up painting for good.

Thomas Wade, *Carting turf from the moss*, undated.

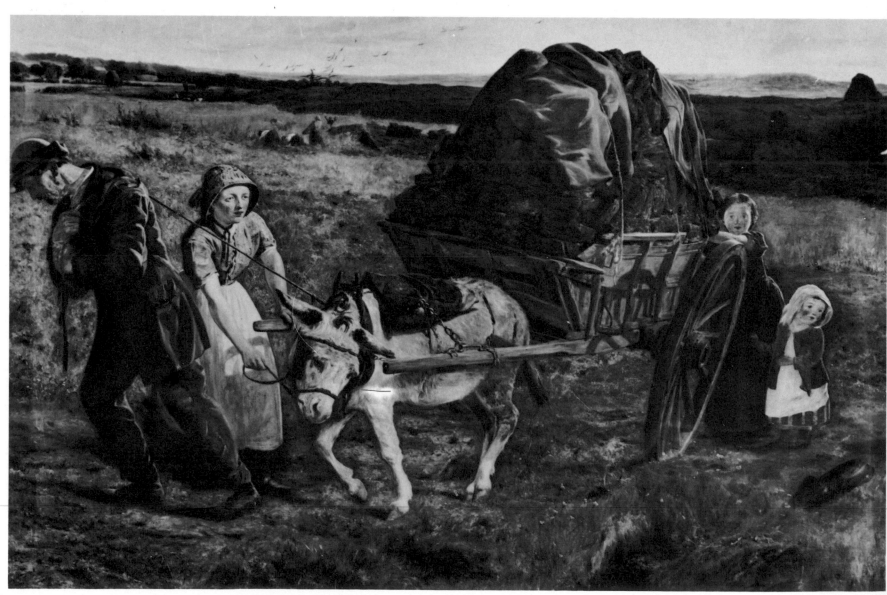

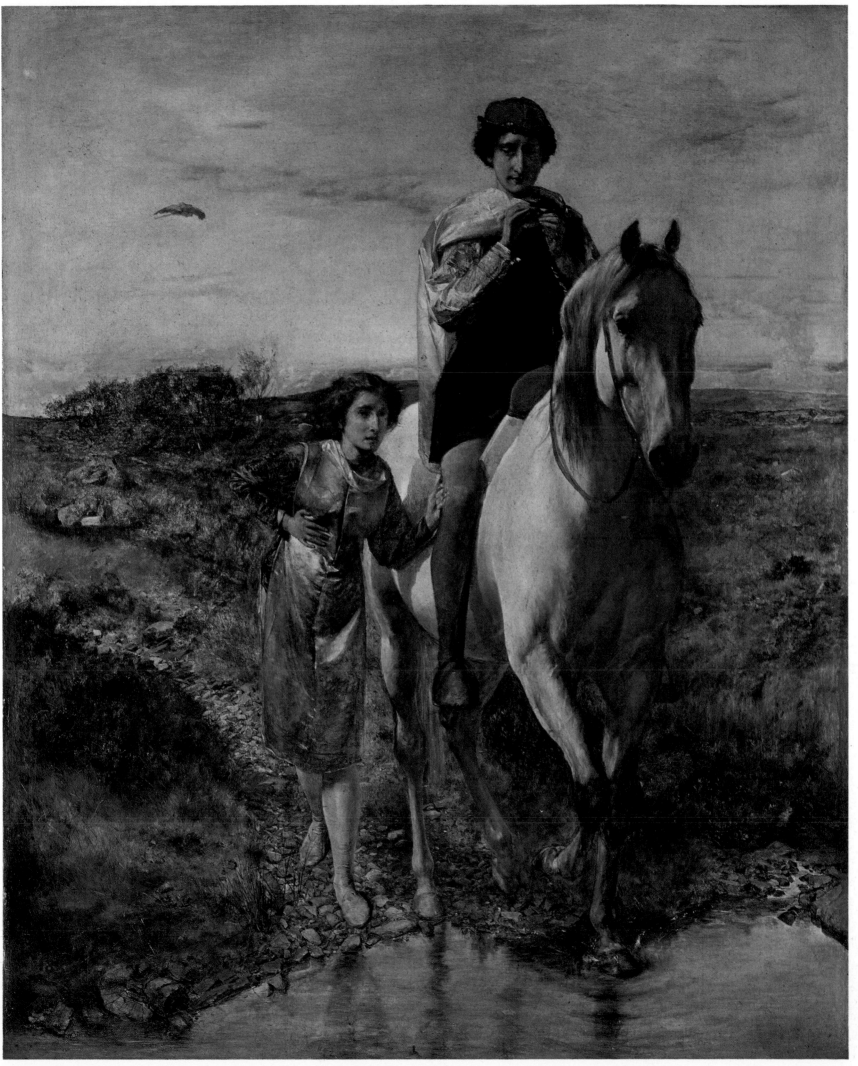

Part II The Pre-Raphaelite Landscape

From the start, landscape was a key element in the Pre-Raphaelite style. The determination of the Pre-Raphaelites to paint with complete truth and honesty, without regard to academic convention or tradition, is clearly reflected in their approach to landscape painting. The most important exponents of Pre-Raphaelite landscape were Hunt, Millais and Madox Brown. Between them they changed the whole direction of English landscape painting in the 1850s and '60s. Rossetti tried landscape painting, but soon tired of it. This resulted in a basic division in the Brotherhood from the very beginning, with Rossetti and his followers pursuing romantic, medieval subjects, far removed from everyday life, and Hunt, Millais and their followers concentrating on greater realism and naturalism.

Although Ruskin did not become aware of the Pre-Raphaelites until 1850, his writings had already exercized an important influence on them. Holman Hunt, in particular, discovered Ruskin's *Modern Painters* in 1847, and wrote later that 'of all its readers none could have felt more strongly than myself that it was written expressly for him'. Ruskin had begun the book as a defence of Turner, but in the second volume, published in 1846, he expanded it into a much wider survey of European art. His purpose was to show that Turner's art was more truthful to nature than that of any of the old masters. Ruskin looked at nature with the eyes of a botanist and geologist. Truth to nature for him meant the detailed recording of the minutiae of nature, painted with the highest degree of finish. He praised such early Italian artists as Perugino, Fra Angelico, Pinturicchio, Giovanni Bellini, 'and all such serious and loving men'. By contrast, he denounced the sloppy and coarse methods of Ribera, Salvator Rosa and Murillo. English modern painters were also heavily criticized for their trivial subject-matter and dishonest execution. In a famous and much-quoted passage, Ruskin exhorted the young artists of England to 'go to Nature in all singleness of heart, and walk with her laboriously and trustingly, having no other thoughts but how best to penetrate her meaning, and remember her instructions; rejecting nothing, selecting nothing, and scorning nothing; believing all things to be right and good, and rejoicing always in the truth.' Ruskin's intense reverence for nature was both passionate and moralistic; he believed that only by trusting completely to nature could an artist produce an art that is truly noble and good.

Ruskin's words found their most responsive echo in Holman Hunt, the most serious-minded and earnest of the Pre-Raphaelites. During 1848 he communicated his enthusiasm for Ruskin to Millais, and they both decided to paint their next pictures according to entirely new principles based on Ruskin's ideas. So what were the principles of Pre-Raphaelite landscape? Firstly, complete fidelity to nature to be achieved by painting out-of-doors in natural day-light. Secondly, painting in clear colours over a white ground with the minimum of shadows. Hunt summarized it thus: 'I purpose after this to paint an out-of-door picture, with a foreground and background, abjuring altogether brown foliage, smoky clouds, and dark corners, painting the whole out-of-doors, direct on the canvas itself, with every detail I can see, and with the sunlight brightness of the day itself.' This microscopic, inch-by-inch delineation of every leaf and flower was an extraordinarily laborious method of painting. It required incredible patience and determination, and also the ability to paint out-of-doors in all weathers; many of the Pre-Raphaelites' letters and diaries complain of long hours out in the fields, tormented by heat, cold, rain, wind or insects. It was also very slow, and a whole day's work might result in an area of only a

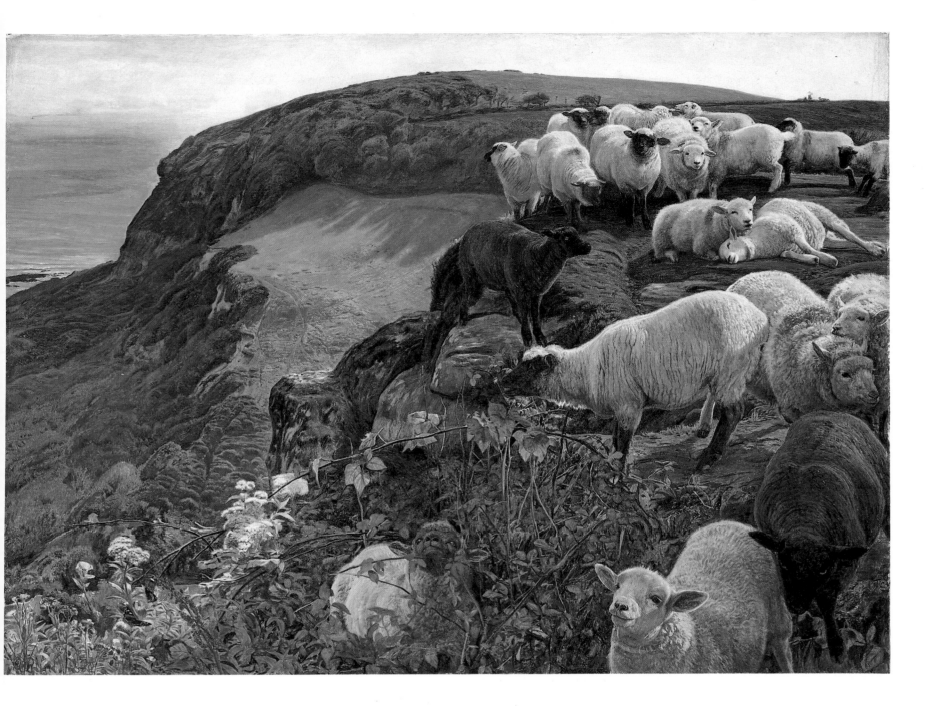

William Holman Hunt
Strayed Sheep (Our English Coasts)

Signed and dated 1852
Canvas 43 × 58 cm/17 × 23 ins
Tate Gallery, London

Painted on the south coast at Fairlight, near
Hastings, in the summer and autumn of 1852, and
exhibited at the Royal Academy in 1853. The
picture was first commissioned as a replica of the
sheep in the background of *The Hireling Shepherd*,
but Hunt decided to make it into a separate picture.
Its brilliant and prismatic colours make it the most
remarkable of all Hunt's landscapes, and it was
greatly admired at the Paris *Exposition Universelle* of
1855; Delacroix wrote in his Journal, 'I am really
astounded by Hunt's sheep.'

few square inches being completed. This often led to a relentless accumulation of
compressed detail at the expense of the overall composition; a common fault with
Pre-Raphaelite landscapes, but a sacrifice they thought was justified in their crusade
for greater truth in art. Many critics argued that to treat every inch of the canvas with
equal importance was in itself unnatural, as the human eye could not take in so much
detail at once. They also criticized the lack of shadow in many Pre-Raphaelite
landscapes, and indeed their brilliant colours do often produce an airless, artificial
effect that is certainly not realistic – in twentieth-century terms, we would call them
surrealistic. However, in their own day the Pre-Raphaelites were doing something
quite new and modern, and their results gave Victorian landscape painting a salutary
shock. They also produced some of the most remarkable and beautiful landscapes in
the whole of English art.

Hunt's first picture painted according to the new principles was *Rienzi*. All the
landscape details were painted from nature, but they are not as brilliant as the
landscape backgrounds for *Valentine Rescuing Sylvia* (p. 21) and *The Druids* (p. 18). In
both these pictures Hunt had begun to paint on a wet, freshly prepared surface each
day, and this technique gave a far greater clarity and brilliance to his colours. Millais
was to take up the same methods in *Ferdinand Lured by Ariel* and *The Woodman's
Daughter* (p. 32), his first attempts at Pre-Raphaelite landscape. It was in May 1851
that Ruskin came to the defence of the Pre-Raphaelites, and in the summer of that

year Hunt and Millais went to the Surrey countryside to paint the landscape backgrounds for their next pictures. These were to be *The Hireling Shepherd* (p. 41) and *Ophelia* (p. 33), two of the most outstanding of all Pre-Raphaelite landscapes. During that same summer Madox Brown was working on the landscape for *The Pretty Baa-Lambs* (p. 50), so it can justifiably be claimed that Pre-Raphaelite landscape came of age in 1851. Hunt was later to write that with *Ophelia* 'a new art was born'.

Millais never became a pure landscape painter. The landscape backgrounds in his pictures are important only as settings for the figures and action. But his landscape details are beautifully observed, and they serve both to echo and to intensify the emotional situation of the figures – a technique closely imitated by Arthur Hughes. This is clearly demonstrated in Millais' *The Huguenot* and *The Proscribed Royalist*, both painted in 1852. His last and most intensely Pre-Raphaelite landscape was the rocky setting for his portrait of Ruskin. After 1853, Millais continued to use the characteristically bright Pre-Raphaelite colours, but cleverly broadened his technique. This meant that his landscapes still looked Pre-Raphaelite from a distance, but on closer inspection did not show the same minuteness of detail as his earlier works. The most outstanding examples of this phase are *Autumn Leaves* (p. 38) and *The Blind Girl* (p. 36). *Sir Isumbras* (p. 39) and *The Vale of Rest* show a similar tendency towards an increasing fluidity of technique. After renouncing Pre-Raphaelitism, Millais rarely returned to landscape painting. He painted a few highland landscapes such as *Chill October*, but in a conventional late Victorian style. His brother, William Henry Millais, was a gifted watercolourist and continued to paint landscapes in Pre-Raphaelite style long after his more famous brother had abandoned them.

Holman Hunt could have been the most brilliant landscape painter of the Brotherhood but, like Millais, he never became a pure landscapist. Landscape backgrounds were, however, a key element in his art, as can be seen in *The Hireling Shepherd* and *The Light of the World* (p. 43). The last, and in some ways the finest of his early landscapes is *Strayed Sheep* (p. 81). Its colours are even more brilliant than *The Hireling Shepherd*, and as an example of Pre-Raphaelite painting of English landscape in full sunlight, there is nothing to equal it. Throughout every inch of the picture Hunt has studied the effect of sunlight and shadow as it falls on every object, even the veins of the sheep's ears. Close examination of the sheep's wool reveals that it is made up of tiny strokes of different colours, and the reflected colours of the shadows are wonderfully observed, full of surprising blues and violets. It is the most minutely observed, and the most scientific of all Hunt's landscapes, and it exercized a great influence over all the other painters who tried to emulate the Pre-Raphaelite landscape style. Later critics pointed out that Hunt's experimentation with light and colour clearly anticipates later developments in French painting, particularly Impressionism and Pointillism. Although *Strayed Sheep* was greatly admired in France, it did not create a new school of Pre-Raphaelite followers there as it had done in England.

Hunt continued to use landscape backgrounds in his pictures, but his most important contributions to Pre-Raphaelite landscape after 1853 were his landscapes of the Middle East. In painting *The Scapegoat* (p. 44) he became the first artist to apply Pre-Raphaelite principles to the landscape of the Holy Land. It remains the most extraordinary and the most eerie of all Pre-Raphaelite landscapes, but it is not painted with the same minute finish as *Strayed Sheep*. Like Millais, Hunt was beginning to broaden and loosen his style, although his interest in light and colour remained the same. The most remarkable feature of the landscape is the background – the mountains beyond the Dead Sea. Hunt deliberately chose to paint them at sunset, and the resulting range of lurid pinks and purples adds greatly to the gloomy and haunting atmosphere of the picture. It has a visionary intensity that only Holman Hunt was capable of, and which has no parallel in the landscapes of Millais

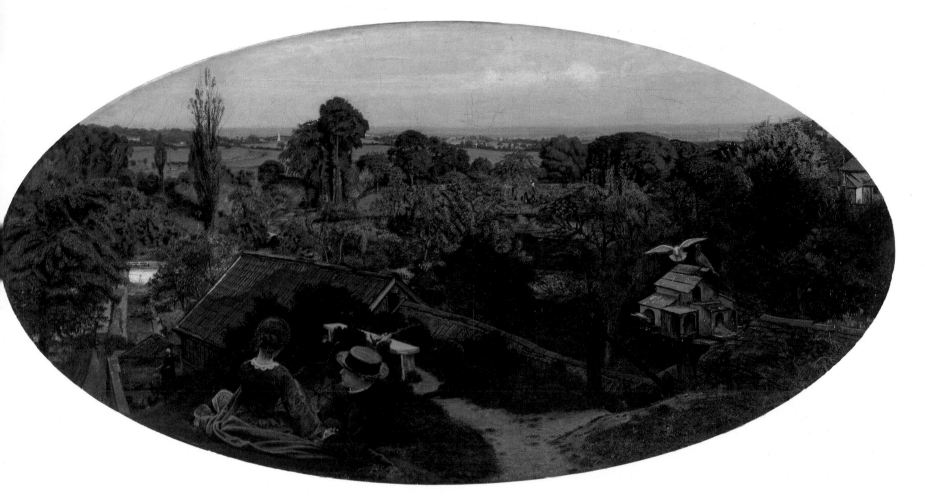

Ford Madox Brown
An English Autumn Afternoon

Signed 1852–55
Canvas, oval, 72 × 135 cm/28¼ × 53 ins
Birmingham City Museum and Art Gallery

A view from the back window of the artist's house in Hampstead, with Kenwood House and Highgate Church in the distance. Brown began the picture in 1852, but continued repainting it until 1855. It is an informal, human landscape, recording simply and without affectation a view from a London window. It was this very quality of unpretentiousness which Ruskin attacked, when he asked Brown one day why he had chosen 'such a very ugly subject?' Brown answered defiantly, 'Because it lay out of my back window.'

or Madox Brown. While in the Middle East, Hunt also produced a number of remarkable watercolour landscapes which have something of the intensity of *The Scapegoat*. He later painted some watercolour landscapes in Italy, but these became progressively looser in technique, and one of them, *Sunset at Chimalditi*, was bought by Ruskin because it reminded him of Turner's work. After about 1870 Hunt gave up serious landscape painting, except for the occasional background, as in *The Triumph of The Innocents* (p. 104). But his importance in the growth of Pre-Raphaelite landscape was crucial, and his own interpretation of it remains a uniquely personal one.

Ford Madox Brown was the only major Pre-Raphaelite to devote himself to pure landscape. He had already painted a few landscapes in the 1840s before coming into contact with the Brotherhood, and under their influence he painted all his major pictures of the 1850s out-of-doors. The first was *The Pretty Baa-Lambs*. Both *Work* (p. 49) and *The Last of England* (p. 11) were painted out-of-doors, but the landscape backgrounds occupy only a small portion of the painting. By far the most important of his landscapes was *An English Autumn Afternoon* (above). Brown was never interested in grandiose or dramatic effects of nature, and the choice of a suburban view out of his back window was characteristic. All Brown's landscapes have this intimate, personal quality; he painted them honestly and directly because they appealed to him. This was not calculated to appeal to Ruskin, who expected artists to choose more interesting and picturesque scenery. But although Brown was never a Ruskinian landscape painter, his more modest landscapes exercized considerable influence over other Pre-Raphaelite landscape painters, especially Seddon, Brett and Hunt, and also the landscape painters of the Liverpool School, such as Daniel Alexander Williamson, William Davis and Thomas Wade. Brown wrote that *An English Autumn Afternoon* was intended as 'a literal transcript of the scenery round London', and although he included two foreground figures, they were not meant to add romantic interest, but only to lead the eye into the landscape. The elliptical shape is highly unusual, and one of Brown's most successful experiments with shaped canvases. The characteristic compositional device employed by the Pre-Raphaelites of placing the figures on a plateau in the foreground, with a distant, panoramic view beyond, was to be much imitated by other landscape painters. This enabled the Pre-Raphaelite landscape painter to concentrate on the landscape, rather than the sky, and to combine a detailed foreground with a distant background. This technique was a particular favourite with the Liverpool landscapist William Davis.

During the 1850s Brown painted several other landscapes. He was more responsive than the other Pre-Raphaelites to the beauties of nature, particularly to unusual effects of colour. One day in 1854, he made a country trip with his wife Emma, and 'got a ride on the top of a bus in the most lovely weather ... one field of turnips did surprise us into exclamation, with its wonderful emerald tints.' His diaries are full of similar passages, but he also complained that 'these little landscapes take up too much time to be profitable ...' Nevertheless, he could not stop painting them; *The Hayfield* of 1855 and *Walton-on-the-Naze* of 1860 are two of his finest – small, unpretentious, but beautiful. What makes them so refreshing is that they are a townsman's view of nature. The landscape is in no way idealized, nor are there ridiculous rustics looking picturesque; instead we encounter one or two middle-class Victorians taking a pleasant stroll in an ordinary bit of British countryside.

Brown was not the only older artist to be converted to Pre-Raphaelite landscape. Three others were William Dyce, William Bell Scott and Edward Lear. Dyce painted his picture of the young Titian in 1857 in retaliation against Ruskin's criticism of his previous picture, *Christabel*. Ruskin was delighted with the change, and gave *Titian's First Essay in Colour* (p. 60) a long and laudatory review, beginning, 'Well done! Mr. Dyce, and many times well done!' The following year Dyce painted his most famous landscape, *Pegwell Bay* (p. 85), and this was followed in 1861 by a picture of the seventeenth-century clerical poet, *George Herbert at Bemerton*. Like *Titian*, this depicts a historical figure set in a minutely detailed landscape. Dyce also painted several biblical subjects set in Scottish highland landscapes, such as *The Man of Sorrows*, and also some Welsh landscapes with figures. These pictures are usually small to medium-sized, and taken as a whole they form a distinguished addition to Pre-Raphaelite landscape painting. They all have a tendency to greyness and coldness of colouring, but their uncompromising seriousness and clarity command respect. Bell Scott also painted a number of Pre-Raphaelite landscapes, especially coastal scenes at sunset. His series of paintings of Northumbrian history at

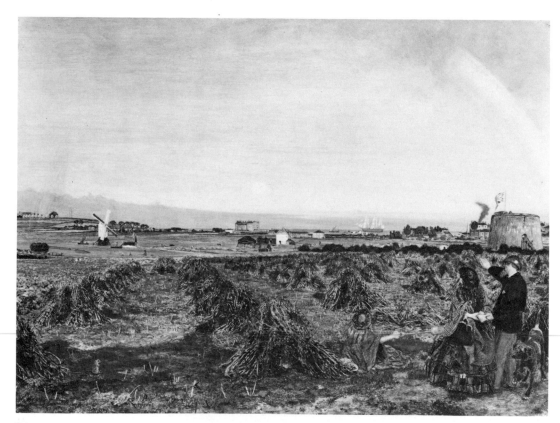

Ford Madox Brown, *Walton-on-the-Naze*, 1880.

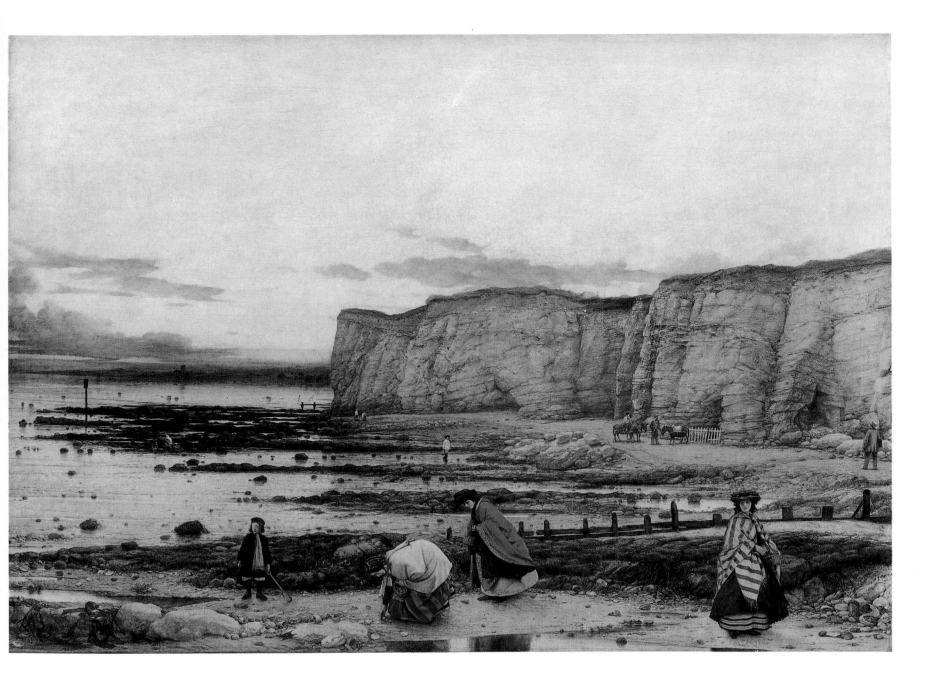

William Dyce

Pegwell Bay, Kent — a Recollection of
October 5th, 1858

1858–60
Canvas 62 × 88 cm/24½ × 34½ ins
Tate Gallery, London

Painted during a holiday Dyce spent with his family
at Ramsgate in Kent in 1858, but not exhibited at the
Royal Academy until 1860. Donati's Comet, which
was visible in 1858, appears in the sky. The figures
in the foreground are Dyce's son, his wife and his
wife's two sisters. It is one of the most
uncompromisingly literal of all Pre-Raphaelite
landscapes, for which reason it has often been
compared to photography. It is unlikely, however,
that Dyce used photographs at all. Although the
landscape is severe and rather colourless, and the
figures strangely melancholy, it has always been one
of the most popular of all nineteenth-century
landscapes.

Wallington includes a number of landscape backgrounds painted on the spot, in
particular one showing Saint Cuthbert at his retreat on the Farne Islands. One of his
last, and most successful sunset landscapes was *The Gloaming* (p. 88). Another
surprising convert to Pre-Raphaelite landscape was the topographer and nonsense
poet, Edward Lear. So impressed was he with *The Hireling Shepherd* that he asked
Hunt, fifteen years his junior, to give him lessons in landscape painting. Together
they visited Fairlight, near Hastings, where Hunt painted *Strayed Sheep*, and Lear
worked on his large *Quarries of Syracuse*. Lear declared himself 'a PRB for ever', but
his later works show a move away from the Pre-Raphaelite style, towards a larger and
more monumental conception of landscape, painted with a broader technique.

Another younger disciple of Holman Hunt was Thomas Seddon. Seddon travelled
with Hunt on his first expedition to the Holy Land in 1853–54. In 1856 he returned
there, but died en route, in Cairo. Seddon painted very few pictures, almost entirely
of the Middle East, of which the best-known is *Jerusalem and the Valley of
Jehoshaphat* (p. 87). Although Seddon's stature as an artist was by no means equal to
that of Hunt, his landscapes are interesting because they are the only pure Pre-
Raphaelite landscapes of the East, mostly without narrative content. Seddon held an
exhibition of his works in London in 1855, and another was organized after his death,
in 1857. Ruskin wrote and spoke favourably of both exhibitions, praising Seddon's
honest and factual approach to Eastern landscape. Because of his premature death,
Seddon has been regarded as the only pure Pre-Raphaelite landscape painter, but had

he lived longer, he would almost certainly have moved away from Pre-Raphaelite landscape, as did so many other artists. Even more obscure is William J. Webbe, who painted a handful of Pre-Raphaelite works between 1853 and 1864, in obvious emulation of Holman Hunt. He painted a number of studies of sheep and other animals set amongst foliage observed in microscopic detail, and in 1862 he also visited the Holy Land. His picture entitled *Twilight* (p. 93) is the only known work by him that shows genuine originality, combining a sinister subject with an almost hallucinatory obsession with detail.

The names of John Brett and John William Inchbold can conveniently be grouped together, since they both suffered the full force of Ruskin's baleful influence. Inchbold was born in Leeds in 1830, and was converted to Pre-Raphaelite landscape in around 1852. His first important picture was *The Chapel, Bolton*, exhibited at the Royal Academy in 1853. In 1855 he followed this with *A Study in March*, generally known as *In Early Spring* (p. 89), one of his finest and best-known works. All Inchbold's early landscapes were exhibited with quotations from Wordsworth, a poet frequently quoted by Ruskin in *Modern Painters*. Ruskin and Inchbold met in about 1854, and in his *Academy Notes* Ruskin regularly praised Inchbold's pictures for their precise detail. He also encouraged Inchbold to visit Switzerland, and the two met in the Alps in the summer of 1858. Ruskin was disappointed with Inchbold's Alpine works, and obviously gave him a thorough lecturing. He wrote to his father: 'At last I think I succeeded in making him entirely uncomfortable and ashamed of himself, and then I left him.' Inchbold struggled doggedly on, and produced at least one memorable Swiss landscape, *The Lake of Lucerne*. He continued to paint Pre-Raphaelite landscapes, often rather gloomy moorland scenes, but also some beautiful views in Devon and Cornwall. He also visited Venice and Spain, and gradually adopted a broader style, like so many other Pre-Raphaelites. Inchbold was constantly harassed by financial troubles, and his later work does not have the quality of his best pictures of the 1850s. He was a sad, rather morose character, and not strong enough to stand up to Ruskin's criticism. He did, however, inspire one other Yorkshire artist, also from Leeds, to take up Pre-Raphaelite landscape painting – John Atkinson Grimshaw. Grimshaw is now best-known for his dock scenes and moonlit landscapes, but in the early 1860s he went through a phase of Pre-Raphaelite landscape painting, producing several very fine works in a style close to that of Inchbold, but usually brighter in colour.

Inchbold was also responsible for the conversion of John Brett. The two met in

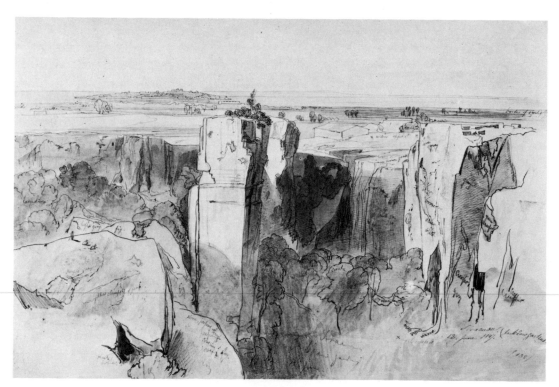

Edward Lear, study for *Quarries of Syracuse*, 1847.

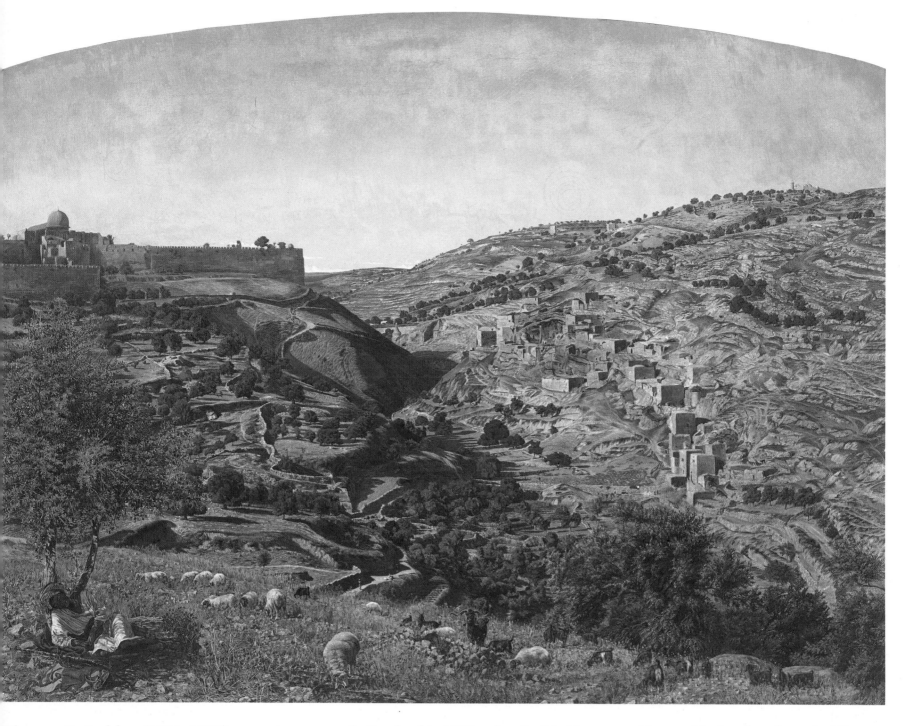

Thomas B. Seddon (1821–1856)
Jerusalem and the Valley of Jehoshaphat from the Hill of Evil Counsel

1854
Canvas, arched top 67 × 83 cm/26½ × 32¾ ins
Tate Gallery, London

Seddon accompanied Holman Hunt to the Holy Land in 1853–54, and this landscape is the best-known product of the journey. It is another extreme example of Pre-Raphaelite attention to detail, painted in full sunlight. Seddon, however, was not as accomplished an artist as Hunt or Madox Brown, and his colours tend to be rather livid and hard. Seddon died in Cairo in 1856, and his works are extremely rare.

Switzerland in 1856, when Inchbold was working on his *Jungfrau from the Wengern Alp*, and Brett on *The Glacier of Rosenlaui*. It was a moment of revelation for Brett, and he finished his *Glacier* picture in impeccable Ruskinian style. His next picture, *The Stonebreaker* (p. 65), was lavishly praised by Ruskin at the 1853 Royal Academy Exhibition, and he exhorted the artist to go to paint the Val d'Aosta. Brett dutifully obeyed, and he and Ruskin met there later that summer. Ruskin once again applied himself to knocking this new pupil into shape, but he found that Brett was made of sterner stuff. He wrote to his father: 'He is much tougher and stronger than Inchbold, and takes more hammering – but I think he looks more miserable every day, and have good hope of making him completely wretched in a day or two more . . .' The result of this joint effort was *The Val d'Aosta* (p. 91), the ultimate Ruskinian landscape, one would have thought; but Ruskin was not happy with it, mainly because Brett had chosen a view lacking in grandeur. Perhaps Ruskin had at last realized that romantic grandeur and factual detail were incompatible, and that totally Ruskinian landscape was an impossibility, for in 1859 he gave up his *Academy Notes*, and stopped encouraging young artists. Reluctantly, he bought the *Val d'Aosta*, but as if acknowledging his mistake, he soon re-sold it. In 1875, Ruskin revived his *Academy Notes*, and criticized what he saw as a decline in Brett's art. This was unjust, as Brett had continued to paint in minute detail, and had produced some fine pictures, such as *Florence from Bellosguardo* (1862–63) and *Etna from the Heights of Taormina* (1870–71). For the rest of his long career, Brett devoted himself to painting coastal scenes, mostly while cruising in his yacht around the British Isles. Many of these smaller works and sketches are delightful, and still contain Pre-Raphaelite effects of colouring and detail. But he became best known for his big panoramas of the sea, such as *Britannia's Realm*, bought by the Chantrey Bequest in 1880, and in 1881 he was elected an Associate of the Royal Academy, the only Pre-Raphaelite after Millais to achieve this honour. Brett's sister, Rosa Brett, also produced a small number of minutely detailed pictures of flowers and landscapes.

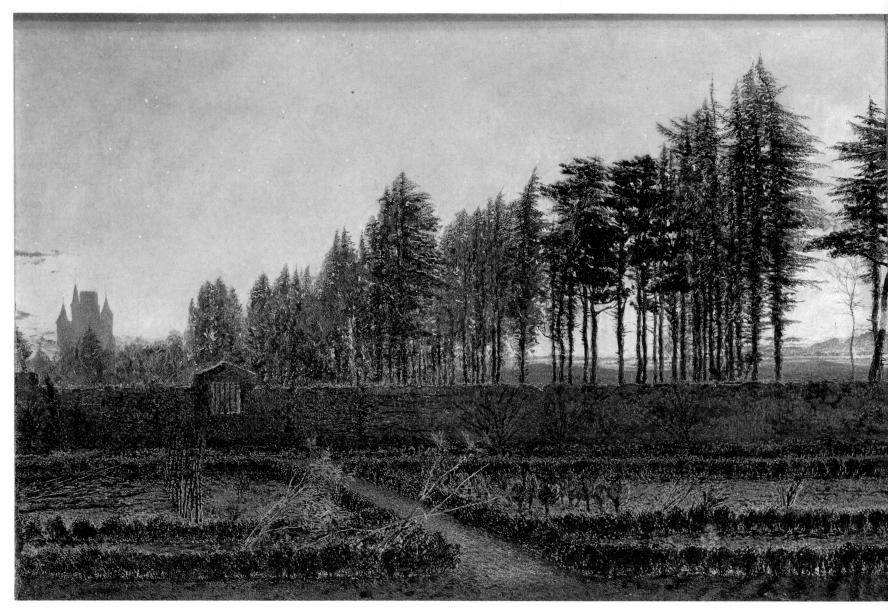

William Bell Scott
The Gloaming – a manse garden in Berwickshire

Signed, 1862
Canvas 33 × 48 cm/13$^{1}/_{16}$ × 19 ins
E.J.McCormick Collection

Although he lived in Newcastle-on-Tyne, Scott was a friend of Rossetti, and kept in close touch with him and several other Pre-Raphaelite artists. During the 1860s he painted a number of Pre-Raphaelite landscapes, many of them sunsets. Scott was also interested in German art, and his landscapes show the influence of such Romantic painters as Caspar David Friedrich.

John William Inchbold (1830–1888)
A Study in March (In Early Spring)

c1855
Canvas 51 × 34 cm/20 × 13$\frac{1}{2}$ ins
Ashmolean Museum, Oxford

Exhibited at the Royal Academy in 1855 with a quotation from Wordsworth: 'When the primrose flower peeped forth to give an earnest of the spring.' In the first volume of *Modern Painters* Ruskin praised Wordsworth for his attention to natural detail, and Inchbold himself wrote Wordsworthian sonnets. Most of his early landscapes contain an astonishing amount of foreground detail, to which the background is subordinated.

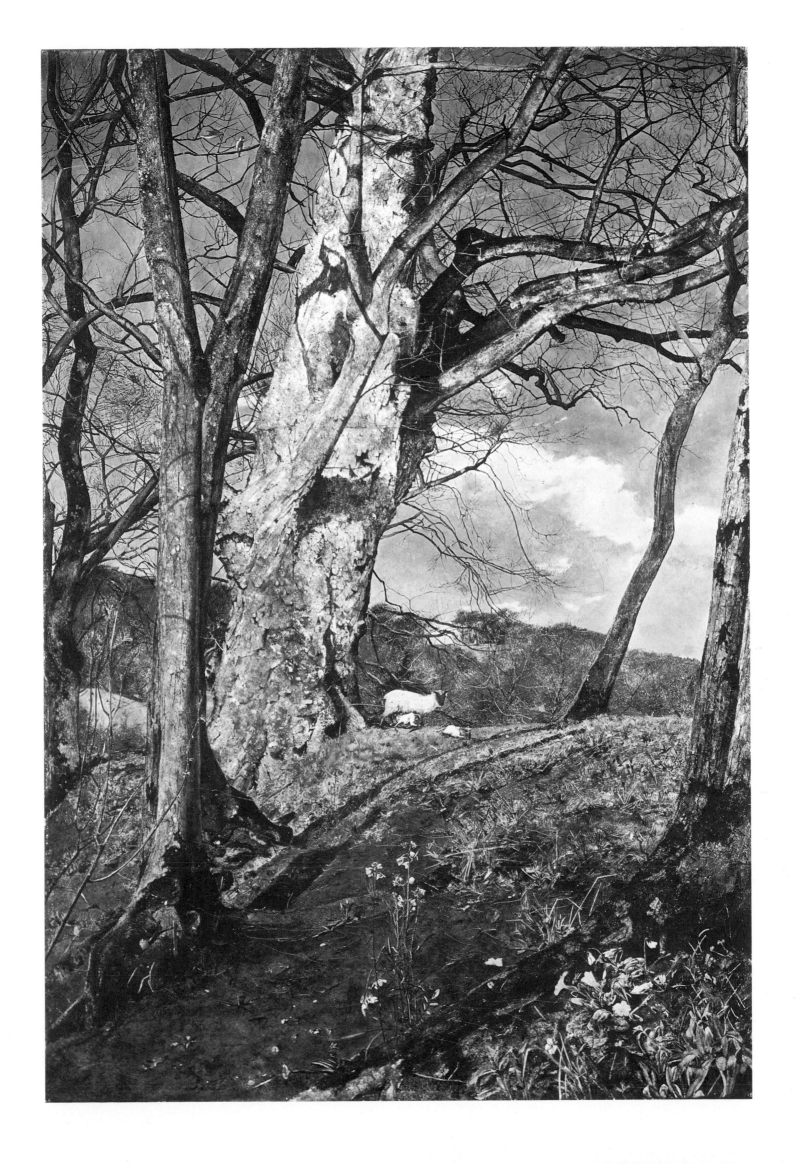

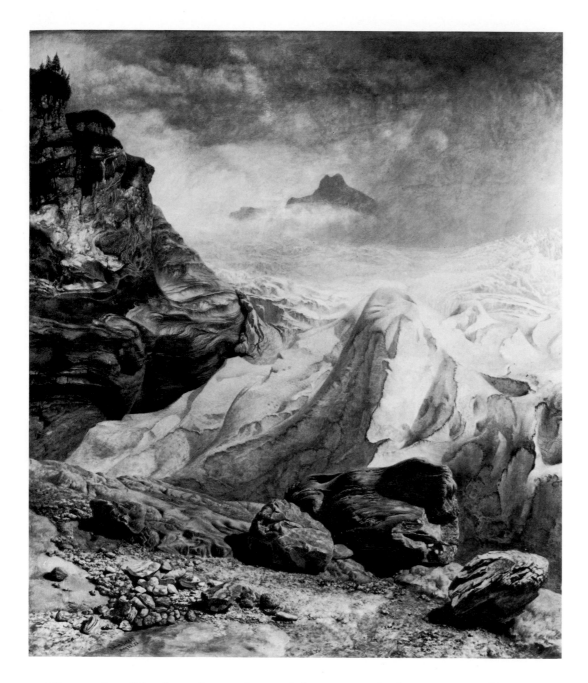

John Brett, *The Glacier of Rosenlaui*, 1856.

Many other friends and associates of the Pre-Raphaelites occasionally painted landscapes. Among them were Alice Boyd, the owner of Penkill Castle, and a friend of Rossetti and Bell Scott, and Michael Frederick Halliday, who shared a studio with Holman Hunt. Ruskin himself was a fine draughtsman and watercolourist, and his own works must be reckoned as a notable contribution to the movement. Another of his devotees was the rather pathetic John Wharlton Bunney, who spent six years painting a picture of St Mark's, Venice. One day the irrepressible Whistler crept up behind Bunney while painting in the Piazza San Marco and pinned a card to his back which read, 'I am totally blind'. Somehow this cruel but funny jest seems appropriate — such slavish devotion to Pre-Raphaelite principles could lead only to absurdity. George Price Boyce, the diarist and friend of Rossetti, painted some beautiful watercolour landscapes in Pre-Raphaelite style. James Smetham, another Rossetti disciple, also attempted Pre-Raphaelite landscapes, but his other work is more visionary, in the tradition of John Linnell and Samuel Palmer. Smetham was an intensely religious man, and this may have led to his breakdown in 1857, and eventual insanity. In one of his notebooks he attempted to illustrate every verse of the Bible. Thomas Matthews Rooke also painted landscapes, usually in watercolour, and was commissioned by Ruskin to paint old buildings in France, Switzerland and Italy. Joseph Noel Paton's works are full of Pre-Raphaelite landscape detail, especially *The Bluidie Tryst* (p. 75), but his brother, Waller Hugh Paton, was much more of a landscapist, both in oil and watercolour. The list of other young landscape

90

John Brett
The Val d'Aosta

Signed and dated 1858
Canvas 88 × 68 cm/34½ × 26⅞ ins
Sir Francis Cooper, Bt.

After the success of *The Stonebreaker*, Brett followed Ruskin's advice: 'What would he not make of the chestnut groves of the Val d'Aosta!' — and left for Italy. Surprisingly, Brett chose a rather insignificant part of the Val d'Aosta for his picture, instead of the Matterhorn or Mont Blanc. Although the result was a landscape of the most extreme Ruskinian type, Ruskin himself praised it in rather guarded terms at the Royal Academy of 1859. Although acknowledging that it was a true 'historical landscape', recording the facts with total honesty he complained that it was 'Mirror's Work, not Man's'.

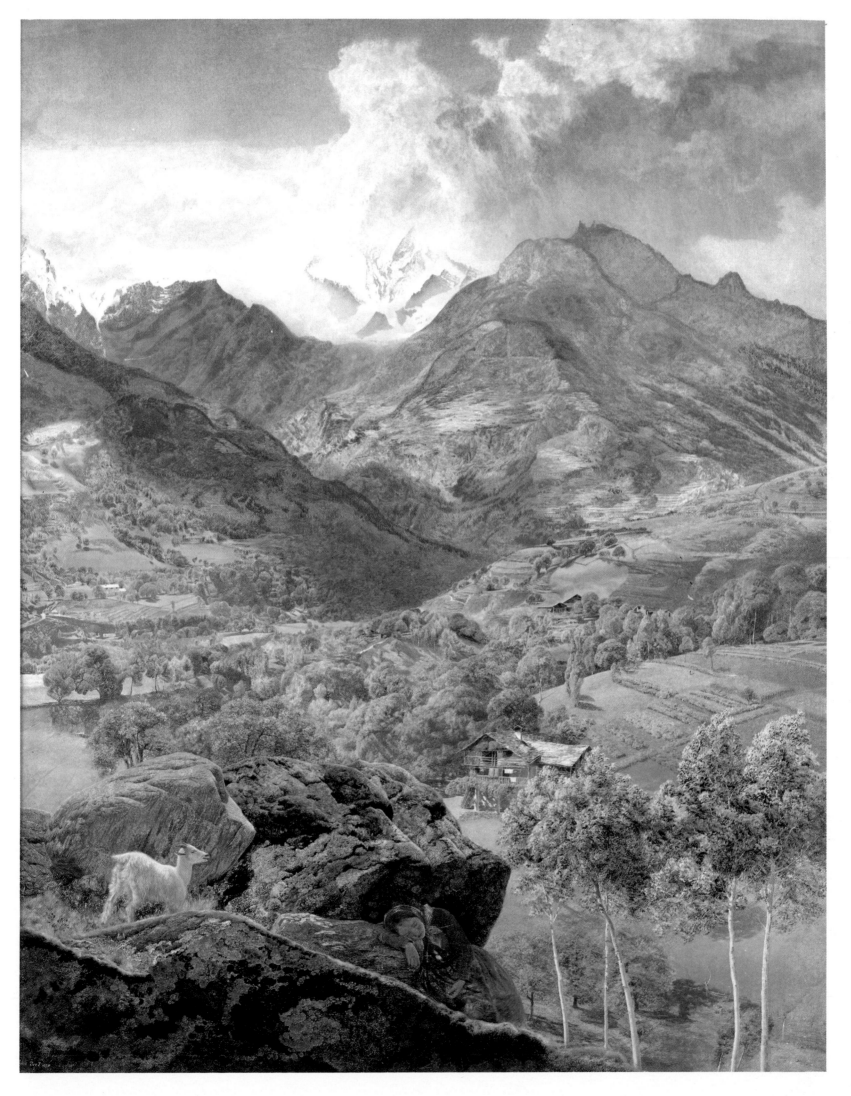

painters who flirted briefly with Pre-Raphaelitism and then moved on is endless, and more are being discovered all the time. Several, such as John Mulcaster Carrick, Edward Charles Booth and John Samuel Raven, are mentioned briefly in Ruskin's *Academy Notes*. Others in this category include Charles Napier Hemy, Henry W. Banks Davis, Andrew MacCallum and George Hastings. Pre-Raphaelite detail can also be detected in some of the early works of Benjamin William Leader and Sidney Richard Percy.

By far the biggest concentration of Pre-Raphaelite landscape painters was to be found in Liverpool. Here Pre-Raphaelite pictures had won several prizes at the local Academy, and had an immense influence on many Lancashire artists. In the case of William Lindsay Windus, the effect was not a happy one, but it did produce at least one outstanding landscape painter, William Davis. His picture, *Hale, Lancashire* (below), is typical of the unpretentious subject-matter combined with literal rendering of detail to be found in most of his pictures. Ruskin criticized Davis for not choosing more interesting subjects, but most of the Liverpool painters seemed to prefer the more modest, informal style of Madox Brown. Daniel Alexander Williamson and Thomas Wade both painted in a style similar to Brown's; other notable landscape painters in Liverpool included John Edward Newton, Henry Mark Anthony, William Joseph Bond, Frederick Clive Newcombe and John Wright Oakes. There were also a number of fine watercolourists, in particular Alfred William Hunt.

During the 1860s and '70s, the Pre-Raphaelite style of landscape painting gradually fell out of favour, partly because it was so laborious and slow, but also because of new influences from the Continent – the work of Jules Bastien-Lepage, Impressionism, and later, Post-Impressionism. The quarrel between the old style and

William Davis (1812–1873)
Hale, Lancashire

Signed with initials, *c*1860
Canvas 33 × 50 cm/13 × 19¾ ins
Walker Art Gallery, Liverpool

Davis was one of the most interesting Liverpool landscape painters to be influenced by the Pre-Raphaelites. He was a retiring and rather unlucky artist, who was almost entirely supported by the Liverpool patron John Miller. His modest but beautifully observed landscapes were admired by Rossetti and Madox Brown. Rossetti brought them to the attention of Ruskin, who wrote a letter of advice to Davis which he unfortunately never received. Ruskin suggested that Davis should choose more interesting subjects.

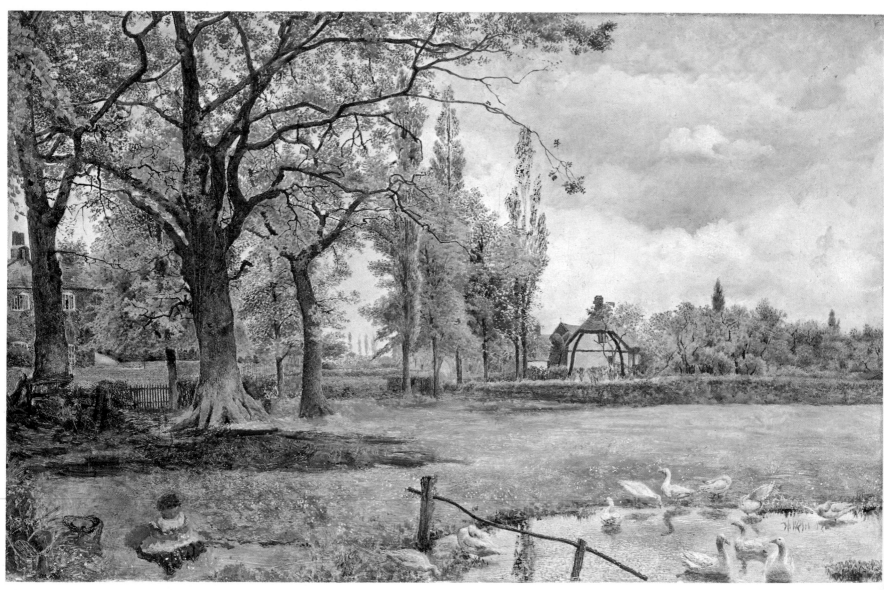

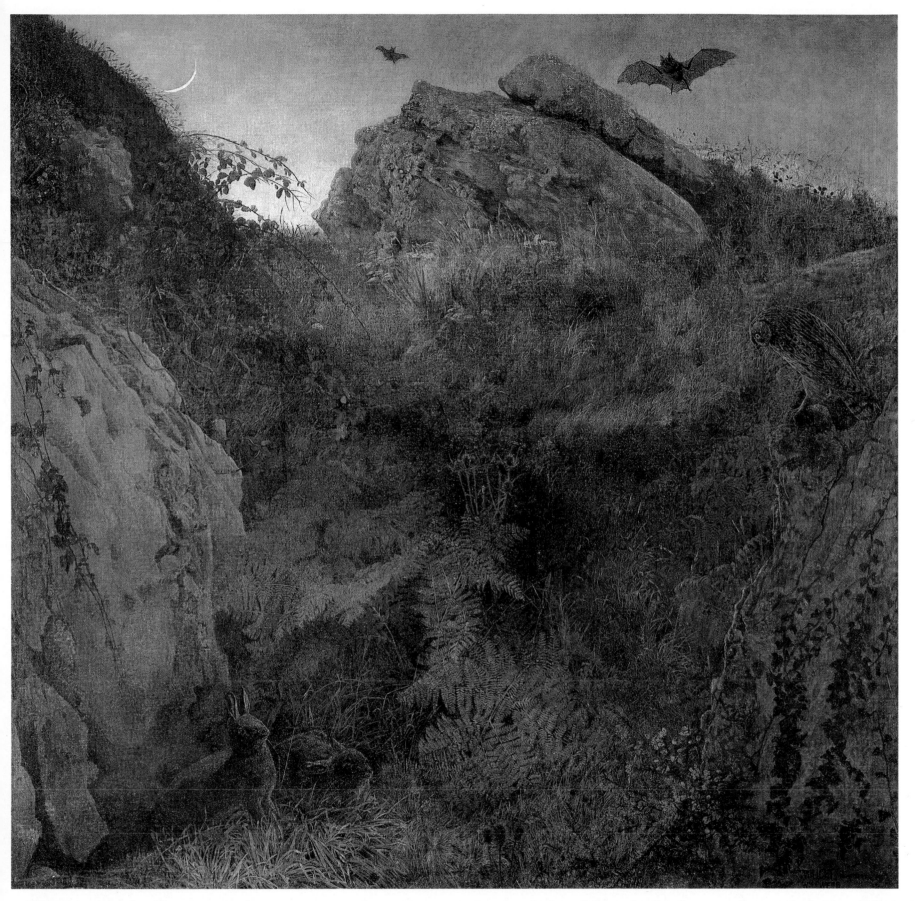

William J. Webbe (fl. 1853–1878)

Twilight

Signed and inscribed with title
Canvas 91 × 91 cm/36 × 36 ins
Private Collection

Very little is known of Webbe's life, but most of his pictures are of sheep and show the influence of Holman Hunt. This extraordinary picture shows that he could also paint imaginative subjects of his own.

the new came to a head with the celebrated Whistler v. Ruskin trial of 1877, and in 1885 Whistler delivered his 'Ten o'clock Lecture'. In it he satirized the Ruskinian principles of naturalist landscape: 'To say to the painter, that Nature is to be taken as she is, is to say to the player that he may sit on the piano.' In terms of the English landscape tradition, as exemplified by Constable, Turner and David Cox, Pre-Raphaelite landscape is an aberration. By breaking completely with tradition, and insisting on total realism, it condemned itself to a dead end. But it is nonetheless historically important, and one of the most interesting side-effects of the Pre-Raphaelite movement.

Part III Later Years

The second phase – Pre-Raphaelitism and the Aesthetic Movement

By 1853, the original Brotherhood was dissolved, and by 1860 the first phase of the Pre-Raphaelite movement was over. After 1859 Ruskin gave up his *Academy Notes* because he could no longer praise or support the work of his friends and protégés. He had already denounced the changes in Millais' art, and he was later to quarrel with Rossetti too. His encouragement of Inchbold and Brett had failed to produce a coherent school of Pre-Raphaelite landscape. Nonetheless, Ruskin remained faithful to the original principles of the Brotherhood of the 1850s, and he felt increasingly out of sympathy with the new developments of the 1860s and '70s. This was to lead to his notorious attack on Whistler in 1877, and the Whistler v. Ruskin libel trial which followed. Although Ruskin won the battle, he lost the war, and his reputation was irreparably damaged. The only Pre-Raphaelite with whom he remained on good terms was Hunt, who did not die until 1910, becoming an immensely respected and prestigious figure. Hunt too remained faithful to his original Pre-Raphaelite principles, and never joined the Royal Academy, unlike Millais, who became its President just before his death in 1896.

The second phase of the Pre-Raphaelite movement really began with the association of three artists – Rossetti, William Morris and Edward Burne-Jones. Under their combined influence, the movement was given a new impetus and a new sense of direction, carrying it far beyond painting, into almost every aspect of Victorian artistic life – furniture, the decorative arts, architecture and interior decoration, book design and illustration, and even literature. For the rest of the century, Pre-Raphaelitism was to become part of the English way of life. Joseph Comyns Carr, one of the founders of the Grosvenor Gallery, wrote that 'even in the 'seventies, when I first actively engaged in the study of painting, the stirring spirit of English art still throbbed to the message that had been delivered by the Pre-Raphaelite Brotherhood more than twenty years before.'

The 1860s was a period of intense artistic and intellectual ferment, and out of it emerged the Aesthetic Movement, which was to shape the course of English painting for the rest of the century. It also completely changed the course of the Pre-Raphaelite movement, for the Aesthetic Movement was, by its very nature, eclectic, and drew on a wide variety of sources of inspiration. Pre-Raphaelitism was one element in the Aesthetic Movement, but by no means the only one, and therefore the second phase of the Pre-Raphaelite movement is far more complex than the first. At first the dominating figure was, once again, Rossetti, but as his health began to decline in the 1870s, the leadership passed to Burne-Jones. The latter's triumph was finally achieved in 1877, with the opening of the Grosvenor Gallery, when he was hailed as England's leading modern artist. Burne-Jones's style was a highly personal fusion of Pre-Raphaelite, Italianate and classical elements, and he did not regard himself as a leader of the Aesthetic Movement, whose more extreme exponents were Whistler, Swinburne, and Walter Pater. Burne-Jones remained faithful to the romantic, Rossettian style of Pre-Raphaelitism; even at the very end of his life in the 1890s he was still painting stories from his beloved *Morte d'Arthur*. His influence on other English artists was immense, and he was the only Victorian artist to gain an international reputation in his own lifetime. He spawned a whole generation of followers, of whom the best-known are John Melhuish Strudwick, Evelyn de Morgan, Spencer-Stanhope and Sidney Harold Meteyard. Echoes of his work are to

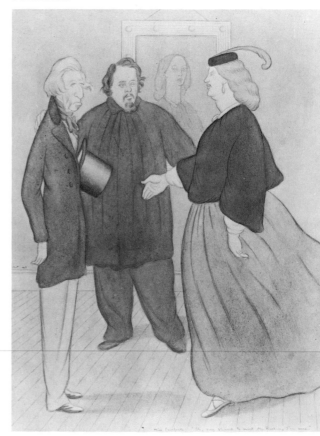

Max Beerbohm, Ruskin, Rossetti and Fanny Cornforth.

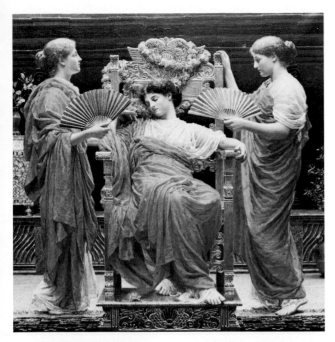

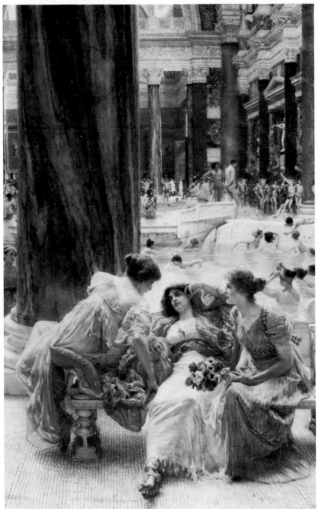

Above: **Albert Joseph Moore**, *Midsummer*, 1887.
Below: **Sir Lawrence Alma-Tadema**, *The Baths of Caracalla*, 1899.

be found in Aubrey Beardsley and many other illustrators of the 1890s, and such later romantic Pre-Raphaelite artists as Waterhouse, Byam Shaw and Cadogan Cowper carried his influence well into the twentieth century.

Parallel with Burne-Jones and the Aesthetic Movement, another movement had emerged from the 1860s, in direct opposition to Pre-Raphaelitism. This was the classical movement, of whom the chief exponents were Frederick Leighton, George Frederick Watts, Edward John Poynter and Lawrence Alma-Tadema. Leighton and Watts both flirted briefly with Pre-Raphaelite ideas in the 1850s, but Leighton became an avowed anti-Pre-Raphaelite in the 1860s. His aim was to lead English art back to its European, classical heritage, and after he became President of the Royal Academy in 1878, the English art world divided into two camps, the Academy championing the classical and more traditional artists, and the Grosvenor representing Burne-Jones, Whistler, and the more progressive elements of the Aesthetic Movement. But taking a broader view, one can see that Leighton too was a high Victorian aesthete, and very much a man of his time. The classical movement is really only another aspect of the Aesthetic Movement. Burne-Jones and Leighton represent the romantic and the classical ends of the same aesthetic philosophy. Both were High Victorian dreamers, one dreaming of Avalon, the other of Parnassus. In the work of many other late Victorian artists, Pre-Raphaelite, classical and aesthetic elements are fused in various degrees, and to separate them is no easy task. In the work of Albert Moore, for example, the classical and the aesthetic are combined in a uniquely subtle and personal way that defies easy definition. To make matters worse, many people still think of Moore as a Pre-Raphaelite, which he certainly was not. Simeon Solomon, on the other hand, was a Pre-Raphaelite, and a follower of Rossetti and Burne-Jones, but in his work one also finds classical and aesthetic elements, combined with his own personal interest in Jewish history and ritual. He is a typical figure of the 1860s, and illustrates perfectly how complex Pre-Raphaelitism had become by this period. The truth is that the second phase of the Pre-Raphaelite movement is part of a tremendously rich and eclectic artistic epoch. In the much-quoted words of Henry James, writing about Burne-Jones in 1877, 'it is the art of culture, of reflection, of intellectual luxury, of aesthetic refinement, of people who look at the world and at life not directly, as it were, and in all its accidental reality, but in the reflection and ornamental portrait of it furnished by literature, by poetry, by history, by erudition.' Pre-Raphaelitism was an expression of the final rich flowering of late Victorian civilization, an epoch that was soon to be swept away for ever by the destructive forces of modernism and the Great War.

The tragic Pre-Raphaelite – the later work of Rossetti

The later career of Rossetti is another strange and tragic chapter in the Pre-Raphaelite story. After the death of Elizabeth Siddal in 1862, Rossetti was a haunted man. The move from Chatham Place to Tudor House, a large eighteenth-century mansion by the river in Chelsea, was not enough to exorcize the past. He was tortured by remorse and insomnia, and became increasingly dependent on chloral and alcohol. The Bohemian disorder of his household and life-style have become in themselves part of the Pre-Raphaelite legend. Various people lived there, including the poet Algernon Swinburne, and, for a time, the author George Meredith. Models came and went, several of them becoming Rossetti's mistresses, notably the vulgar and grasping Fanny Cornforth, with whom he maintained an easygoing relationship for years. There was also the sinister Charles Howell, an extraordinary rogue who became Rossetti's unofficial agent and dealer. The house was full of old English furniture, blue-and-white china and endless bric-à-brac collected by Rossetti in local junk shops. Both house and garden swarmed with pets – owls, wombats, wallabies, parrots, peacocks, even at one time a Brahmin bull whose eyes reminded him of Jane Morris. As time went on, Rossetti became more eccentric and more of a recluse, seeing only a few close friends and patrons. After Robert Buchanan's attack on him in his notorious pamphlet, *The Fleshly School of Poetry* (1871), Rossetti suffered from persecution mania, and even attempted suicide the following year. But in spite of all this, he remained a witty, intelligent and fascinating man, and he cast his spell over many younger artists. Meetings at Tudor House could be relied on to produce good conversation, stimulating ideas, interesting people and abundant merriment and it remained a focal point for many of the vital artistic developments of the 1860s.

Rossetti's own creative genius was by no means exhausted. He continued to paint and write during the last twenty years of his life, and it was only his long final illness that prevented him from working. His famous picture *Beata Beatrix* (p. 97), painted in memory of Elizabeth Siddal, shows the new direction in which his art was moving. Instead of the small, intense watercolours of the 1850s, he was now beginning to paint in oils, and on a larger scale. *Beata Beatrix* was the first of the female half-length figures that were to become the recurring theme of his art. It has now deservedly become one of the most famous of all Pre-Raphaelite images, and it is certainly one of the most remarkable pictures of the century. In it painting, poetry and personal sorrow are combined in a uniquely powerful and intense way, and the picture vibrates with emotion. It is impossible to stand in front of it and not be moved. Rossetti was only ever to paint one other subject from Dante, his *Dante's Dream* of 1871, and that was based on a much earlier watercolour. He also abandoned Arthurian and Tennysonian subjects. Thereafter there was to be one subject, and one subject alone in his art – women. Rossetti was a love poet and a love painter, and there has been no greater worshipper of female beauty in English painting.

But there were other reasons for Rossetti's change of style. He was extremely sensitive to, and aware of, artistic trends in the 1860s. Some of his small watercolours of the late 1850s, such as *The Blue Closet*, anticipate the aesthetic interest in musical subjects later explored by Whistler and Albert Moore. Rossetti took a keen interest in what his younger contemporaries were doing, and during the 1860s he painted a few classical subjects and even occasional female nudes. He also responded to the vogue for Italian Renaissance painting, and his pictures of women owe an obvious debt to such Venetian portrait painters as Titian, Giorgione and Palma Giovane. Two pictures of 1872 illustrate just how Rossetti's new style had evolved, *The Bower Meadow* (p. 99) and *Veronica Veronese* (p. 100). The same mood of dreamy sensuality pervades both pictures, which are painted in rich, exotic colours. The models conform to the classic Rossetti type, with their pouting red mouths, wistful expressions and long wavy hair. These pictures were extremely popular with

Dante Gabriel Rossetti
Beata Beatrix

Signed with monogram 1864–70
Canvas 86 × 66 cm/34 × 26 ins
Tate Gallery, London

Painted as a memorial to Rossetti's wife, Elizabeth Siddal, who died in 1862. Rossetti had in fact begun the picture many years before, but took it up again in 1864 and completed it by 1870. It is one of his most intensely visionary, Symbolist pictures, and marks a new direction in his art. Once again, it represents the death of Beatrice in Dante's *Vita Nuova*. Beatrice sits in a death-like trance, while a bird, the messenger of Death, drops a poppy into her hands. In the background the figures of Love and Dante gaze at each other, with the Ponte Vecchio and the Duomo of Florence silhouetted behind them.

Left: **Dante Gabriel Rossetti**, *Dante's Dream*, 1871. Below: *Proserpine*, 1877.

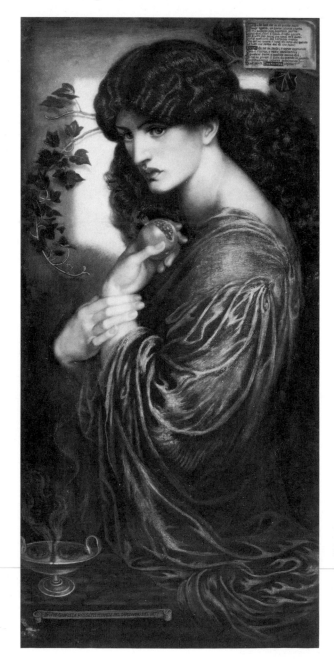

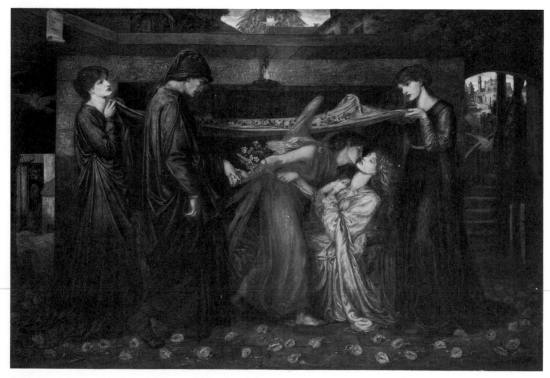

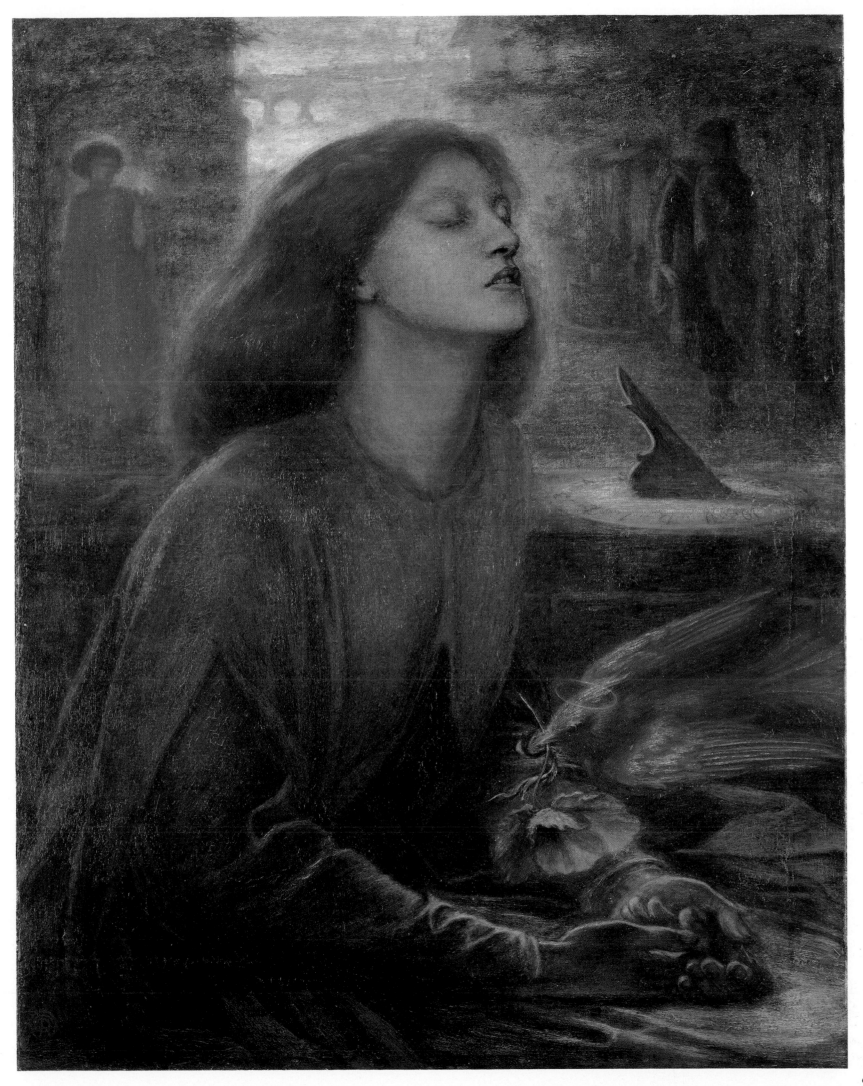

Rossetti's patrons, mostly northern businessmen, and no major collection in Birmingham, Liverpool or Manchester was complete without one.

There is one woman, however, whose name is inseparable from that of Rossetti during his last years – Jane Morris. Born Jane Burden, she was the wife of Rossetti's former pupil and protégé, William Morris. The marriage had not proved a happy one, and during the 1860s she and Rossetti found increasing solace in each other's company. Between 1871 and 1874 Rossetti and Morris shared the tenancy of Kelmscott Manor in Oxfordshire, and as Morris was frequently abroad or away, Rossetti and Jane spent long periods there together. It was a melancholy, despairing kind of love affair, and is certainly one of the strangest artist-model relationships in art history. Bernard Shaw described Jane Morris as 'the most silent woman I have ever met', and as Rossetti's health and mental state grew steadily worse during the 1870s, his love for Jane, and his dependence on her, became an obsession. Just as he had immortalized Lizzie Siddal, so now he was to immortalize Jane Morris. He drew and painted her continually. Again and again her face stares out from Rossetti's canvases; she was the *femme fatale* of his life as well as his art. Photographs which Rossetti took of her in his garden show that she really did look the way Rossetti painted her. The masses of black, wavy hair, the sad eyes, the curved mouth, the columnar neck – they are all there; Rossetti only developed and accentuated them. Of all Rossetti's many pictures of Jane, none is more remarkable than the large *Astarte Syriaca* (p. 102). Its unreal lighting, lurid colours and mood of heavy melancholy and longing reflect the claustrophobic atmosphere of their relationship. It has been compared to an icon, and as a hymn to female beauty, and it certainly has an intensity of devotion that is usually reserved for religious art. Even to those familiar with Pre-Raphaelite art, Rossetti's works have a strangeness and an obsessive sensuality, that are unique in English art. There is nothing quite like them, and although he had

Dante Gabriel Rossetti
The Bower Meadow
Signed and dated 1872
Canvas 85 × 67 cm/33½ × 26½ ins
Manchester City Art Gallery

The models for the two girls in the foreground were Maria Stillman (also a painter) and Alexa Wilding. The rich colours and languorous mood of the painting are typical of Rossetti's work at this period. The landscape background was originally painted in November 1850 at Knole, near Sevenoaks, Kent, for a picture of *Dante and Beatrice in Paradise*.

Left: **Dante Gabriel Rossetti**, Jane Morris in a study for *Daydream*, 1878. Below: A photograph of Jane Morris by Rossetti.

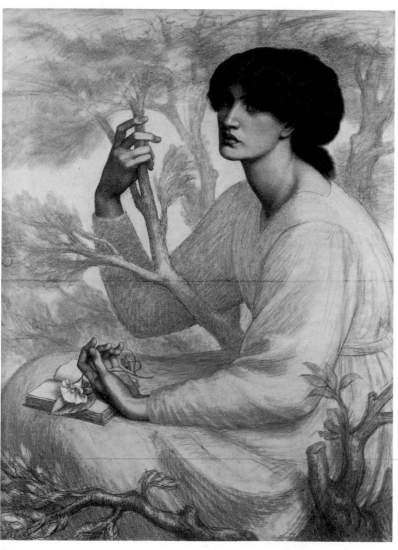

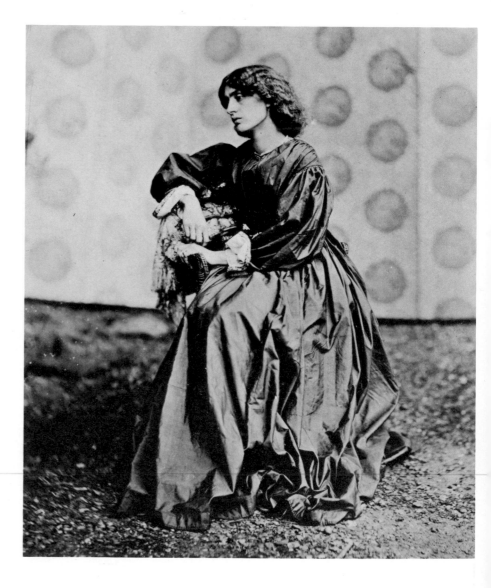

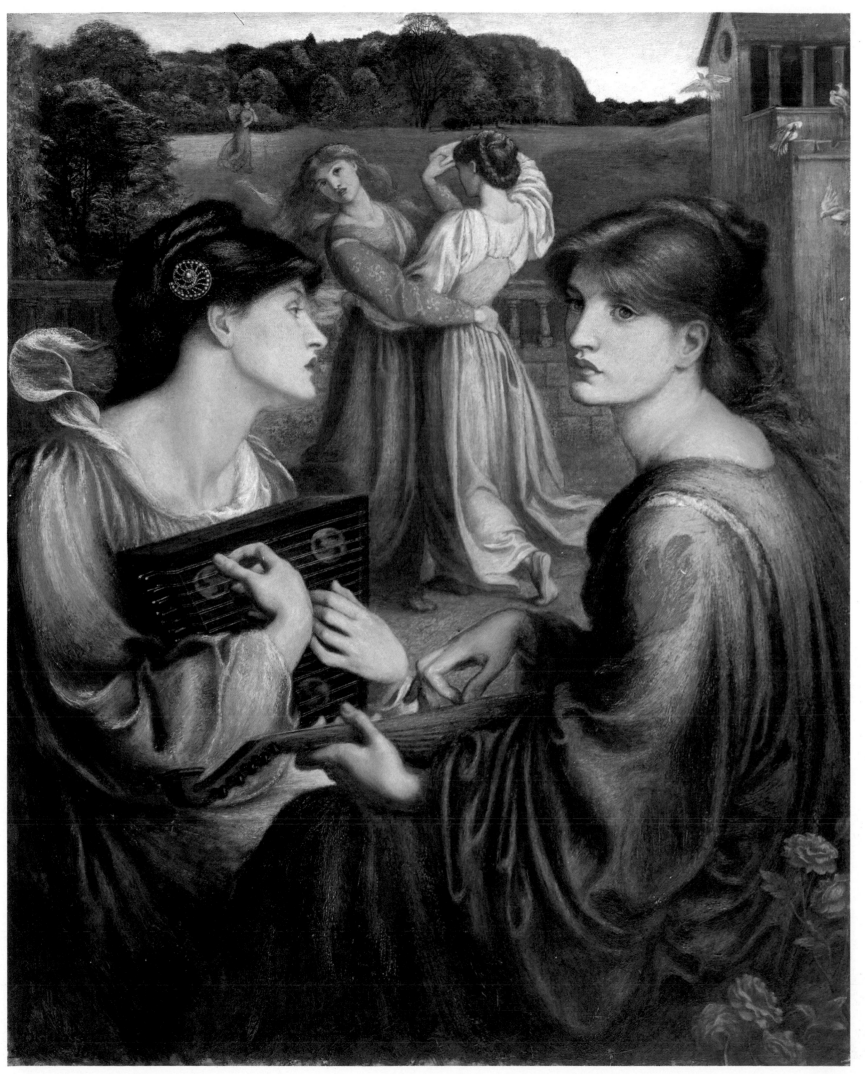

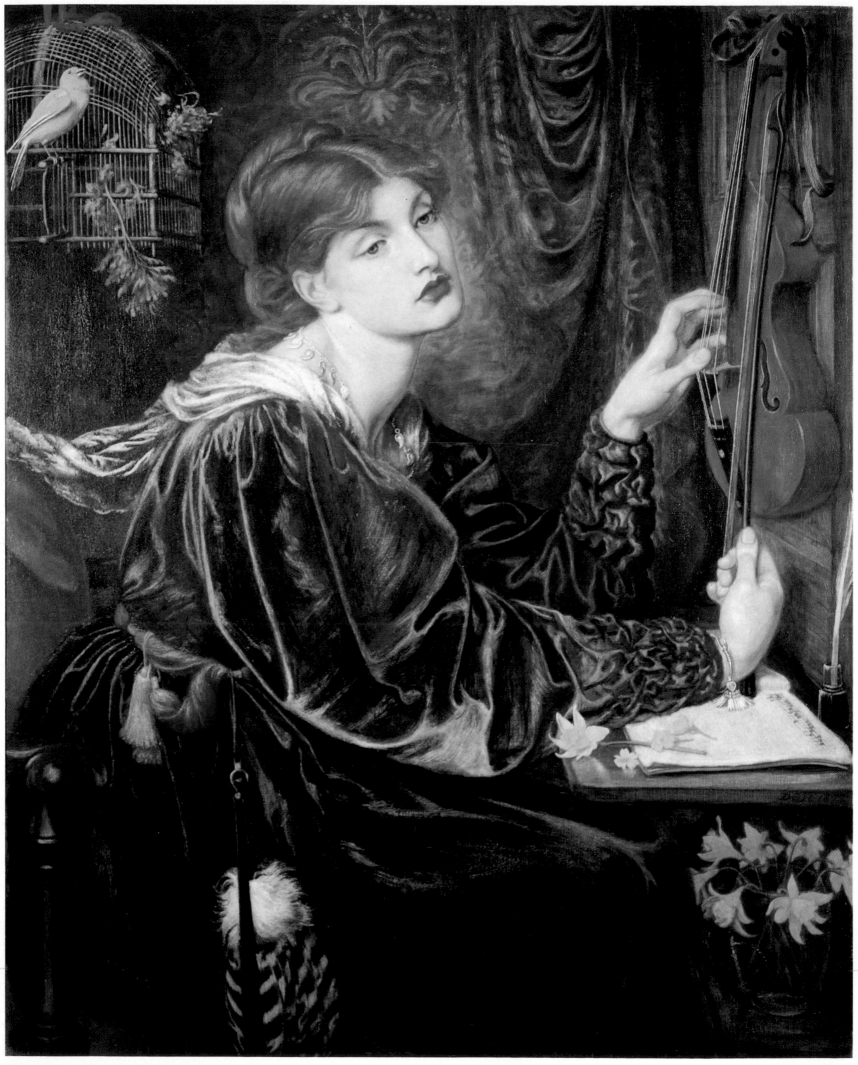

Dante Gabriel Rossetti

Veronica Veronese

Signed and dated 1872
Canvas 109 × 89 cm/43 × 35 ins
Bancroft Collection, Wilmington Society of Fine Arts,
Delaware

The model, once again, was Alexa Wilding, one of Rossetti's favourite sitters. The picture was painted for F.R.Leyland in 1872, and Rossetti wrote to him describing it: 'The girl is in a sort of passionate reverie, and is drawing her hand listlessly along the strings of a violin which hangs against the wall, while she holds the bow with the other hands, as if arrested by the thought of the moment, when she was about to play. In colour I shall make the picture a study of varied greens.'

many admirers and followers, his style was inimitable. His real descendants were the Symbolist and decadent painters of the *fin de siècle*; his brooding and monstrous images of women are the direct ancestors of the endless *femmes fatales* of Art Nouveau. Another of his greatest late works is *The Blessed Damozel* (p. 103), commissioned in 1871 but not completed until 1879. This time the model was Alexa Wilding, and although the picture does not have the haunting quality of *Astarte Syriaca*, it is one of the richest and most decorative of all Rossetti's late works. Fittingly, it illustrates his poem of the same title, first published in *The Germ* in those far-off days of 1850.

By 1878, Rossetti's long, slow and sad decline had begun. He stopped painting or writing, and became almost a permanent invalid. His consumption of drugs had become appalling. In 1880 he told the novelist Thomas Hall Caine, later his biographer, that he was taking 180 grains of chloral a day, washed down with neat whisky. At last he died, paralysed and partially deaf, at the age of only 54. It was a sad end for the one truly original genius of the Pre-Raphaelite movement.

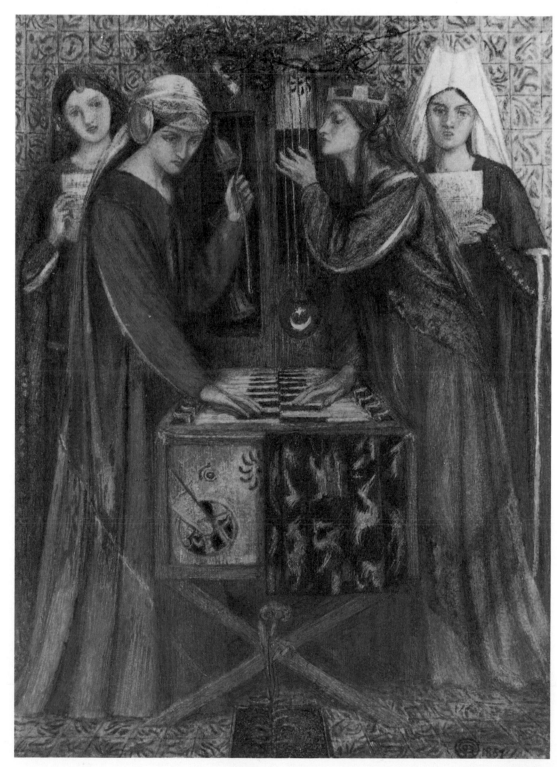

Dante Gabriel Rossetti, *The Blue Closet*, 1857.

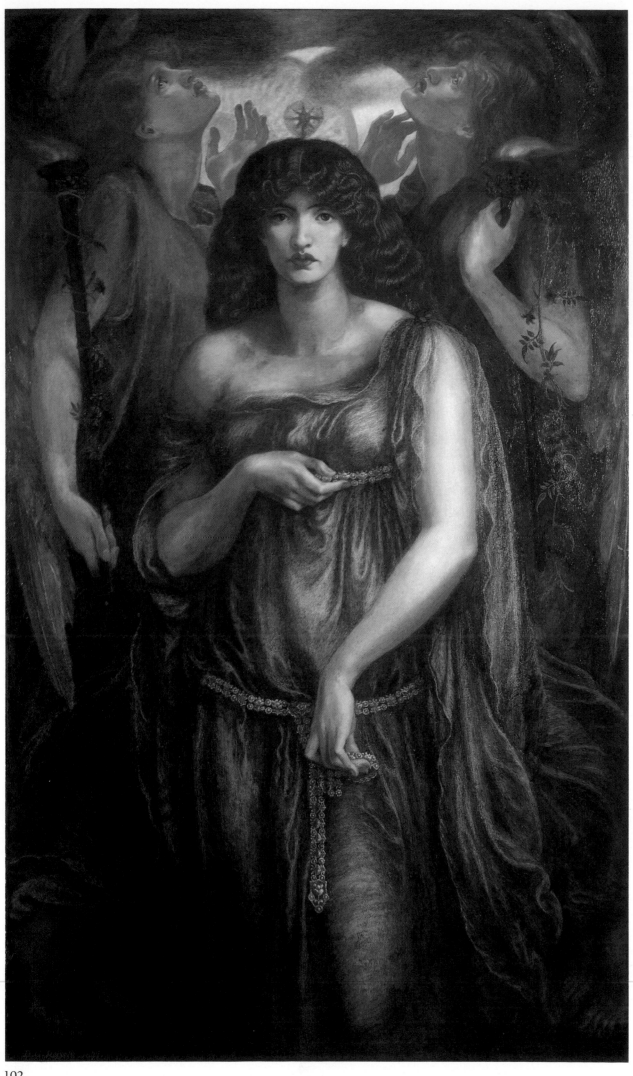

Dante Gabriel Rossetti
Astarte Syriaca

Signed and dated 1877
Canvas 183 × 107 cm/72 × 42 ins
Manchester City Art Gallery

One of the largest and most
extraordinary of all Rossetti's pictures
of Jane Morris. She is portrayed as
Venus Astarte, with two torch-bearing
attendants, in a composition full of
tension and mannerism, glowing with
deep and mysterious colours. This is
the very epitome of the Rossettian Pre-
Raphaelite love goddess, and Rossetti
wrote a poem describing it, which
ends:

> That face, of Love's all-penetrative spell
> Amulet, talisman and oracle –
> Betwixt the sun and moon a mystery.

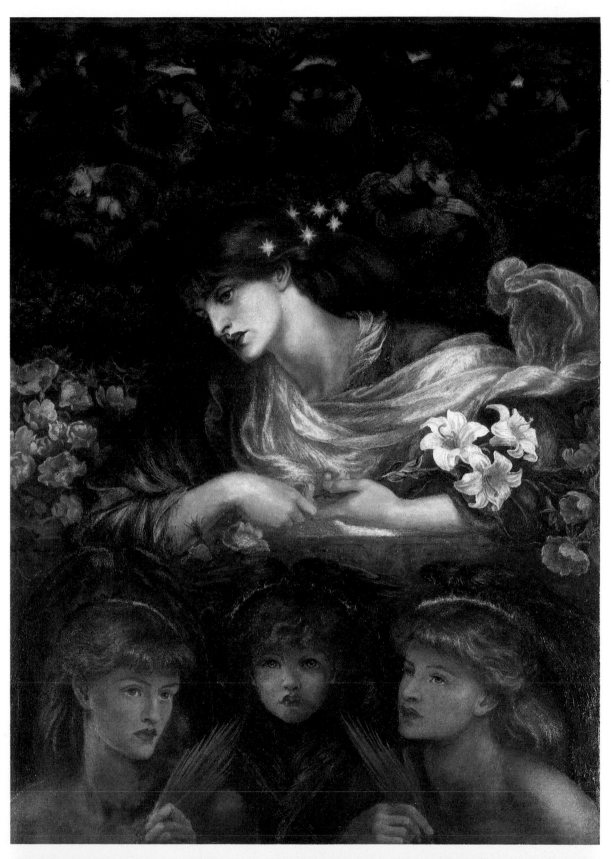

Dante Gabriel Rossetti
The Blessed Damozel

Canvas 174 × 94 cm/68½ × 37 ins, with predella
Fogg Museum of Art, Harvard University

An illustration to Rossetti's poem of the same title, which begins:

The blessed damozel leaned out
From the gold bar of Heaven;
Her eyes were deeper than the depth
Of waters stilled at even;
She had three lilies in her hand,
And the stars in her hair were seven.

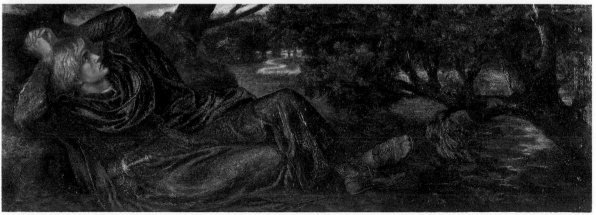

The faithful Pre-Raphaelite – Holman Hunt

Meanwhile, Rossetti's old friend and colleague, Holman Hunt, was pursuing his own very individual path. He lived to a ripe old age, and was to become much more famous and well-known in his lifetime than Rossetti ever did. This was mainly due to his reputation as a serious religious painter, which spread his name far and wide, through the countless engravings and prints made after his work. Hunt was the only one of the original Brotherhood to remain faithful to its principles, and his later pictures are all developments of ideas formulated much earlier. In spite of the difficulties he always experienced with technique, Hunt laboured more and more over his pictures, sometimes taking years to complete them. He also became the first Pre-Raphaelite to write a history of the movement; his *Pre-Raphaelitism and the Pre-Raphaelite Brotherhood* was published in 1905. Although Hunt tried to claim rather too much of the glory for himself, it remains one of the few prime sources of information about the Brotherhood.

Hunt's *Isabella and the Pot of Basil* (p. 105) of 1867 shows his mature style developing. Like *The Finding of the Saviour in the Temple* (p. 45), the picture is an elaborate, highly-wrought composition, crammed with detail. Hunt's interest in the Middle East is reflected in many of the accessories, especially the prie-dieu in the foreground. The subject is from Keats, one of the Brotherhood's favourite poets, and recalls Hunt's own *Eve of Saint Agnes*, painted nearly twenty years earlier in 1848. The figure of Isabella is a portrait of Hunt's first wife, and he painted a number of portraits of friends and relations during the 1860s and 1870s in this elaborate and robust manner.

Hunt returned to the Holy Land from 1869 to 1872, and this trip provided the genesis of his two last major religious pictures, *The Shadow of Death* (p. 107) and *The Triumph of the Innocents* (below). Both these pictures, which occupied him for nearly

William Holman Hunt
The Triumph of the Innocents

Signed and dated 76–87
Oil on linen 157 × 248 cm/62 × 97½ ins
Walker Art Gallery, Liverpool

The second and most ambitious of Hunt's biblical pictures of the 1870s and '80s. It was begun in Jerusalem on his second trip to the Middle East, 1869–72, and continued on his third trip, 1875–78. The subject is a curious mixture of the real and the allegorical. It represents the Holy Family, at night, on the Flight from Egypt. They have seen a vision of the spirits of children murdered in the Massacre of the Innocents, who float in strange, watery auras intended to symbolize the streams of eternal life. This symbolism is carried further by the bubbles, or 'airy globes' as Hunt called them, in which are reflected various biblical allegories symbolizing the Jewish millenium. The picture was not finally finished until 1887, and meanwhile Hunt painted another replica, now in the Tate Gallery. Ruskin proclaimed it 'the greatest religious painting of our time', but Hunt's fellow Pre-Raphaelite, Frederick George Stephens, criticized its 'strange mixture of real and unreal' which he found 'self-contradictory and puzzling' and declared the picture a noble failure.

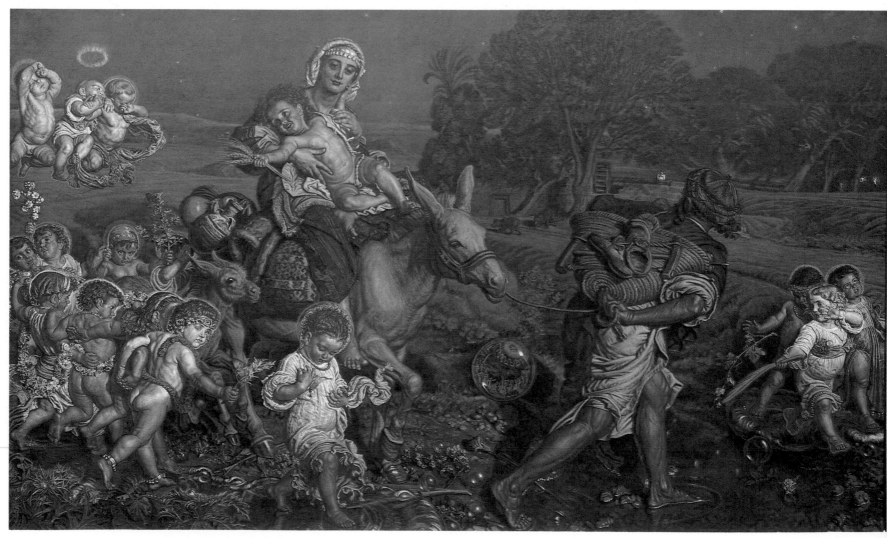

William Holman Hunt
Isabella and the Pot of Basil

Signed and dated Florence 1867
Canvas 185 × 113 cm/72¾ × 44½ ins
Laing Art Gallery, Newcastle

Begun as a portrait of Hunt's first wife, Fanny Waugh, who died in Florence in 1866. The picture was then finished in London between 1867 and 1868. The subject is from *Isabella* by Keats, one of Hunt's favourite sources for literary themes. The inlaid prie-dieu belonged to the artist. He accumulated a large collection of Middle Eastern and other objects in his studio, and frequently made use of them in his paintings.

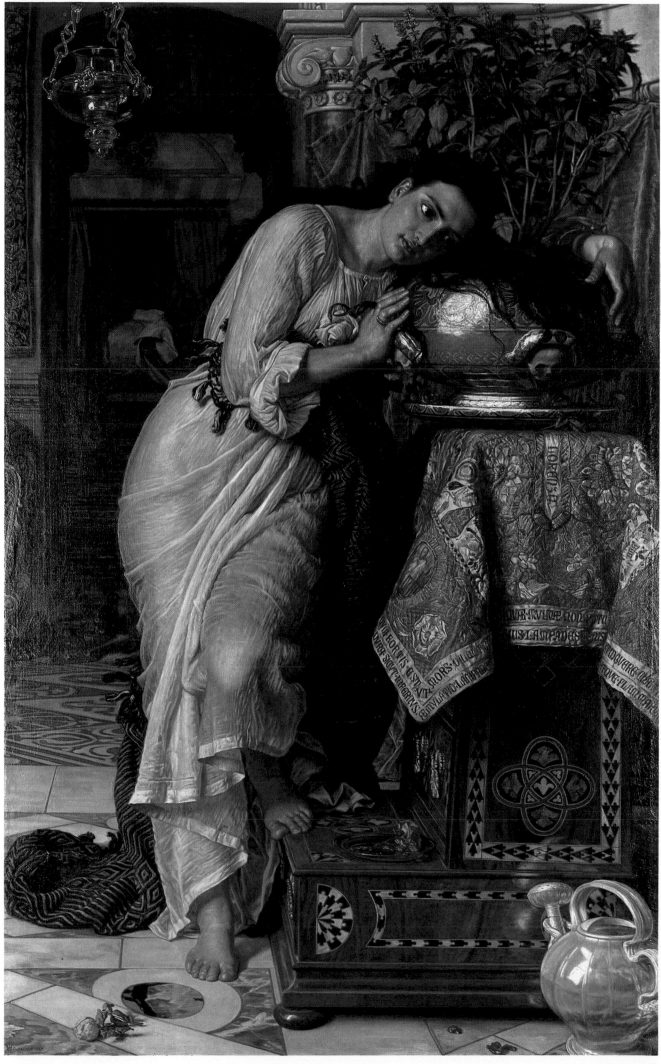

twenty years, consolidated his reputation as England's greatest religious artist, and prints and reproductions of them can still be found in churches, schools and colleges all over the world. Hunt's immense standing usually ensured a polite critical reception of his religious works – it would have seemed almost profane to criticize, especially considering how long the artist had toiled to produce them. But for us, a hundred years later, it is not easy to find these pictures artistically satisfying. Impressive, certainly, but the painting of the face and the body of Jesus in *The Shadow of Death* is harsh and unattractive, and basically at odds with the artist's strongly realistic style. Even the solidity of his modelling is somehow reminiscent of the heavy oppressiveness of the worst kind of Victorian furniture.

Hunt's religious pictures are symbols of Victorian faith; to our sceptical, twentieth-century eyes, they seem too laboured, too sentimental and too evocative of the very kind of Victorian religiosity and humbug we have deliberately rebelled against. But Hunt's reputation can rest securely on his last great work, the *Lady of Shalott* (p. 108). As Burne-Jones was also to do in the 1890s, Hunt here returned to the romantic Tennysonian themes of his youth, and in doing so, created his greatest masterpiece, and a key Pre-Raphaelite image. In this wonderful picture, Hunt's elaborate symbolism, decorative richness, and the swirling Art Nouveau figure of the red-haired model are successfully combined to produce a powerful and effective composition. One wishes that Hunt could have painted more pictures like this, and

William Holman Hunt

The Shadow of Death

Signed with monogram and dated 1870–73, Jerusalem
Canvas 212 × 166 cm/83½ × 65½ ins
Manchester City Art Gallery

The first major biblical picture to result from Hunt's second trip to the Holy Land, 1869–72. The picture was begun in a carpenter's shop in Bethlehem, and Hunt took immense pains to get every detail of the tools and the workshop historically correct. Later he continued painting it on a rooftop in Jerusalem, to make sure of the effects of full sunlight. The picture was not finished until 1873, when it was bought and exhibited by Agnews of London. A long pamphlet was published explaining the subject, in particular the pose of Christ, who stretches himself after his labours in the worshop, and unwittingly presages the crucifixion, which his mother sees in his shadow on the wall. The critics were respectful and appreciative, and the picture toured Oxford and the North of England with great success.

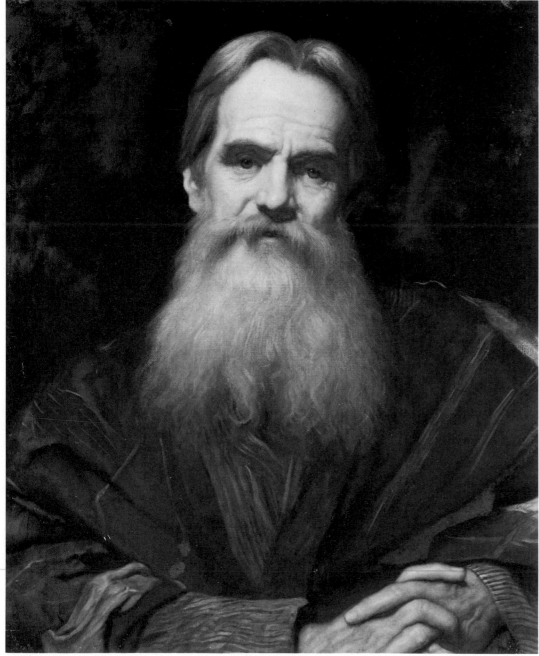

Sir William Blake Richmond, portrait of William Holman Hunt, 1900.

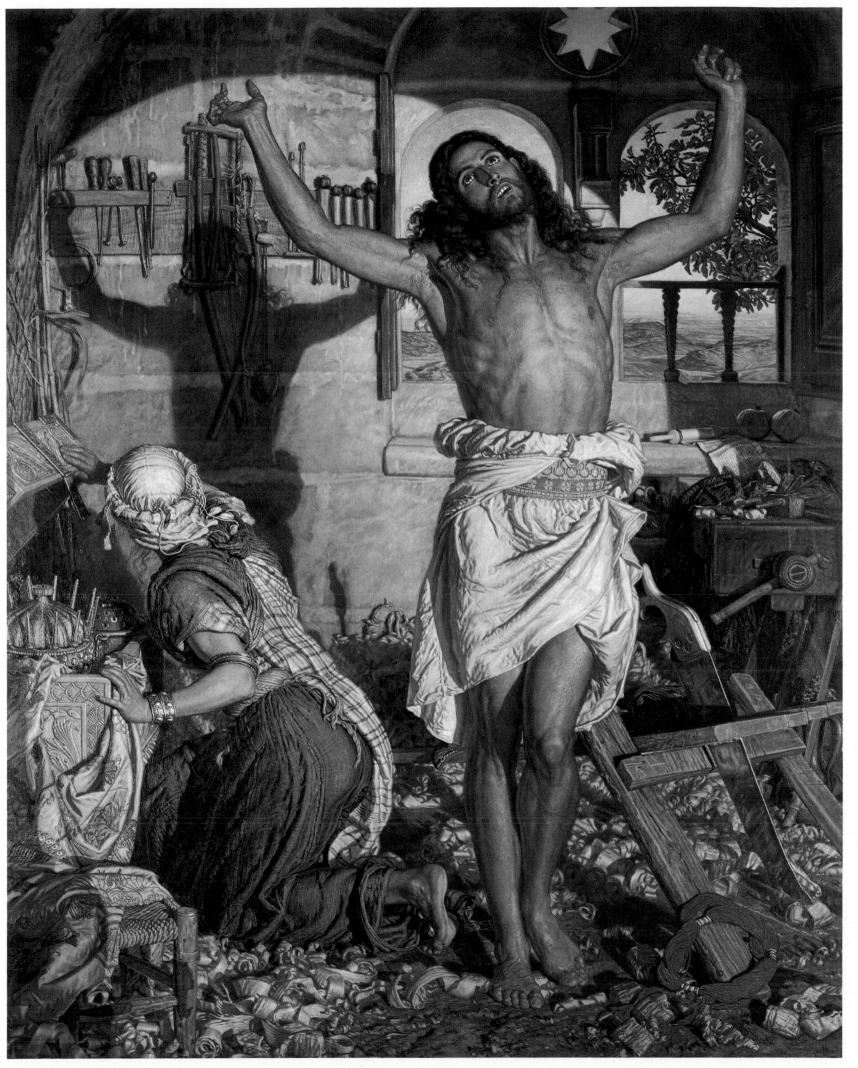

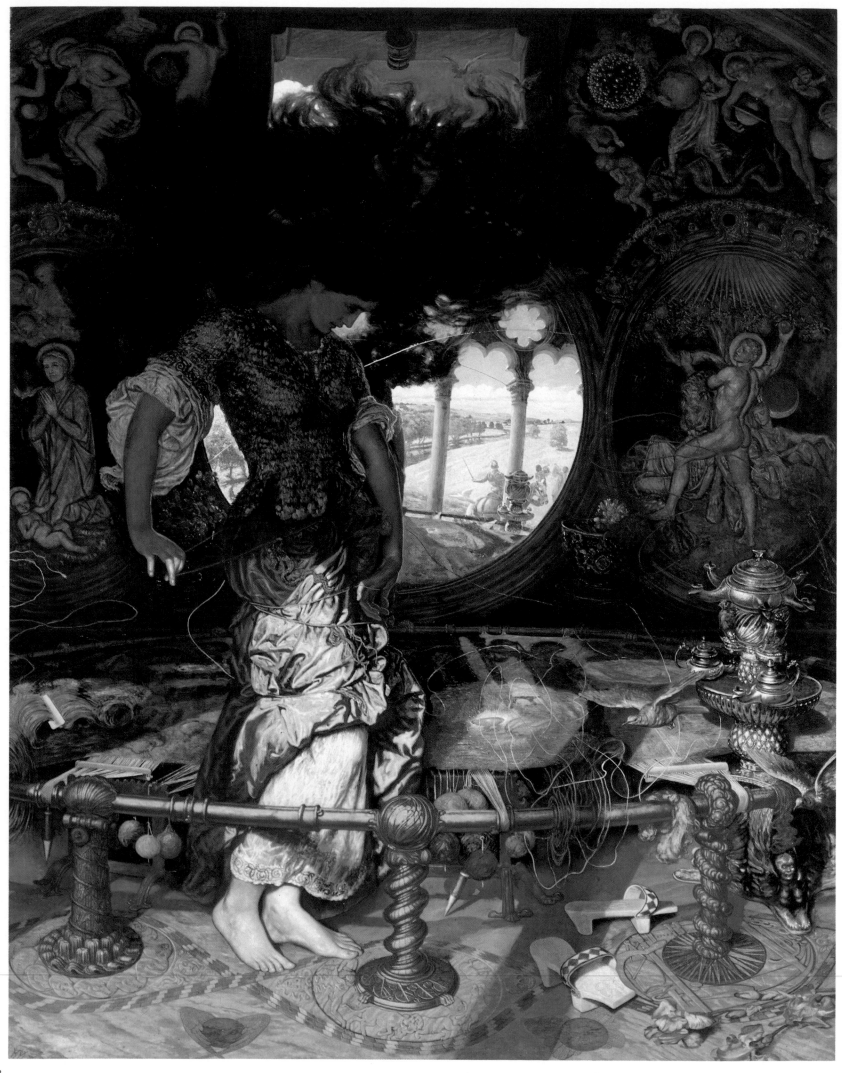

William Holman Hunt
The Lady of Shalott

Signed 1886–1905
Canvas 188 × 146 cm/74 × 57½ ins
Wadsworth Athenaeum, Hartford, Connecticut

The last and greatest of Hunt's Pre-Raphaelite pictures, begun around 1886 and not completed until 1905, by which time his eyesight was beginning to fail. The picture depicts the fatal moment when the Lady of Shalott, weaving her tapestry, sees the reflection of Sir Lancelot in the mirror, and looks out of the forbidden window on to the world outside, thus breaking her vow. The design goes back to Hunt's illustration for Moxon's edition of Tennyson (1857), and even back to a drawing of 1850. The picture was intended as an elaborate fable representing the conflict between the forces of good and evil, and in the background are reliefs representing the Virgin and Child, Hercules in the garden of the Hesperides, and a frieze of cherubs. The hair was modelled by a Mrs Amelia Milnes, and took three years to finish. It was draped over an easel to get the windblown effect that Hunt wanted.

fewer religious ones. But Hunt's moral earnestness and his religious faith are key elements in his character, and he alone of the Brotherhood achieved their aim of painting pictures which would have wide popular appeal. In any assessment of the Pre-Raphaelites, Hunt must be accorded equal status with Rossetti and Millais, although he lacked the imagination of the one and the natural talent of the other. In his own way, Hunt was a totally individual and original artist with a highly personal vision; his art must be counted as one of the most remarkable achievements of English nineteenth-century painting.

The Palace of Art – William Morris and Edward Burne-Jones

Morris and Burne-Jones first met, appropriately, in Oxford, that most medieval of English towns. Both men intended to study for the Church. It is no coincidence, therefore, that their main contribution to Pre-Raphaelitism was to lead English art and design back to the spirit of the Middle Ages. Morris was to become famous as a designer and decorator, Burne-Jones as a painter, but their lifelong artistic collaboration forms an integral part of the Pre-Raphaelite story.

In appearance and character, the two men could hardly have been more different. Burne-Jones was tall, thin, sensitive and withdrawn; Morris short, stocky, boisterous and energetic, with dark curly hair and beard. Their backgrounds were very different too; Burne-Jones was the son of a frame-maker and gilder in Birmingham; Morris's father was a wealthy London businessman. But when it came to art, literature and views about life, Ned and Topsy, as they called each other, quickly discovered they were kindred spirits. After their first meetings at Exeter College in 1853, they soon became the centre of a group of high-minded and idealistic young men, united by their enthusiasm for poetry, the Middle Ages, and gothic architecture, and by their hatred of the industrial revolution, materialism, trains, and just about everything created in the nineteenth century. They read Keats, Shelley, Tennyson, and above all Chaucer. Later they discovered Malory's *Morte d'Arthur*, which was to have the biggest impact in shaping the course of their artistic careers. Among modern writers they admired Carlyle, and, of course, Ruskin. From reading Ruskin they first learnt of the existence of the Pre-Raphaelite Brotherhood, and at the house of Thomas Combe in Oxford they were able to see for the first time works by Millais, Hunt and Rossetti. It was Rossetti's watercolour of *Dante Drawing an Angel* (p. 25) that made the deepest impression on the two young Oxford students. From the start it was the romantic, medievalizing side of Pre-Raphaelitism that appealed to them, and it was therefore Rossetti who became their hero.

In 1855 the time came for Morris and Burne-Jones to leave Oxford. After a trip through northern France to look at medieval churches and cathedrals, they both decided to dedicate their lives to the arts, Morris to architecture, Burne-Jones to painting. Morris entered the office of the architect George Edmund Street, and Burne-Jones met Rossetti at the Working Men's College, and became his pupil. Later both Morris and Burne-Jones moved into the rooms in Red Lion Square that had been occupied by Rossetti and Deverell in the historic days of the PRB. Rossetti encouraged Morris to become a painter, but soon discovered that he had little aptitude for it. More importantly, in Red Lion Square he began to design his own furniture, 'tables and chairs like incubi and succubi', as Rossetti described them. Several of these pieces were painted with medieval scenes by Rossetti and Burne-Jones. With Rossetti's help, Burne-Jones obtained his first commission to design stained glass.

It was against this background that the episode of the Oxford murals took place in 1857. This was to be the last, and the happiest, group effort by the Pre-Raphaelites since the days of the Brotherhood. 'What fun we had! What jokes! What roars of laughter!' recalled the painter Val Prinsep later. Rossetti 'was the planet around which we revolved ... we copied his very way of speaking. All beautiful women were "stunners" with us. Wombats were the most beautiful of God's creatures.

Medievalism was our *beau idéal*, and we sank our individuality in the strong personality of our adored Gabriel.' Together they painted ten different scenes from the *Morte d'Arthur*; Morris chose to illustrate *Sir Palomides watching Tristram and Iseult*. Prinsep records that the figures were poorly and clumsily painted, but the background of leaves and flowers were more suited to Morris's talents. Unfortunately, the murals today are no more than a shadow of what they must have been after that joyous Pre-Raphaelite summer of 1857.

The Oxford episode had one other important result for Morris. It was here that he met the beautiful Jane Burden, with whom he fell in love. Both he and Rossetti made drawings of this new and wonderful 'stunner', who seemed to epitomize the type of romantic, medieval beauty that they were looking for. She was the model for Morris's only known finished oil painting, *Queen Guinevere* (p. 111). The following year they married. By Victorian standards, it was an unconventional marriage, and ultimately it was to be an unhappy one. Jane was the daughter of an ostler, and Morris's parents did not approve. But it appealed to Morris's ideas of medieval chivalry; many Victorian artists married girls far beneath them in the social scale. Also Morris was financially independent, and free to do what he wanted. So the young couple decided to go their own way, and the first step was to build their own house, a house in which everything was to be designed and made by them and their friends. That was to be the celebrated Red House at Bexley in Kent, designed by Philip Webb. This was their 'Palace of Art', a temple with Jane as its high priestess. Finding that everything on the market was ugly and badly designed, Morris, Burne-Jones and their friends set about designing everything themselves – furniture, carpets, tapestries, stained glass and metalwork.

Out of all this activity, and through the prodigious enthusiasm and energy of Morris, grew 'the Firm'. This was the celebrated firm of Morris, Marshall, Faulkner and Company, first established in Red Lion Square in 1861, and later to become simply Morris & Co. Morris and Burne-Jones were the most important designers, but almost everyone in the Pre-Raphaelite circle was involved – Madox Brown, Arthur Hughes, William de Morgan, who was in charge of the pottery and tiles, and many others. Morris's most important contribution to Pre-Raphaelitism was this involvement of artists in design and decorative work. This was to become one of the

William Morris (1834–1896)
Queen Guinevere (La Belle Iseult)

1858
Canvas 71 × 51 cm/28⅛ × 20 ins
Tate Gallery, London

Painted in 1858, while Morris was working on the Oxford Union frescoes. It is a portrait of Jane Burden, whom he married the following year. While working on the picture, Morris is said to have written on his drawing, 'I cannot paint you, but I love you', and then shown it to her. Morris was encouraged to take up painting by Rossetti, but this is his only known picture to survive.

Max Beerbohm, 'Topsy and Ned Jones settled on the settle in Red Lion Square'.

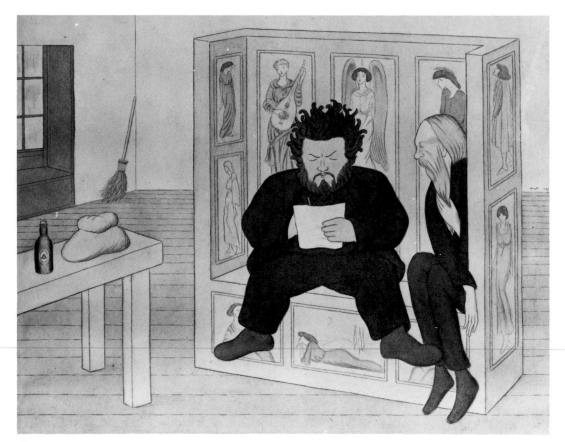

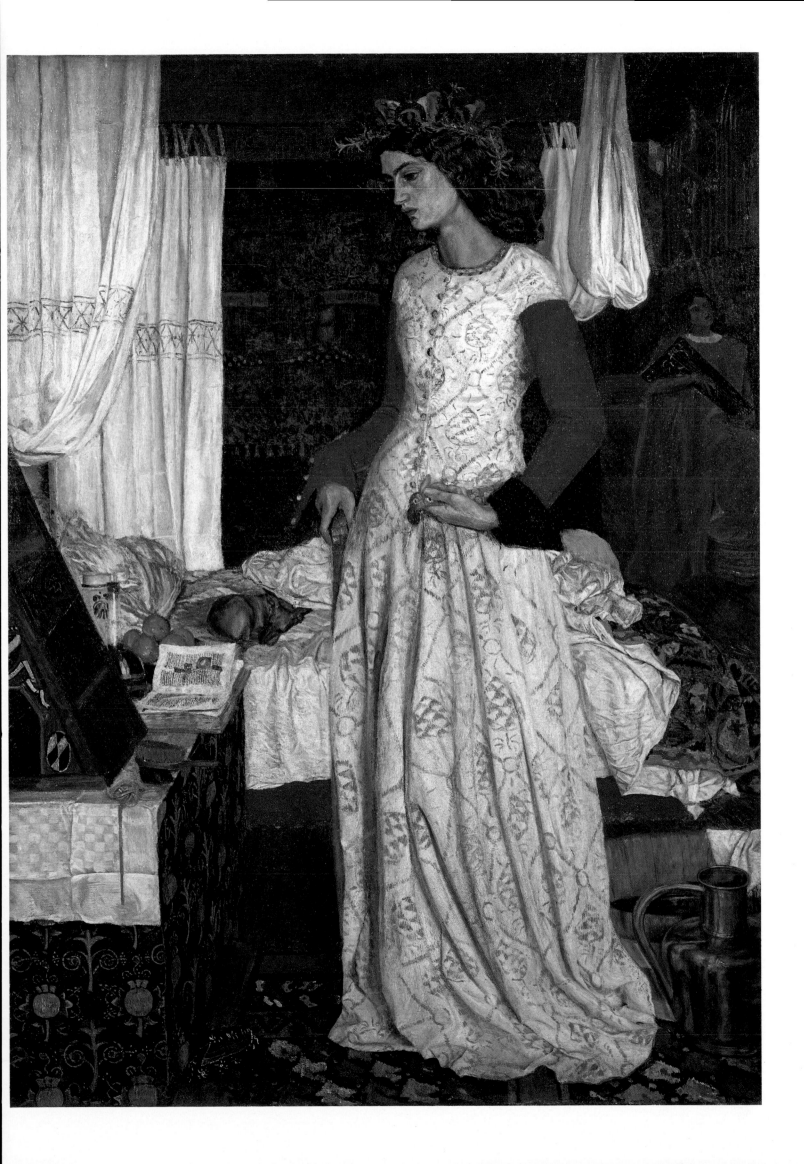

key tenets of the Aesthetic Movement, and almost all young artists of the 1860s first made their living by doing decorative and illustrative work. As the architect Thomas Graham Jackson was to write in 1873, 'Henceforth, instead of architects, painters and sculptors, let us have artists.' The most important part of the Firm's business was their stained glass, but they also produced beautiful tapestries, carpets, wallpapers, tiles, pottery, jewellery and metalwork. On top of all this, Morris was a prolific poet, and his first books of poetry, *The Defence of Guinevere* (1858) and *The Earthly Paradise* (1868–70), enjoyed considerable popular success. Almost single-handedly, this remarkable dynamo of a man, a true Victorian polymath, revolutionized English taste. His famous dictum, 'Have nothing in your house that you do not know to be useful, or believe to be beautiful', heralded a complete change of attitude in England towards interior decoration, and was to become the battle-cry of the Arts and Crafts Movement.

The Firm was a success, but Morris became disillusioned that he was merely working for the rich. His goods were too expensive for ordinary people. His answer, like Ruskin, was to become a Socialist. During the 1880s he threw himself with typical energy into Socialism, but this too ended in bitterness and further disillusionment. At the end of his life he turned for consolation to book printing, and founded the Kelmscott Press. Together again, he and Burne-Jones designed some of the most beautiful books ever printed, and finally in 1896, the year of Morris's death, the Kelmscott *Chaucer*, surely one of the greatest achievements of Pre-Raphaelitism, and as Yeats called it, 'the most beautiful book in the world'.

Edward Burne-Jones 1833–1898

With Burne-Jones we come to the most important artist of the second generation Pre-Raphaelites, and one of the major English artists of the nineteenth century. Burne-Jones was internationally famous in his own lifetime; now he is famous once again, and indelibly associated in the public mind with the romantic, other-worldly atmosphere of late Pre-Raphaelitism. His lifelong friendship and artistic association with William Morris have already been described; now it is appropriate to turn to his own career as a painter.

Burne-Jones came from a humble, middle-class background in Birmingham. His mother died a week after his birth, so he was inevitably a lonely and introspective child. He began to draw at a very young age, but his imagination was shaped above all by literature – Shakespeare, Homer, the Greek myths, and such romantic poets as Byron, Scott, Keats and Coleridge. When he later became a painter, the world of romantic poetry was to colour his whole vision of art. His pictures were full of knights 'alone and palely loitering', fair damsels in distress, and *belles dames sans merci*. The second great influence on his character was the Catholic writer John Henry Newman. Burne-Jones was later to write that Newman had taught him 'so much that I do mind – things that will never be out of me. In an age of sofas and cushions he taught me to be indifferent to comfort, and in an age of materialism he taught me to venture all on the unseen'. Burne-Jones went up to Oxford intending to enter the Church and, although he never became a clergyman, or even a regular churchgoer, he continued to think of the best and highest form of life as a religious life. He transmuted his religious ideals into artistic ones. Beauty was his goddess, and he was her disciple. Beauty was synonymous with truth and goodness; it was the Holy Grail. 'Only this is true', he wrote, 'that beauty is very beautiful, and softens, and comforts, and inspires, and rouses, and lifts up, and never fails'. There was a kind of missionary fervour about Burne-Jones's art that remained with him to the end of his life. He was a serious, earnest, mid-Victorian moralist who wanted to improve the lot of mankind and leave the world a better place than he found it. Although he was looked to as the leader of the Aesthetic School, he could never really accept the aesthetic philosophy that art existed only for art's sake, and for no other purpose at all.

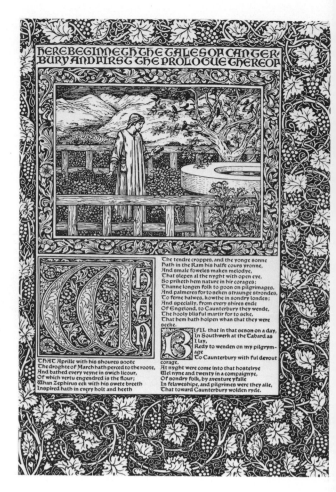

First page of the Kelmscott *Chaucer*, 1896.

George Howard, Burne-Jones drawing, *c*1875.

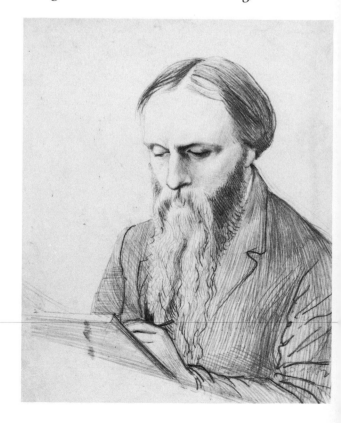

Sir Edward Burne-Jones (1833–1898)
Sidonia von Bork

Signed and dated 1860
Gouache 84 × 43 cm/33 × 17 ins
Tate Gallery, London

One of the finest of Burne-Jones's early
watercolours, painted while he was still very much
under the influence of Rossetti. The subject is taken
from Wilhelm Meinhold's *Sidonia the Sorceress*,
published in 1847. It tells of a high-born but cruel
sorceress, Sidonia von Bork, whose fatal beauty
causes men to fall in love with her. The book was
greatly admired by Rossetti and his circle, and
Morris reprinted it at the Kelmscott Press in 1893.
Sidonia is shown plotting her next crime at the court
of the Dowager Duchess of Wolgast, who is seen to
the right. The design of the dress was taken from
Giulio Romano's *Portrait of Isabella d'Este* at
Hampton Court, also a picture with a distinctly
menacing and sinister mood.

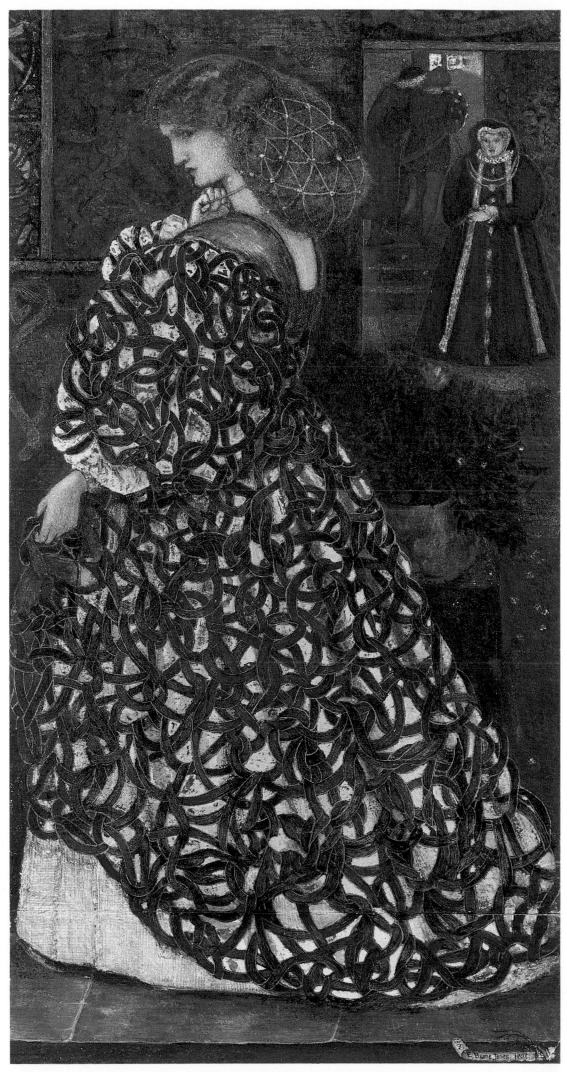

Once up at Oxford, both Morris and Burne-Jones were soon disillusioned by the religious atmosphere. Instead they conceived an almost mystical passion for the art and literature of the Middle Ages. At one point they discussed forming an order devoted to the service of Sir Galahad. About 1855 they discovered the book that was to influence Burne-Jones more than any other – Sir Thomas Malory's *Morte d'Arthur*. The legends of King Arthur and the Round Table made an immediate and profound appeal to the romantic and poetic side of Burne-Jones's character. The beauty and mystery of these ancient legends appealed to him also because they were Christian legends, concerned with the battle between good and evil, and sin and salvation. Like many Victorians who had lost their faith, Burne-Jones retained a passionate belief in the Christian virtues. Also, Malory's stories were about romantic, courtly love, and the spirit of chivalry, both of which appealed deeply to the Victorian imagination. Although Burne-Jones was to paint religious and classical subjects, it was the Arthurian legends that retained the deepest hold on his imagination, right up to the end of his life. A year or two before he died, he wrote 'Lord, how that San Graal story is ever in my mind and thoughts . . . was ever anything in the world beautiful as that is beautiful?'

It was also in 1855 that Morris and Burne-Jones discovered the paintings of the Pre-Raphaelites, in the house of the Oxford publisher Thomas Combe. Later in the year, the two of them visited northern France, looking at medieval churches and cathedrals. The spectacle of High Mass in Beauvais Cathedral was a particularly moving experience for both of them, and on the return journey, they made their joint decision to devote their lives to art. 'That was the most memorable night of my life', wrote Burne-Jones later. Back in London, the problem was how to devise a way of meeting his hero, Rossetti. 'I was two and twenty,' he wrote, 'and had never met, or even seen, a painter in all my life. I knew no-one who had ever seen one or had been in a studio, and of all men that lived on earth, the one that I wanted to see was Rossetti.' He went to hear him lecture at the Working Men's College, met him, and arranged to visit his studio. Rossetti declared that young Ned Jones was 'one of the nicest young fellows in Dreamland', and agreed to take him on as a pupil. Burne-Jones was to remain Rossetti's pupil for only about two years, but the effect on him was both profound and long-lasting. He was always generous in praise of his 'glorious Gabriel' to the end of his life, and still thought him the greatest artist he had known. Under Rossetti's direction, he began to make pen and ink drawings, mainly of medieval subjects, in the spiky, gothic style of Rossetti's work at this period. At this stage, their work is almost indistinguishable.

In 1858 Burne-Jones fell ill, and went to recuperate at Little Holland House, that celebrated meeting-place of the Victorian art world, presided over by the hospitable and motherly Mrs Prinsep. Here Burne-Jones came under the influence of George Frederick Watts, who lived at Little Holland House for nearly thirty years. Watts, who remained something of a father-figure for Burne-Jones, encouraged him to study the Elgin marbles and Italian painting, in order to expand and improve his style. He also encouraged him to visit Italy for the first time in 1859.

By about 1860 he was starting to work in watercolours, on a small scale, and in this year painted *Sidonia von Bork* (p. 113), one of his best early works. Although strongly Rossettian in character, it already shows signs of Burne-Jones's developing powers. By this time Burne-Jones had met Ruskin as well as Watts, both of whom were worried by Rossetti's excessive influence over his young pupil. Ruskin complained of the 'stiffness and quaintness and intensity' of Rossetti's followers, and thought they needed more 'classical grace and tranquillity'.

Burne-Jones was to make three more trips to Italy, with Ruskin in 1862, and finally in 1871 and 1873. The effect of these trips on Burne-Jones's style was immense; the influence of Italian painting was to become a key element in his art.

As for so many young artists of that generation, the 1860s was to be a crucial period of artistic ferment. Burne-Jones, like all great painters, had unusual powers of

Sir Edward Burne-Jones
The Madness of Sir Tristram

Signed with initials and dated 1862
Coloured chalks, watercolour and bodycolour
58 × 61 cm/23 × 24 ins
Private Collection

A scene from Burne-Jones's beloved *Morte d'Arthur*, in which Sir Tristram discovers false evidence of Iseult's love for Sir Kay Hedius. Sir Tristram is driven to madness, and retreats to a forest, where he lives like a wild man, fed by herdsmen and shepherds. The design comes from a set of thirteen stained glass panels, illustrating the story of Sir Tristram, which Burne-Jones designed for Morris and Company. He had become a partner in the firm in 1861.

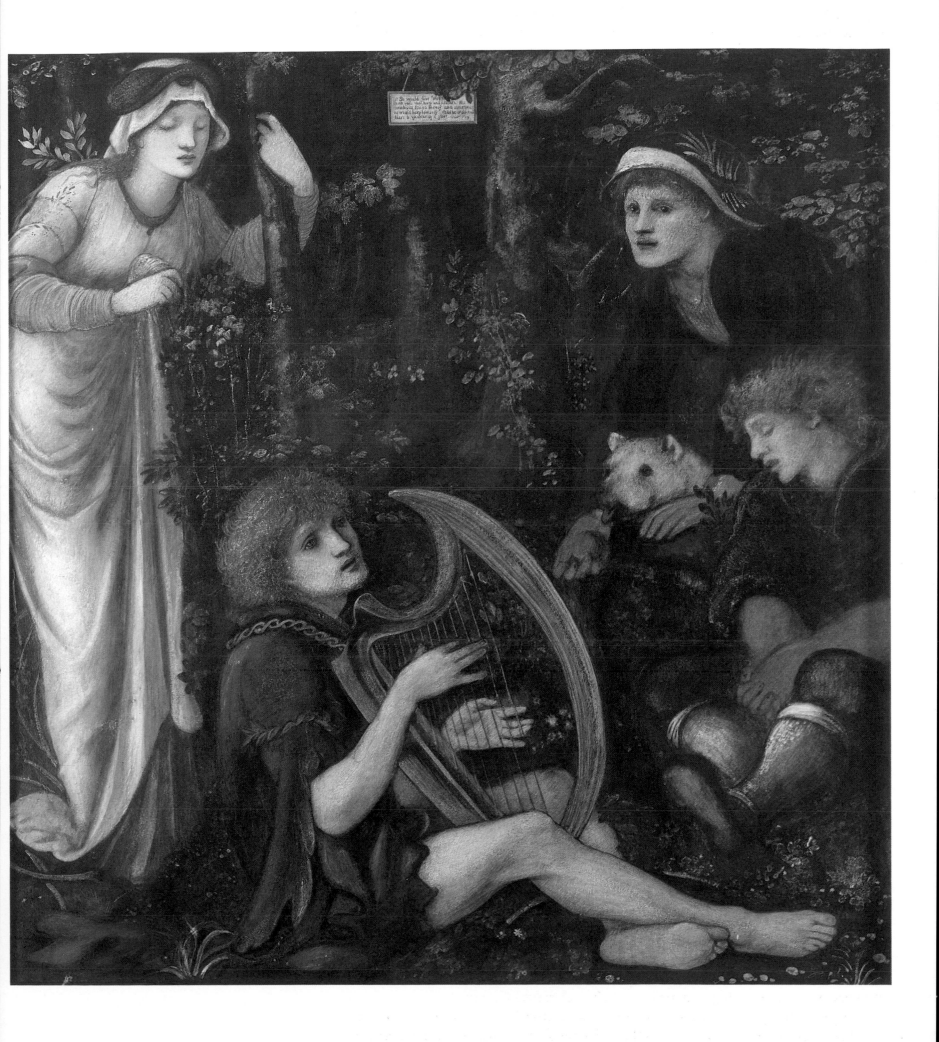

115

assimilation, and was highly receptive to all the complex prevailing currents of the 1860s. During this decade, his style began to move away from the narrow gothicism of Rossetti and his circle, towards a more personal interpretation of Pre-Raphaelite, Italianate and classical ideas. By 1861 Burne-Jones was beginning to paint mythological subjects, many of which were derived from his friend William Morris's *The Earthly Paradise*, a long Chaucerian poem, which combines classical and medieval legends. This poem was to furnish Burne-Jones with subjects for the rest of his career. In *The Madness of Sir Tristram* (p. 115) of 1862, one can already see Burne-Jones's figures beginning to acquire more elegance and refinement. The figures and draperies have a classical look, and the mood and colour reflect the influence of his first Italian journey. Like both Watts and Ruskin, Burne-Jones was a great admirer of the Venetian School, especially Titian, Giorgione, Tintoretto and Carpaccio, but he also liked Botticelli, Mantegna and Signorelli. In several of Burne-Jones's pictures of the 1860s, such as *Green Summer* of 1864, one can detect Giorgionesque echoes, and also a move towards more aesthetic subjects. In such pictures as *The Lament* of 1866, or *The Four Seasons* of 1869, the influence of Albert Moore is also evident. Moore and Burne-Jones were never close friends, but they had several friends in common, such as Simeon Solomon, Henry Holiday, Rossetti, Whistler and Swinburne. In 1866 Swinburne dedicated his *Poems and Ballads* to Burne-Jones, so there can be little doubt that Burne-Jones had begun to imbibe the doctrines of the Aesthetic Movement.

Another key element in Burne-Jones's art was his involvement in design and decorative work. From 1857 he was increasingly involved in designing stained glass, and in 1861 he became a partner in Morris, Marshall, Faulkner & Company. From the start, Burne-Jones was the Firm's best and most prolific designer, and as a result there is a constant interaction and exchange of ideas between his paintings and his design work. Nearly all his pictures have their origin in a design for some other medium, sometimes stained glass, but also tapestries, tiles, mosaic, books, furniture, pianos, embroidery, even clothes and shoes. None of the aesthetic artists was more involved in decorative work than Burne-Jones. His set of four pictures of *Pygmalion*, for example, originate from drawings for Morris's *Earthly Paradise*. Although the subjects are classical, and the colours Italianate, Burne-Jones has invested the Pygmalion story with an atmosphere of medieval courtly love, rather than classical legend. Such subjects as Pygmalion, The Sleeping Beauty and King Cophetua appealed to Burne-Jones and other late Victorian artists because they symbolized the medieval ideals of chivalry and courtly love, and also the rejection of nineteenth-century materialism, in the search for higher ideals of love and beauty.

Between 1868 and 1871 Burne-Jones was involved in a romance of his own with the beautiful Greek sculptress Maria Zambaco. He made many lovely drawings of her, and she also appears in several of his pictures of this period, such as *Venus Epithalamia, The Garden of the Hesperides,* and *Phyllis and Demophoön*. The last of these was exhibited at the Old Watercolour Society in 1870, and the nude figure of Demophoön was strongly criticized on grounds of indecency. Burne-Jones's work had been continually attacked by the critics since his election to the Society in 1864, so he indignantly withdrew the picture, and resigned. In the following year, 1871, Robert Buchanan's notorious tirade, *The Fleshly School of Poetry*, was published, and Burne-Jones must have felt that the attack was partly directed against him. In 1873, poor Simeon Solomon was arrested on charges of homosexuality, and thereafter became a complete social outcast, shunned by all his former friends. The Palace of Art was under siege, and Burne-Jones's response was to go to ground. Between 1870 and the opening of the Grosvenor Gallery in 1877 he did not exhibit in public at all, preferring to work for such faithful patrons as William Graham and Mrs Casavetti. He revisited Italy twice, in 1871 and 1873, in search of reassurance and renewed inspiration. This time he concentrated on Florence, Siena and Rome, and wrote to a friend in 1871, 'I love da Vinci and Michelangelo most of all.' In many of his later

Sir Edward Burne-Jones, two scenes from the *Pygmalion* series. Above: *The Hand Refrains*. Below: *The Soul Attains*.

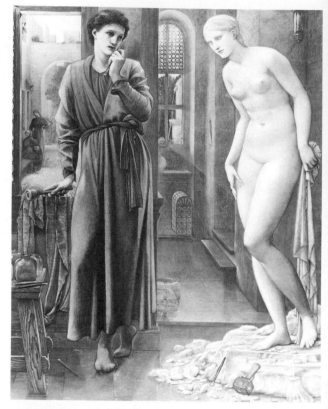

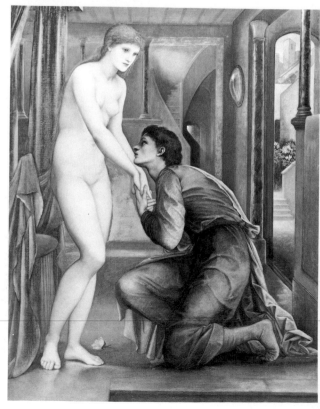

Sir Edward Burne-Jones
The Beguiling of Merlin

Signed and dated MDCCCLXXIV (1874)
Canvas 186 × 111 cm/73 × 43¾ ins
Lady Lever Art Gallery, Port Sunlight

This was one of the pictures exhibited by Burne-Jones at the historic opening of the Grosvenor Gallery in 1877, which established his reputation overnight. The picture was commissioned by F.R.Leyland for his famous interior at 49 Prince's Gate, where Whistler painted the Peacock Room. It illustrates an episode from the French medieval *Romance of Merlin* in which Merlin is lulled to sleep by the enchantress Nimue, in a hawthorn bush in the forest of Broceliande. The scene had also been described by Tennyson in *The Idylls of the King* (1859).

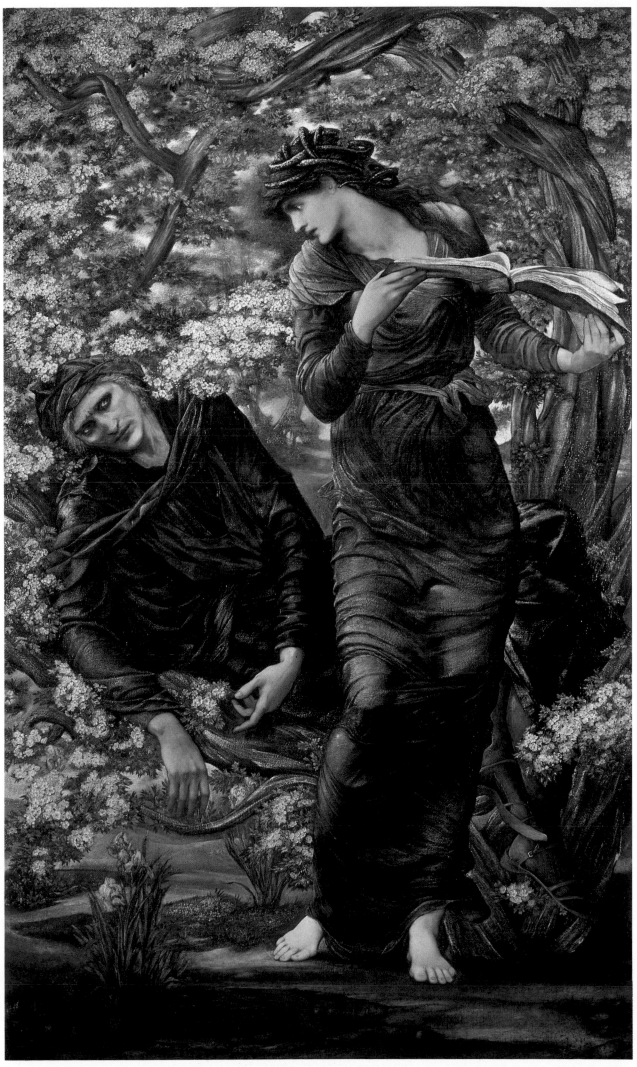

works, one can see his trying to combine Michelangelesque figures with the enigmatic, androgynous faces of Leonardo. The 1870s were to be a period of intensely creative activity for Burne-Jones, and it was at this stage that his mature style finally evolved, resulting in some of his finest works, such as *Laus Veneris, The Days of Creation, Pan and Psyche, Love Among the Ruins, The Beguiling of Merlin* (p. 117), and *The Mirror of Venus* (p. 119). Out of the artistic melting pot of the 1860s, the master had at last forged his own unique brand of aesthetic Pre-Raphaelitism.

In 1877 Sir Coutts Lindsay, a rich dilettante married to a Rothschild heiress, founded the Grosvenor Gallery in Bond Street. The gallery was intended to rival the Royal Academy, and to act as a forum for the work of the more progressive artists of the day. The rooms were spacious and impressive, and the pictures were hung much more tastefully than the usual Royal Academy jumble. The works of each artist were grouped together, to give the public a better chance to appreciate them as a whole. The money and the social connections of Sir Coutts ensured the support of the rich and fashionable, and the opening was a glittering event, recorded in many memoirs of the period. It must be to Sir Coutts's credit that he persuaded Burne-Jones to emerge from his self-imposed exile, and send a total of eight pictures to the opening exhibition, including *The Days of Creation, The Beguiling of Merlin* and *The Mirror of Venus*. The pictures were all hung together, on one wall. Both critics and public were astounded. They suddenly realized that they had a genius in their midst. The name of Burne-Jones was on everyone's lips; overnight he had become famous, hailed as one of the leading artists of the day. Henry James, normally a caustic critic of English art, was one of the first to recognize Burne-Jones's originality. In his review of the 1877 exhibition, he singled out the pictures of Burne-Jones as 'by far the most interesting things in the Grosvenor Gallery', and concluded his long and perceptive analysis thus: 'in the palace of art there are many chambers, and that of which Mr Burne-Jones holds the key is a wondrous museum. His imagination, his fertility of invention, his exquisiteness of work, his remarkable gifts as a colourist . . . all these things constitute a brilliant distinction.'

Sir Edward Burne-Jones, study for *The Mirror of Venus*.

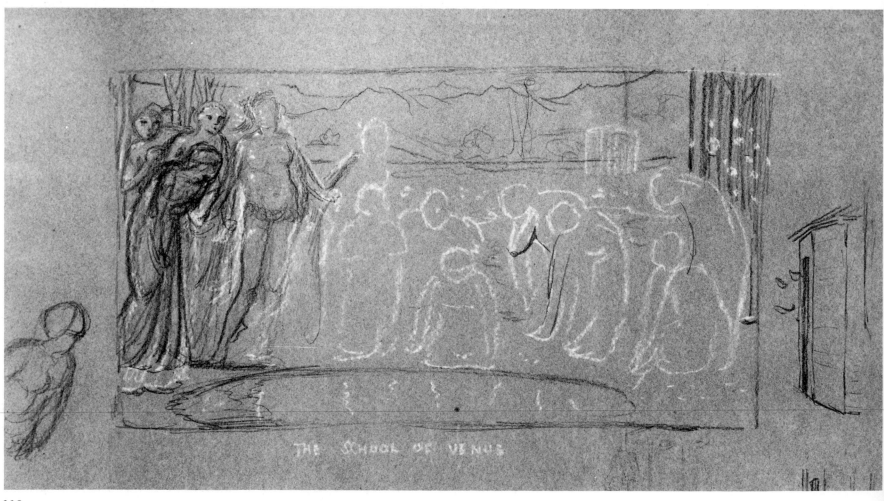

THE SCHOOL OF VENUS

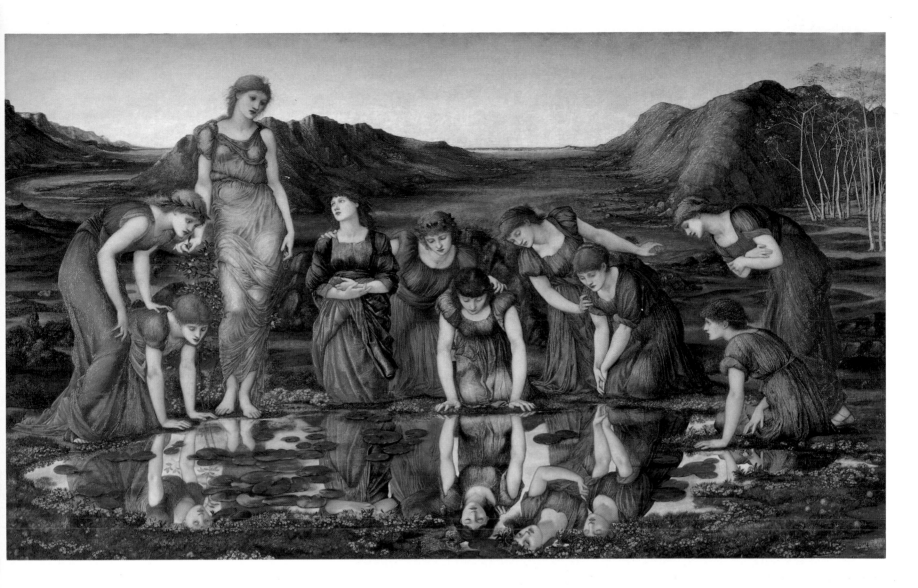

Sir Edward Burne-Jones
The Mirror of Venus

1898
Canvas 120 × 200 cm/47¼ × 78¾ ins
Gulbenkian Foundation, Lisbon

Another of the pictures exhibited at the Grosvenor
Gallery in 1877, also commissioned by F.R.Leyland.
It is a beautiful example of Burne-Jones's mature
style, combining classical, Italianate and aesthetic
elements into something entirely personal and
original.

No picture illustrates better Burne-Jones's unique genius for blending together the
two traditions of Pre-Raphaelitism and the Italian Renaissance into a new aesthetic
style than *The Mirror of Venus*. The scene is purely imaginary, and shows Venus and
her maidens gazing at their reflections in a pool of water. The landscape is arid and
rocky; these strangely lunar landscapes were to become a recurring feature of his art,
widely imitated by his followers. The mood and the colour are Pre-Raphaelite, but
the conscious sweetness and elegance of the figures recall the Italian Renaissance, and
in particular, Botticelli, an artist greatly admired by Burne-Jones, and later to become
a cult among fashionable aesthetes. The conception is purely aesthetic – a ring of
beautiful girls in lovely draperies, with the minimum of narrative or historical
content. The draperies are pseudo-classical, and the title is Venus, but the picture
could equally well have been given a vague allegorical title. Through the faces of the
girls and their wistful expressions Burne-Jones conveys that feeling of intense
sadness and nostalgia for the past that pervades so many late Pre-Raphaelite pictures.
Whether he is painting classical, religious, Arthurian, or simply make-believe subjects, Burne-Jones's work is highly individual. A picture such as *The Mirror of Venus*
is intended above all to be beautiful, and to appeal to the poetic imagination of the
spectator. In Burne-Jones's often-quoted definition, 'I mean by a picture a beautiful romantic dream of something that never was, never will be – in light better than
any light that ever shone – in a land no-one can define, or remember, only desire . . .'
It is a deliberately romantic, introspective art, the aim of which, if it has one at all, is
to awaken our sense of beauty, and arouse a mood of nostalgia, reverie and
introspection. It is a mood common to much of late Victorian art, especially the work
of the later Pre-Raphaelites.

Burne-Jones's great success at the Grosvenor was marred by the ensuing Whistler
v. Ruskin trial, in which he was reluctantly forced to appear as a witness for Ruskin.

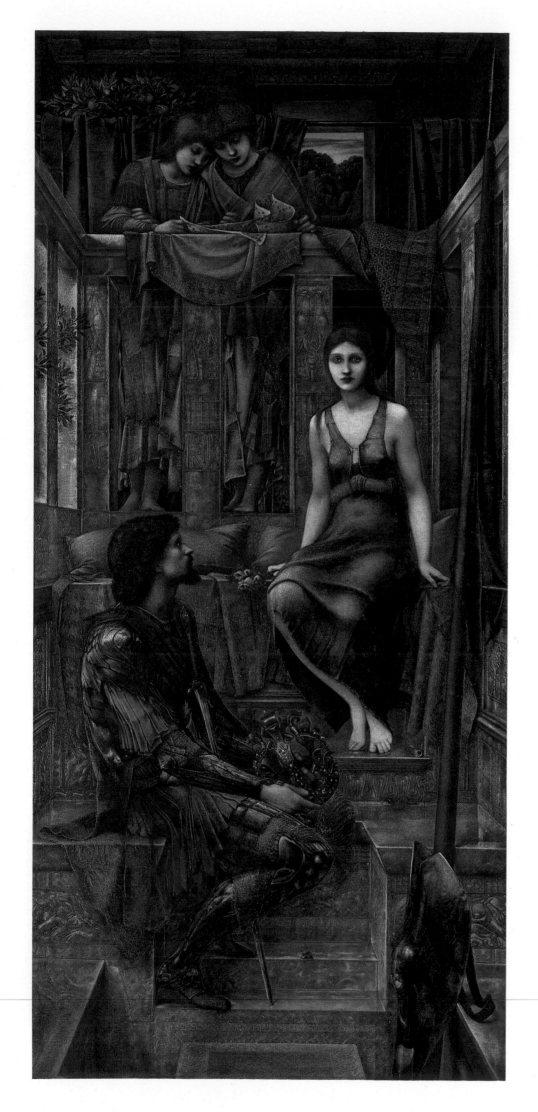

Sir Edward Burne-Jones
King Cophetua and the Beggar Maid

Signed with initials and dated 1884
Canvas 281 × 136 cm/110½ × 53½ ins
Tate Gallery, London

The story of King Cophetua, and his marriage to a beggar maid, comes from an Elizabethan ballad, which also inspired Tennyson's poem, *The Beggar Maid*. The idea of giving up all worldly honours for love strongly appealed to Burne-Jones, and the result is one of his finest and best-known paintings. It was exhibited at the Grosvenor Gallery in 1884, and was also widely praised at the *Exposition Universelle* in Paris in 1889. Burne-Jones was one of the few English artists to enjoy a European reputation, even influencing the young Picasso in Barcelona.

(Opposite)
Danaë and the Brazen Tower, 1887–88.

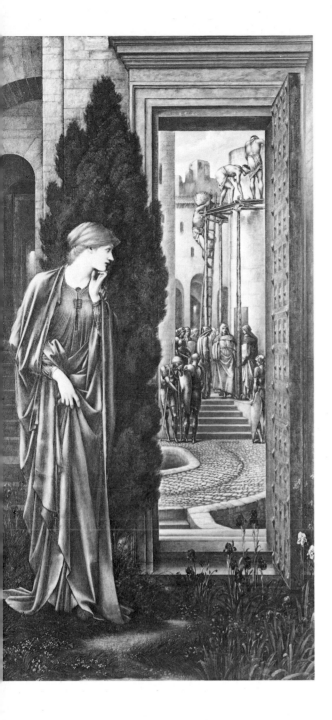

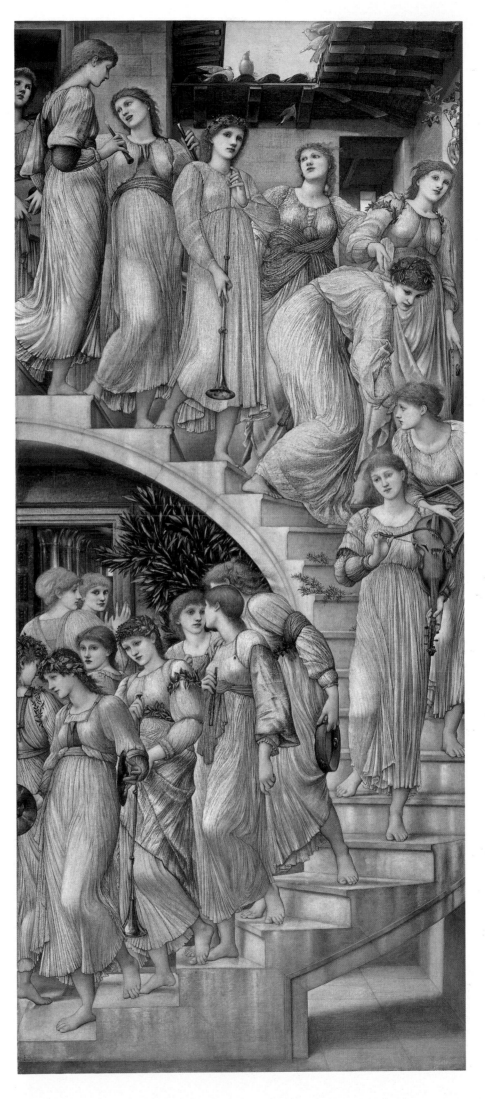

Sir Edward Burne-Jones
The Golden Stairs

Signed with initials and dated 1880
Canvas 279 × 117 cm/110 × 46 ins
Tate Gallery, London

Burne-Jones's later style became increasingly formal
and classical, concentrating more on line, colour and
overall design, than on narrative detail. The
vagueness of the title, rather like Whistler's musical
titles, is also deliberate. The narrow upright shape of
the canvas, reminiscent of Italian altarpieces, was
increasingly favoured by Burne-Jones in his later
years. The picture was exhibited at the Grosvenor
Gallery in 1880.

121

But the combined effect of the Grosvenor opening and the trial was to make Burne-Jones the acknowledged leader of the Aesthetic Movement. He suddenly found himself the centre of a new fashionable cult. Women began to cultivate the Burne-Jones 'look', wearing long, flowing dresses of olive-green, curiously embroidered. Kensington became known as 'Passionate Brompton', where lived the beautiful people of the 1870s and 1880s, known as 'PBs'. The satirists were soon at work, for there were plenty of philistines who found the pictures of Burne-Jones 'queer' and 'unhealthy'. George du Maurier, in particular, created in his cartoons Mrs Cimabue Brown and a whole world of passionate aesthetes, brilliantly caricaturing the more ridiculous excesses of the PBs. In 1880 Gilbert and Sullivan composed their celebrated operetta, *Patience*, making fun of the whole 'greenery-yallery Grosvenor Gallery' craze, and creating that archetypal Aesthetic character, 'Bunthorne, the fleshly poet'.

In the midst of all this, Burne-Jones remained detached. He was flattered by the attentions of Society, but his natural modesty and complete devotion to his art prevented him from becoming spoiled. Among his close friends, he could be a fascinating and amusing conversationalist, and almost all accounts of him in contemporary letters and diaries speak of the quiet but delightful charm of his character. He wrote long and beautiful letters, especially to children, illustrating them with copious drawings and witty caricatures. At the time of the Grosvenor Gallery opening, Burne-Jones was already in his mid-forties, and success was not to change him. He left the leadership of the more outrageous aesthetes to Oscar Wilde, who did not miss the chance to jump on the new bandwagon. Success for Burne-Jones gave him confidence to engage in new commissions and projects, and to work on a larger and larger scale. These last twenty years of his life were to see an increasing preoccupation with very large pictures, and cycles of pictures, although Burne-Jones considered them a poor substitute for the walls he would have covered if he had lived in fifteenth-century Florence. He also began to employ an increasing number of assistants. The best-known among these were Thomas Matthews Rooke and John Melhuish Strudwick, both of whom became fine painters in their own right. Burne-Jones's idea was to create a kind of Renaissance workshop, with a number of gifted and like-minded pupils turning out a large quantity of work under his general supervision.

During the 1880s, Burne-Jones continued to develop many of the themes that had preoccupied him during the previous twenty years. Among his finest classical subjects were *The Garden of Pan, Danaë and the Brazen Tower*, and the remarkable *Perseus* cycle. He also painted religious subjects, such as his *The Annunciation* of 1879, but as he grew older, he tended to revert increasingly to Arthurian and medieval legends, the great inspiration of his youth. This was to result in some of his most famous works, such as *King Cophetua and the Beggar Maid* (p. 120) and *The Last Sleep of Arthur in Avalon* (p. 127). Parallel with this was a tendency to revert to subjects based on fairy tales, such as the famous *Briar Rose* series (p. 124), illustrating the legend of *The Sleeping Beauty*, or subjects based simply on his own private dream world, such as *The Golden Stairs* (p. 121) or *The Depths of the Sea* of 1886.

It was interest from rich private patrons that enabled Burne-Jones to paint his two greatest cycles, *Perseus* and *The Briar Rose*. Arthur Balfour, a rich bachelor politician and later Conservative Prime Minister, was a leading member of that cultivated group of high society known as 'The Souls'. Many of them were friends and admirers of Burne-Jones, and as a result Balfour commissioned Burne-Jones in 1875 to paint a series of pictures for the music room of his London house, 4 Carlton Gardens. The story of Perseus had been described in *The Doom of King Acrisius*, part of Morris's *Earthly Paradise*, so once again Burne-Jones was looking at classical antiquity through the distorting mirrors of medieval literature and the Italian Renaissance. The cycle was at first conceived by Burne-Jones as a set of eight pictures, but only four were actually completed: *Perseus and the Graiae, The Rock of Doom, The Doom*

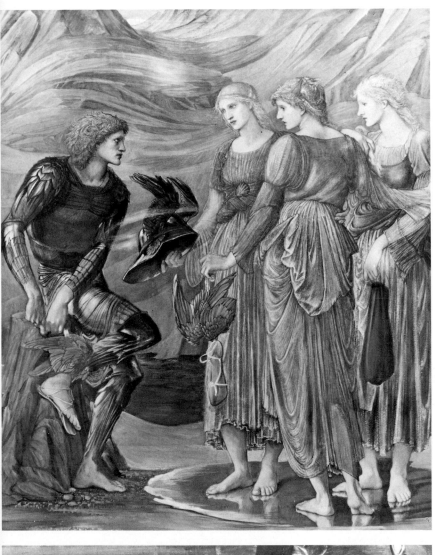

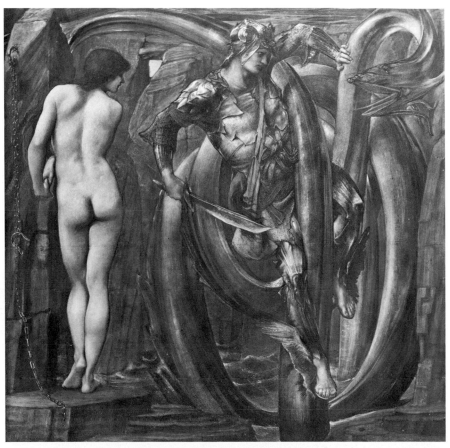

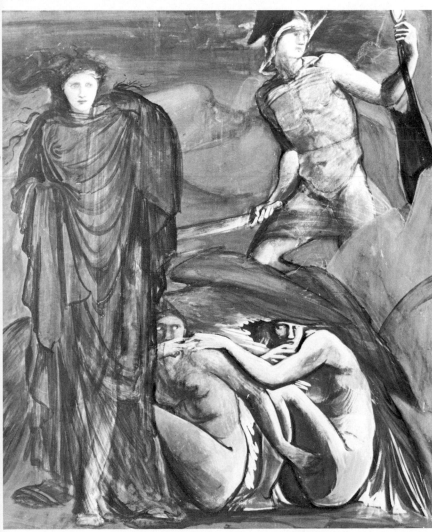

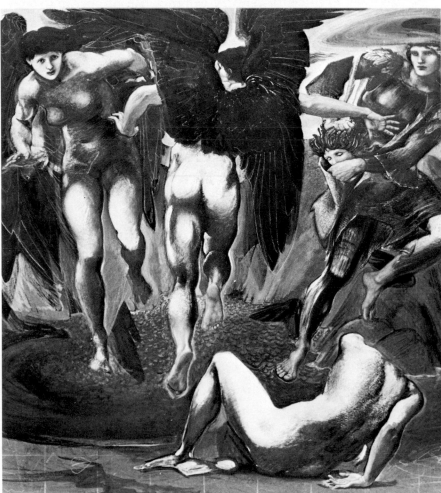

Fulfilled and *The Baleful Head* (p. 125). Four others survive as full-sized cartoons in gouache. The pictures were painted over a period of 17 years, and clearly show Burne-Jones's style developing from his rich, Italianate, tapestry-like style of the 1870s, towards his austere, hard, almost monochromatic style of the 1880s. Taken as a whole, the *Perseus* series represents a unique achievement in Burne-Jones's work, wholly original and brilliantly inventive. The writhing, convoluted sea-monster in *The Doom Fulfilled* has a weird and menacing quality quite unequalled in Victorian art. Only in Gustave Moreau and the Symbolist painters of Europe can one find comparisons. The unfinished cartoons have an even more unearthly, ghostly feeling, partly because of their raw surface, and the extreme angularity of the figures.

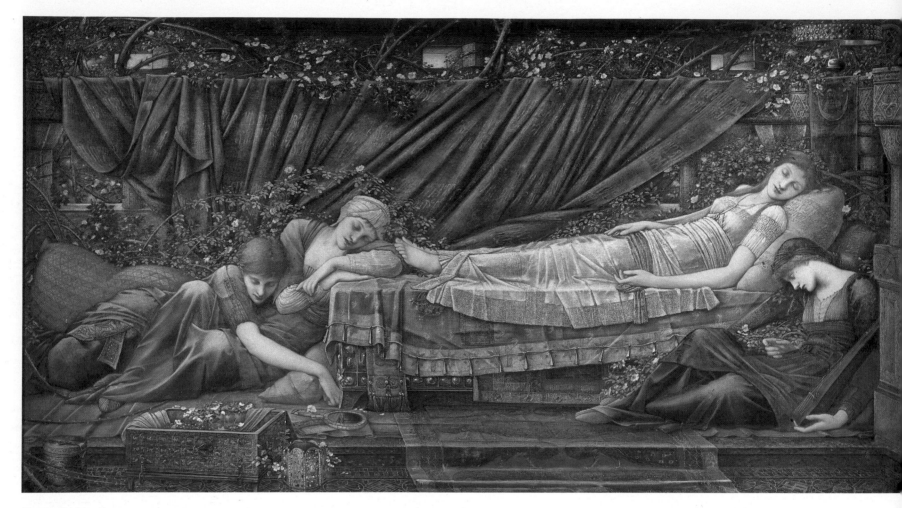

Sir Edward Burne-Jones
The Sleeping Princess (Briar Rose series)

1873–90
Canvas 122 × 229 cm/48 × 90 ins
Faringdon Collection trust, Buscot Park, Faringdon, Berkshire

A panel from the now celebrated Briar Rose series, Burne-Jones's best-known cycle of pictures. The idea began as a set of tiles designed by Burne-Jones to illustrate Perrault's *Sleeping Beauty*. He first painted a small set of three oils, then in 1873 began the large set of four, of which this is one. The other scenes show the Prince entering the briar wood, the King and his courtiers asleep, and a group of servant girls asleep. The whole set was bought by Alexander Henderson, the 1st Lord Faringdon, and installed in his dining room at Buscot Park. Burne-Jones later painted some smaller decorative panels to connect the whole set into a continuous frieze.

Sir Edward Burne-Jones
The Baleful Head

1886–87
Canvas 155 × 130 cm/61 × 51¼ ins
Staatsgalerie, Stuttgart

This is one of the pictures from the Perseus series, commissioned by Arthur Balfour for the music room of his London house at 4 Carlton Gardens. Like so many of Burne-Jones's pictures, the story comes from *The Earthly Paradise* by William Morris. It tells how Perseus kills the Medusa and rescues Andromeda. In this picture Perseus shows Andromeda the head of the Medusa reflected in a well. The Perseus series was Burne-Jones's biggest and most ambitious cycle of pictures. Only four were completed, and another four survive only as large cartoons.

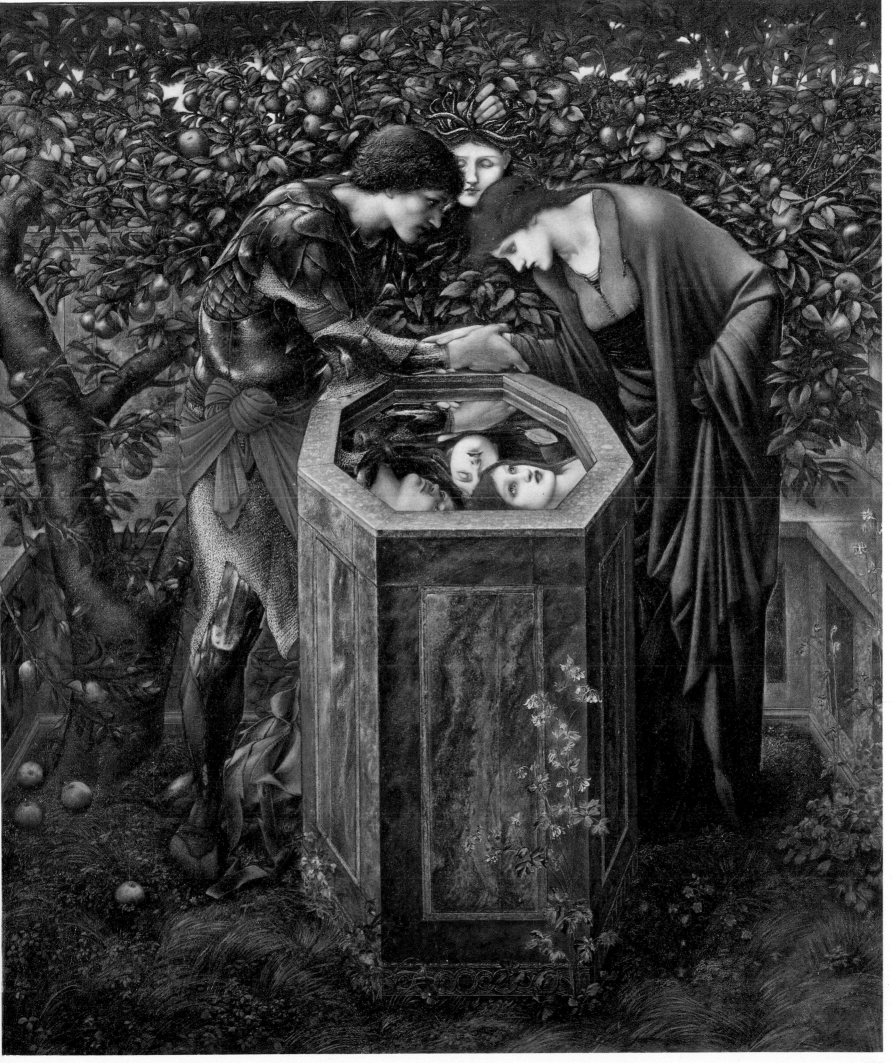

Looking at the whole set, we really feel we are witnessing gods and goddesses enacting a cruel myth on a remote, barren planet. No other Pre-Raphaelite, or even classical Victorian painter, could interpret classical myth with the same imaginative power as Burne-Jones. The *Briar Rose* series is equally remarkable, but has become better-known and more popular because it hangs in England in a National Trust house, whereas the *Perseus* series was sold to a German museum only in the last decade. The *Briar Rose* series is a set of four pictures, showing the Prince entering the Briar Wood, the King and his courtiers asleep, the Sleeping Princess, and finally the Garden Court, showing the servant girls asleep at their work. The four pictures were bought in 1890 by Alexander Henderson, First Lord Faringdon, a rich financier, and installed in his dining room at Buscot Park, Berkshire. Burne-Jones later painted connecting panels to form the whole into a continuous frieze. The Buscot dining room is a temple to which all lovers of Pre-Raphaelite art must make the pilgrimage, for the *Briar Rose* series is not only one of the greatest manifestations of Burne-Jones's genius – it is also one of the masterpieces of High Victorian art.

By this time Burne-Jones's status as one of England's greatest artists was already recognized, both in England and on the Continent. In a belated attempt to heal the rift between the Royal Academy and the Grosvenor Gallery, Lord Leighton and his fellow Academicians elected Burne-Jones an Associate in 1885. Burne-Jones was never consulted, and accepted with the greatest reluctance. He was never happy in the role of ARA, and exhibited only once at the Academy, in 1886. In 1893 he resigned, to Leighton's great disappointment. It had been a well-meaning, but misguided gesture. Burne-Jones was, by his own admission, quite unsuited to any kind of Academy system; he was persuaded, however, to accept a baronetcy in 1894.

Burne-Jones remained faithful to the Grosvenor Gallery until its closure in 1887, when he transferred his allegiance to the New Gallery in Regent Street, founded by Joseph Comyns Carr and Charles Hallé. It was here that he exhibited many of the finest pictures of his late years, such as *Love and the Pilgrim* and *The Wedding of Psyche*. In this last phase his work becomes increasingly austere, monumental and withdrawn. His figures move as if hypnotized in stark, barren landscapes, their robes glittering as if woven from metallic thread. Henry James, who remained a faithful admirer, noted how his late work was growing 'colder and colder', and 'less and less observed', the pictures becoming almost 'abstractions'. Burne-Jones's last and greatest work, *The Last Sleep of Arthur in Avalon*, occupied him for nearly twenty years, but was still left unfinished at his death. Burne-Jones regarded it as the culmination of his life's work, a final statement of his aims and beliefs. To our lasting shame, this great picture was exported from England only about twenty years ago, after selling for a derisory sum at Christie's. It now hangs in the museum at Ponce, Puerto Rico, where few English people are ever likely to see it.

Perhaps Burne-Jones would not be surprised if he could know the fate of *The Last Sleep of Arthur*, for in all his late work, one can detect a growing sense of sadness, resignation and withdrawal from the world. Like so many Victorian moralists, Burne-Jones felt that he had failed. His conception of art as a lofty, noble calling, whose duty was to uplift and inspire mankind, had done little or nothing to check the spread of materialism and ugliness in the nineteenth century. The decadence of the 1890s appalled him, particularly Aubrey Beardsley's illustrations to his beloved *Morte d'Arthur*. Burne-Jones was essentially a mid-Victorian, and retained to the end of his life, as David Cecil has put it, 'the sense of a highly cultured, refined spirit, living a sheltered life at the end of a long tradition of civilization'. Much the same could be said of the other late Pre-Raphaelites, but Burne-Jones was certainly the greatest romantic, and the greatest artist, of them all. His reaction to the failure of his ideals was to retreat even further into the recesses of his own dream world. His late work becomes steadily more remote and withdrawn, and has little to do with Chaucer, or Malory, or the Bible, or any of the literature that provided its initial inspiration. The art of his last years is overwhelmingly nostalgic, wistful and

126

Sir Edward Burne-Jones
The Last Sleep of Arthur in Avalon (detail)
1881–98
Canvas 282 × 645 cm/111 × 254 ins
Museo de Arte, Ponce, Puerto Rico

Burne-Jones's last great masterpiece. He began it in 1881, and continued to work on it right up to his death, leaving it still unfinished. Into it Burne-Jones poured all his artistic ideas and beliefs, and he regarded it as the most important picture he ever painted. In the last years of his life Burne-Jones reverted once more to the Arthurian legends which had inspired much of his art.

Philip Burne-Jones, portrait of Sir Edward Burne-Jones in his studio, 1898.

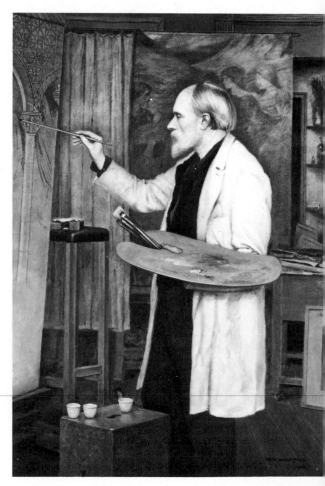

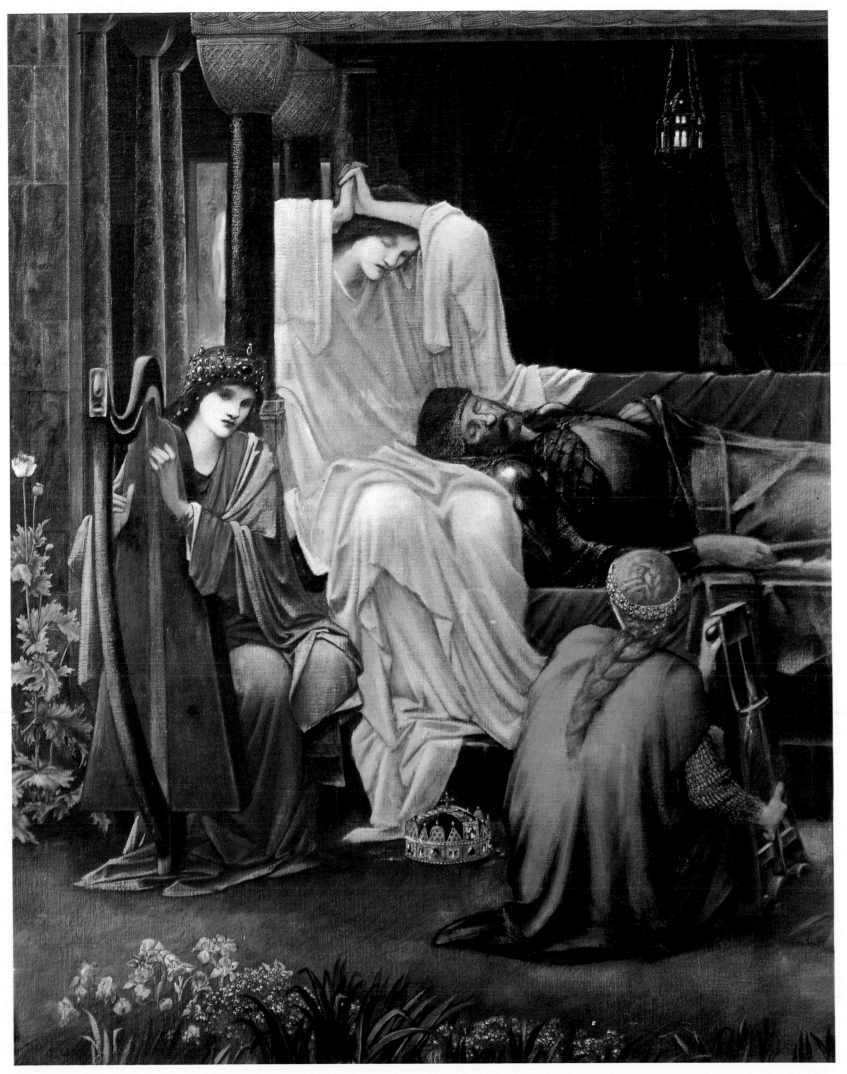

melancholy; it is obsessed with the greatness of the past and with the lost traditions of European art. It has a preference for scenes of disappointed love, and personal tragedy, rather than heroic actions or great battles. It is passive, brooding, introspective; if there are heroes in Burne-Jones's pictures they are passive, hesitant, almost effeminate. The world of Burne-Jones is a Victorian dream world, and epitomizes the spirit of late Victorian civilization. And, as Burne-Jones said of the story of Christ, 'it is too beautiful not to be true'.

Some Pre-Raphaelite followers 1860–1890

William Morris died in 1896, Burne-Jones in 1898. Although Holman Hunt, William Michael Rossetti and Frederick George Stephens all survived into the twentieth century, the death of Morris and Burne-Jones signalled the beginning of the end for Pre-Raphaelitism. Although Pre-Raphaelite influence is detectable in English art right up to 1914, notably in the work of John William Waterhouse, it was largely a spent force by the end of the century. But during their lifetimes, Rossetti, Burne-Jones and Morris all had a tremendous influence on other artists. Some of these painters were only brief converts to Pre-Raphaelitism; some adopted Pre-Raphaelite ideas and grafted them to their own; some were more attracted by Burne-Jones, others by Rossetti. The story of Pre-Raphaelitism and the story of the Aesthetic Movement are not exactly the same, but the two are inextricably interwoven. To define exactly where Pre-Raphaelitism ends, and Aestheticism begins remains a tricky problem for future art historians to solve. For the moment we

Frederick Sandys (1829–1904)
Morgan-le-Fay

1862–63
Panel 63 × 44 cm/24¾ × 17½ ins
Birmingham City Museum and Art Gallery

Sandys was one of Rossetti's closest followers, and also a superb draughtsman. Most of his pictures are half-length or full-length pictures of *femmes fatales*, usually Arthurian or classical heroines. Morgan-le-Fay was a sorceress in the *Morte d'Arthur* and the model may be Keomi, a gypsy girl who posed for Rossetti in *The Beloved*, and was also for a time Sandys' mistress.

Henry Holiday (1839–1927)
Dante and Beatrice

1883
Canvas 140 × 199 cm/55 × 78½ ins
Walker Art Gallery, Liverpool

Henry Holiday spent much of his career designing stained glass, and also teaching at the South Kensington Schools. He did however produce a few pictures, of which this is by far the most famous, due to its frequent illustration in Victorian history books.

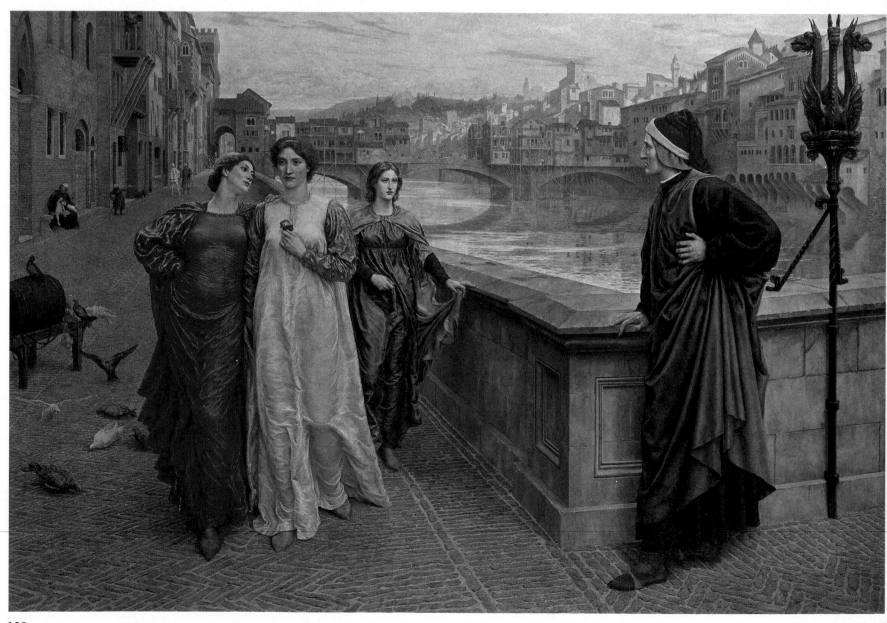

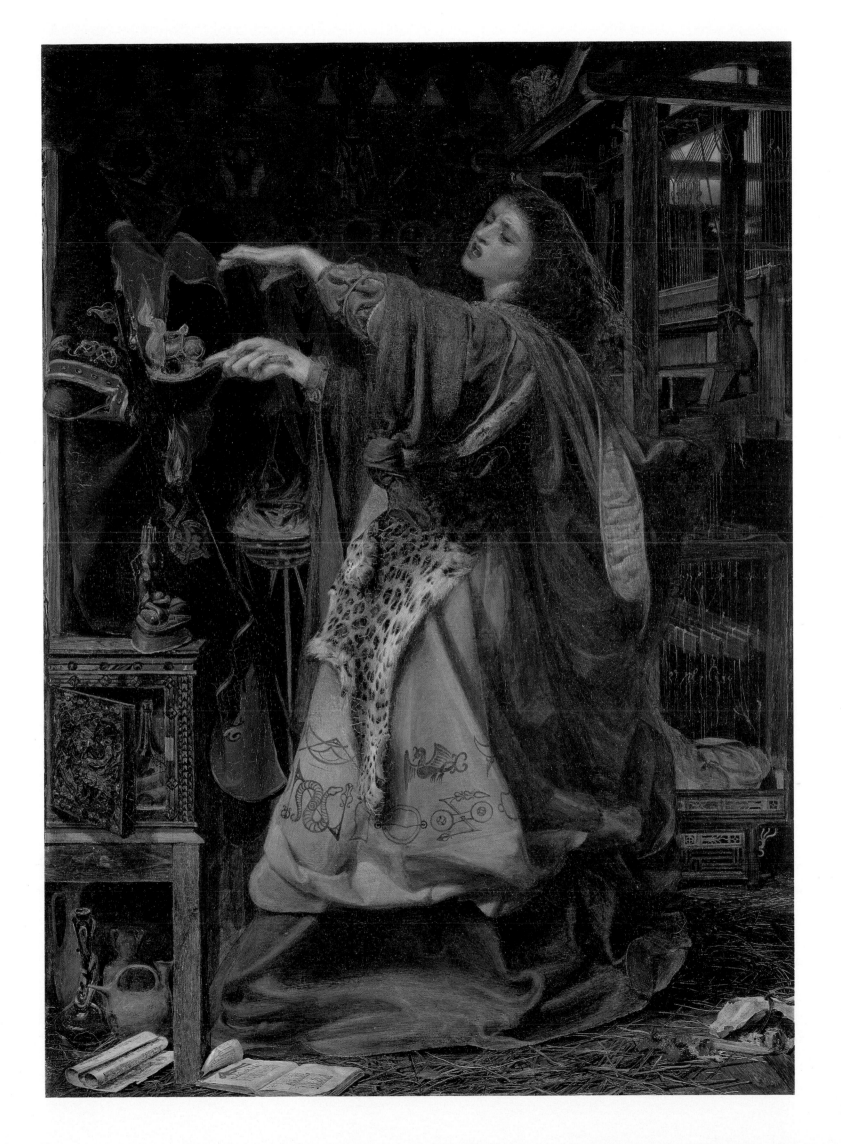

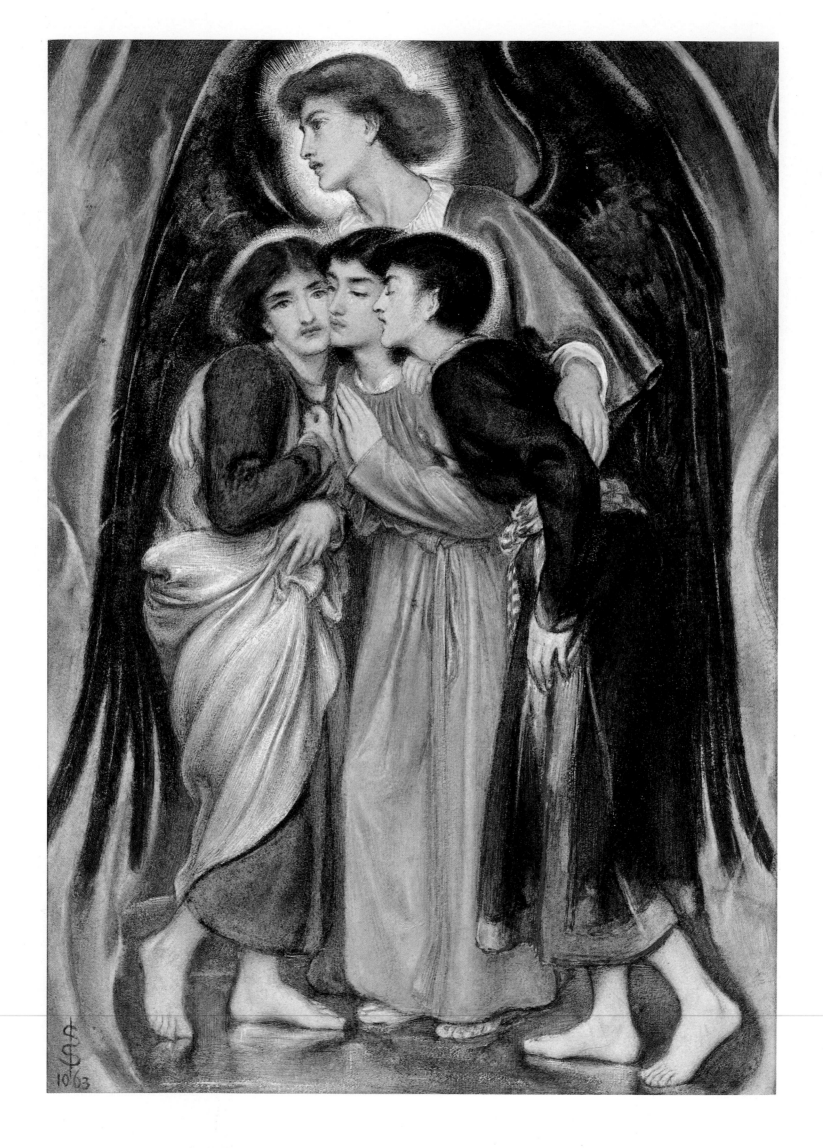

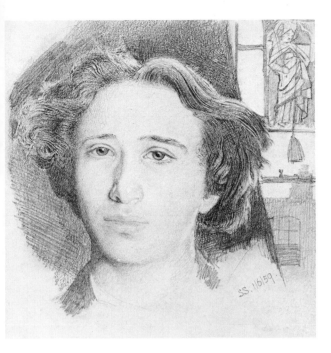

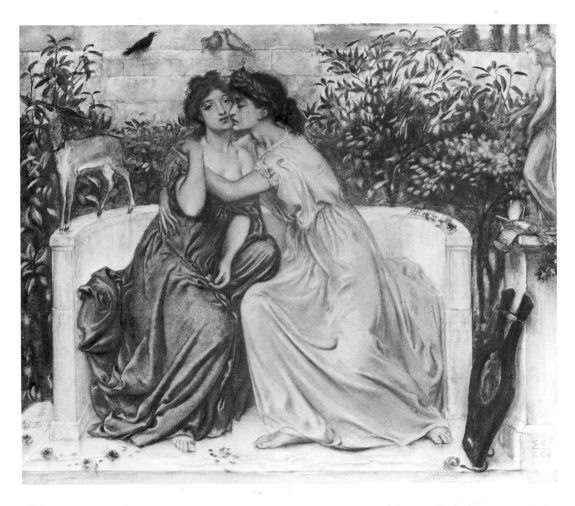

Above: **Simeon Solomon**, self-portrait, 1859. Right:
Sappho and Erinna at Mytelene, 1864. Below right:
Study for the head of Sappho, 1862.

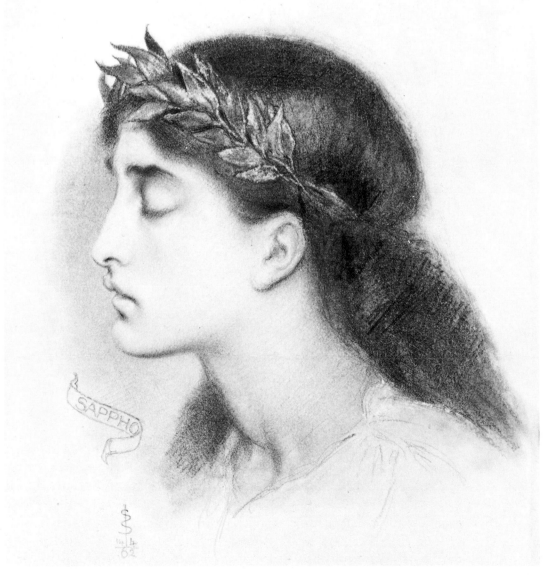

Simeon Solomon (1840–1905)
Shadrach, Meschach and Abednego
preserved from the Burning Fiery Furnace

Signed with monogram and dated 10.63
Watercolour and bodycolour 32 × 23 cm/12¾ × 9 ins
Private collection (Photo: Sotheby's Belgravia)

The young Simeon Solomon was befriended by both
Rossetti and Burne-Jones, and his early work
reflects the influence of both artists. Solomon's
style, however, has a mystical intensity which is
quite distinctive, especially when combined with
his interest in Jewish history and ritual.

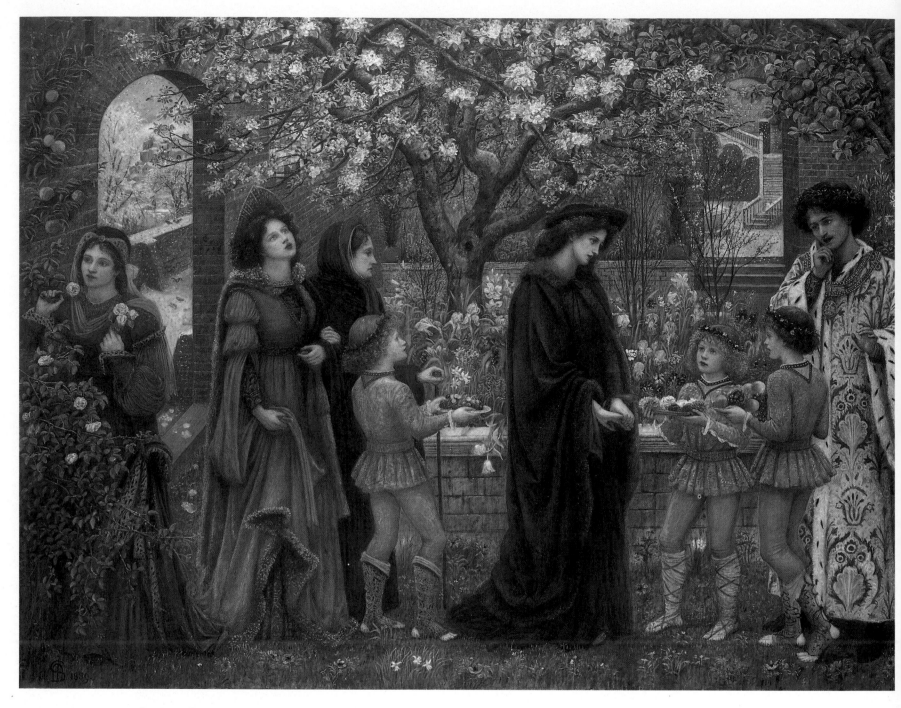

must content ourselves with surveying the work of some of the individuals who fell, to some degree or other, under Pre-Raphaelite influence.

One of Rossetti's most devoted disciples was Frederick Sandys. Sandys was the son of a minor Norwich School artist, and began to exhibit at the Royal Academy in 1851. He first came to notice by producing a print entitled *The Nightmare*, satirizing Millais' picture *Sir Isumbras at the Ford*, and containing caricatures of Millais, Rossetti, Hunt and Ruskin. As a result of this he met Rossetti and Swinburne, and was introduced to the Pre-Raphaelite circle. Most of his pictures, like Rossetti's, are half-length figures of beautiful, and usually destructive women, with titles like *Medea, Fair Rosamund* or *La Belle Ysonde*. Sometimes he attempted more elaborate, full-length figures, such as *Morgan-le-Fay* (p. 129). Unlike Rossetti, however, Sandys was a superb technician and a wonderfully precise draughtsman. His mastery of Pre-Raphaelite techniques is equal to that of Millais or Holman Hunt, and his portraits have rightly been compared with those of the finest early Flemish and German artists. He also produced chalk drawings of exceptionally high quality and his studies of girls, such as *Proud Maisie*, are among the very finest pictures of Pre-Raphaelite 'stunners'. He was also an important illustrator, and worked for the *Cornhill, Good Words* and *Once A Week* magazines, and also illustrated poems by Swinburne and Christina Rossetti. His illustrations combine Pre-Raphaelite subjects

Maria Stillman (1844–1927)
Messer Ansaldo showing Madonna Dianova his Enchanted Garden

Signed with monogram, dated 1889
Gouache 76 × 102 cm/30 × 40 ins
The Pre-Raphaelite Trust

Maria Stillman was born Maria Spartali, the daughter of a Greek family living in London. She was a celebrated beauty, and modelled both for Rossetti and the photographer Julia Margaret Cameron. Her own paintings particularly show the influence of Rossetti, although she was a pupil of Ford Madox Brown. She married an American journalist and photographer, William J. Stillman. The subject of this picture is from Boccaccio, a poet very popular with late Pre-Raphaelite artists.

John Atkinson Grimshaw (1836–1893)
Elaine

Signed and dated 1877
Canvas 83 × 122 cm/32½ × 48 ins
Private Collection

The subject is from Tennyson's poem *Elaine and Lancelot*, in which Elaine dies of unrequited love for Sir Lancelot. She is shown floating down to Camelot in her funeral barge, steered by the shadowy figure of a boatman. Although best-known for his remarkable pictures of moonlit docks, streets and suburban lanes, Grimshaw also painted a number of poetic, allegorical and fairy subjects. He particularly admired the poetry of Tennyson, and owned a copy of Gustave Doré's illustrated version of *Elaine*, published in the same year as this picture.

with a Dürer-like precision, and the Pre-Raphaelites themselves greatly admired his powers as a draughtsman. Like Rossetti, he painted *femmes fatales* and also suffered from them. In Sandys' case the *femme* was a gypsy, Keomi, with whom he had a lengthy affair. To have an affair with a working girl was part of many Victorian artists' code of chivalry.

Another artist to fall under Rossetti's spell, this time with disastrous consequences, was Simeon Solomon. Solomon was a member of an artistic Jewish family; both his elder brother Abraham and his sister Rebecca were artists. He entered the Royal Academy Schools in 1855 and exhibited his first picture there in 1860. His work showed a brilliantly precocious talent, and he was soon befriended by Rossetti, Burne-Jones, Swinburne, and others in the Pre-Raphaelite circle. During the 1860s he produced a number of fine drawings, gouaches and oil paintings, mainly of religious subjects, especially depicting Jewish ritual, but also classical and allegorical subjects which combine Pre-Raphaelite and aesthetic ideas in a highly individual way. Although Solomon's pictures obviously owe much to Rossetti and Burne-Jones, especially his allegorical female figures, they have a strong individuality which makes them instantly recognizable. Unfortunately the corrupting influence of Rossetti, and more particularly, Swinburne, encouraged Solomon to explore the forbidden subjects of homosexuality and lesbianism, both of which feature, more or less overtly, in his work, as in his fine gouache of 1864, *Sappho and Erinna at Mytelene*. On 11 February 1873 he was arrested for homosexual offences, after which he was completely shunned by all his former friends, including Swinburne. Before condemning such extraordinary hypocrisy, one has to remember just how powerful the full weight of the Victorian moral code still was in the 1860s.

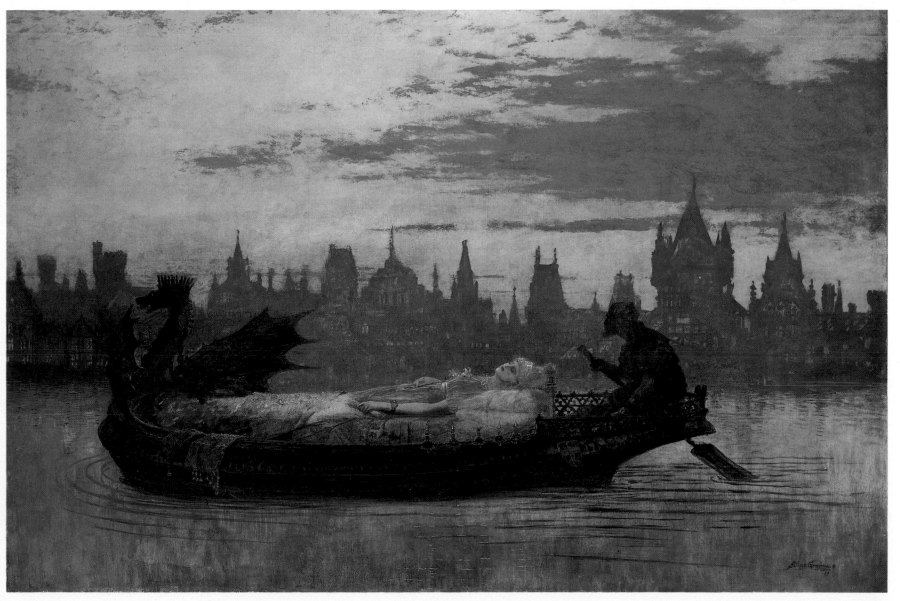

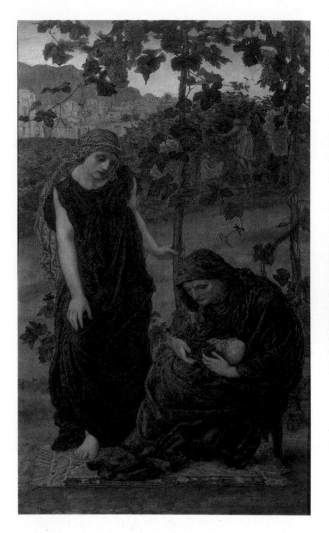
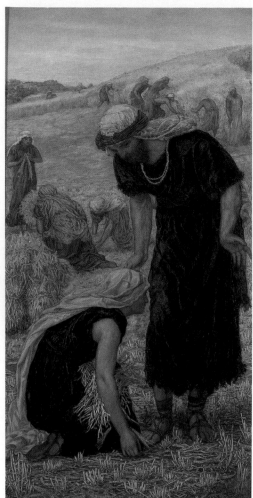
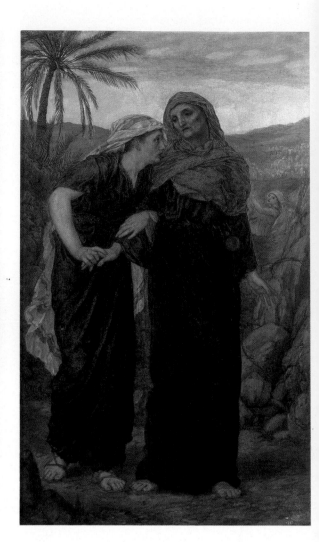

Also Rossetti, Swinburne, Burne-Jones and others were still smarting from the puritanical attacks of Robert Buchanan in *The Fleshly School of Poetry*, which particularly criticized Solomon's paintings on account of their 'unhealthy tendencies'. The disgrace of young Simeon Solomon undoubtedly played into the hands of Buchanan and the other critics of Rossetti and his followers.

The remainder of Solomon's career is one of the minor tragedies of the Pre-Raphaelite story. A complete social leper, he steadily gave away to drink and dissipation, ending his days as an alcoholic in the St. Giles Workhouse in 1905. During his last years he supported himself by making drawings and pastels, usually allegorical heads of a peculiarly androgynous type. These were popular among Oxford undergraduates in the heyday of Walter Pater. Although they are sometimes beautiful, many are weak and repetitive, and not up to the standard of his 1860s work. Occasionally they recapture the air of mystical sensuality that is the distinguishing feature of Solomon's best work.

Another member of Rossetti's circle was the beautiful Greek artist, Maria Spartali, later Mrs William J. Stillman. She actually studied with Ford Madox Brown, but her pictures show much stronger Rossettian influence, particularly her half-length allegorical female figures. It was also Rossetti who encouraged her to paint Italian subjects from Dante and Boccaccio, such as *Messer Ansaldo showing Madonna Diànova his Enchanted Garden* (p. 132), one of her largest and most ambitious pictures. As a young man, Henry Holiday was also a friend of Rossetti, and under his influence painted his best-known picture, *Dante and Beatrice* (p. 128), a familiar image due to its reproduction in countless Victorian history books and anthologies. Holiday became involved in stained-glass design, and also teaching, and produced only a few paintings during the rest of his career.

Two provincial artists to come under Pre-Raphaelite influence were Frederic Shields of Manchester, and John Atkinson Grimshaw of Leeds. Shields was

Thomas Matthews Rooke (1842–1942)
The Story of Ruth

1876–77
Canvas, three panels, 66 × 39 cm/26 × 15½ ins; 22 × 34 cm/26 × 13¼ ins; 66 × 39 cm/26 × 15½ ins
Tate Gallery, London

Rooke was for many years Burne-Jones's chief studio assistant, and his own work reflects the influence of his master. He painted a number of biblical subjects like this one, often using a narrative sequence of several panels in one frame. Rooke was also a noted topographer and painter of old buildings, especially in watercolour, which he painted under the supervision of Ruskin.

John Melhuish Strudwick (1849–1937)
The Music of a Bygone Age

1890
Canvas 79 × 61 cm/31 × 42 ins
The Pre-Raphaelite Trust

Strudwick worked as a studio assistant to both Spencer-Stanhope and Burne-Jones, and his style reflects the influence of both. His subjects are usually poetic and allegorical, and his style a highly personal variation of the Burne-Jones idiom. Like Burne-Jones, he was an admirer of Italian Renaissance painting, and his pictures have a distinctly Italianate flavour, both in their general composition and colouring.

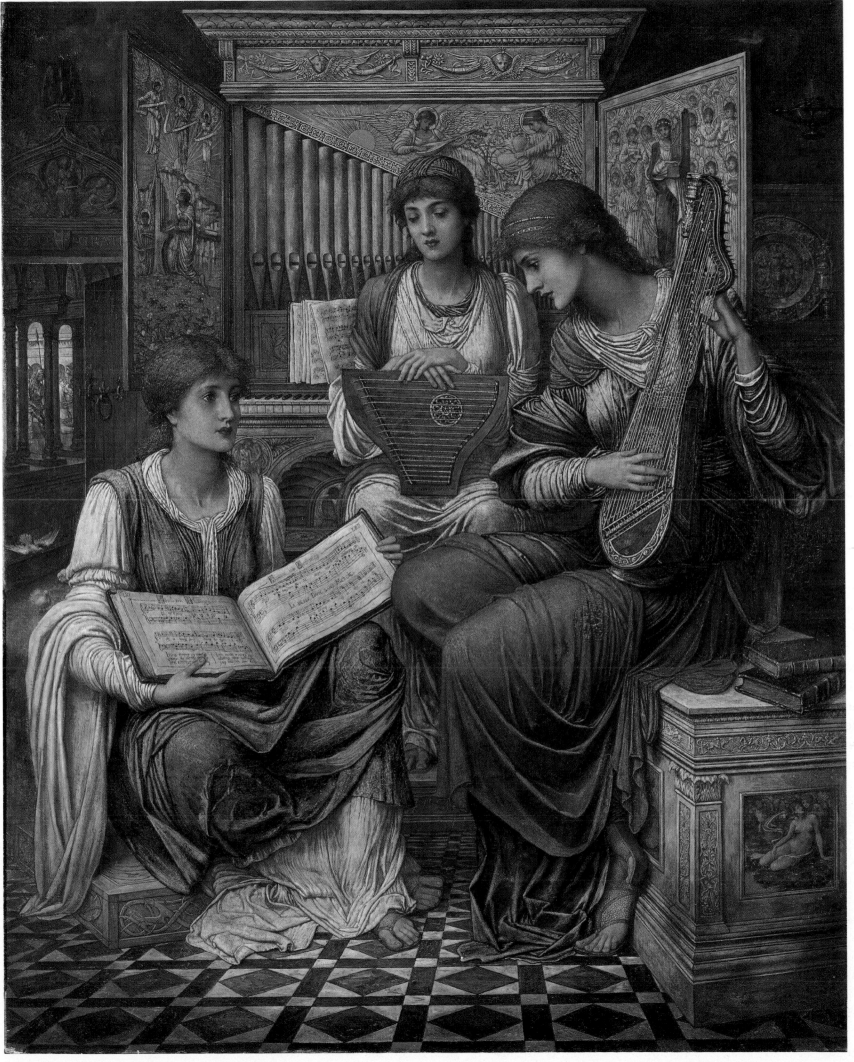

135

converted to the Pre-Raphaelite cause after seeing the Manchester Art Treasures exhibition in 1857, and subsequently became a close friend of Rossetti and Madox Brown. He was a deeply religious man, and most of his pictures are of biblical subjects, painted in a strongly realistic style that is more akin to Holman Hunt than Rossetti. He worked mainly in watercolour and was also a fine draughtsman and illustrator who carried out mural decorations in several churches. Atkinson Grimshaw was never a member of the Pre-Raphaelite circle, although he was acquainted with John William Inchbold, but many of his pictures of the 1870s, particularly his interiors, show an awareness of the Aesthetic Movement. He was also a great admirer of Tennyson, and painted one or two highly Pre-Raphaelite pictures such as *The Lady of Shalott* and *Elaine* (p. 133), based on Tennyson poems. Until recently, Grimshaw was thought of only as a painter of moonlit street and dock scenes, but a recent exhibition at Leeds City Art Gallery has done much to explore the full artistic range of this remarkable and imaginative painter.

Evelyn de Morgan (1855–1919)
Hope in the Prison of Despair
Signed with monogram, undated
Oil on panel, 58 × 65 cm/23 × 25½ ins
Private collection

Evelyn de Morgan was the niece and pupil of Spencer-Stanhope and the wife of the celebrated potter, William de Morgan. She painted allegories, often very large, in the aesthetic Burne-Jones idiom. Her subjects are highly poetic and allegorical, and she is one of the very few Pre-Raphaelite artists whose work can be described as Symbolist.

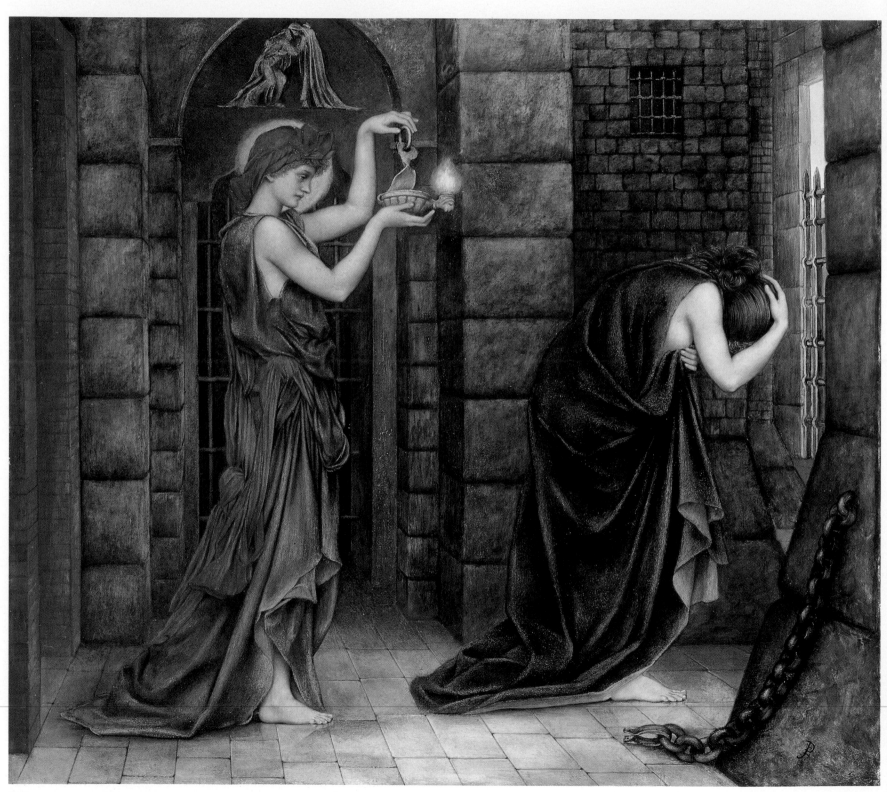

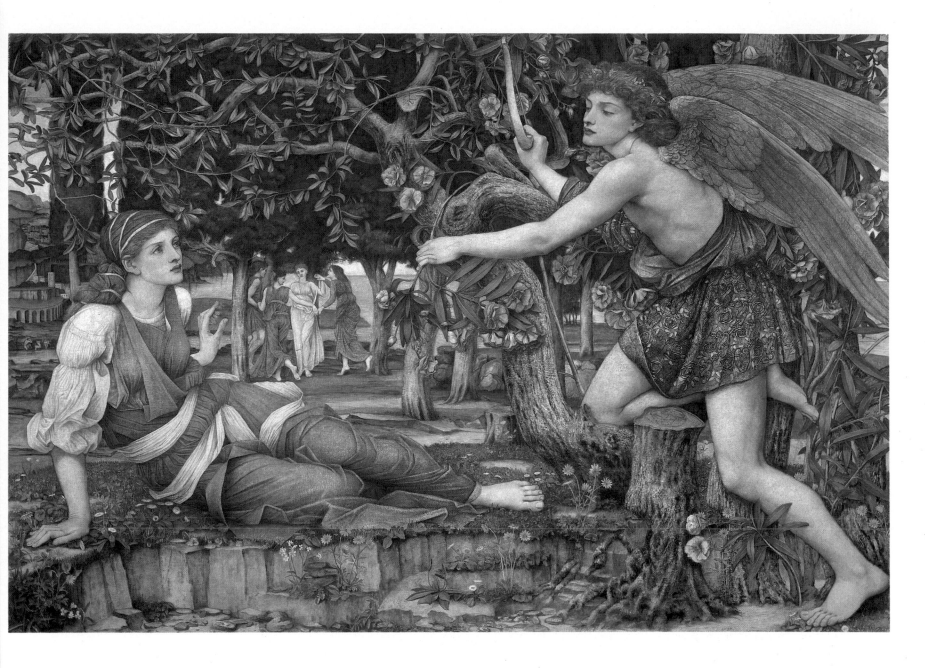

John Roddam Spencer-Stanhope
(1829–1908)

Love and the Maiden

Undated
Canvas 138 × 201 cm/54¼ × 79¾ ins
Private Collection

Spencer-Stanhope was one of the many late
Victorian painters to be influenced by Burne-Jones.
But his style is distinctly personal, and also highly
Italianate. From 1880 onwards, he lived
permanently in Florence and his pictures reflect his
obvious admiration for Florentine Renaissance art,
especially Botticelli. He was the uncle, and also the
teacher, of Evelyn de Morgan.

As Rossetti became more and more of a recluse during the 1870s, it was inevitable
that the leadership of the Pre-Raphaelites should pass to Burne-Jones, particularly
after his triumph at the Grosvenor Gallery in 1877 which established him as one of
England's leading artists. His house in Fulham, The Grange, became increasingly a
focal point for young artists of the 1870s and 1880s, attracted by Burne-Jones's great
reputation and his almost mystical devotion to his art. Burne-Jones's wife, Georgiana
MacDonald, was one of the four remarkable MacDonald sisters; of the other three,
one married the artist Edward John Poynter, later President of the Royal Academy,
and the other two became the mothers of Rudyard Kipling and the Prime Minister,
Stanley Baldwin. Burne-Jones was therefore uncle to both Kipling and Baldwin, a
curious combination from any point of view.

The followers of Burne-Jones have tended to be lumped together as one
amorphous group, and dismissed as mere imitators. It is now clear, however, that
many of them developed artistic personalities of their own, worthy of separate
consideration. This is particularly true of Burne-Jones's two actual pupils, Thomas
Matthews Rooke and John Melhuish Strudwick. Rooke helped Burne-Jones with
much of his design work for Morris and Company, but he also produced paintings of
his own, which are more than mere imitations of Burne-Jones's. His drawings too
have the sensitivity and delicacy of those of his master. Strudwick also produced his
own highly personal version of the Burne-Jones style. His technique was much more
minute than that of Burne-Jones, and he painted in a flat linear style, with great
attention to detail and colouring. His subjects are usually deliberately allegorical, and

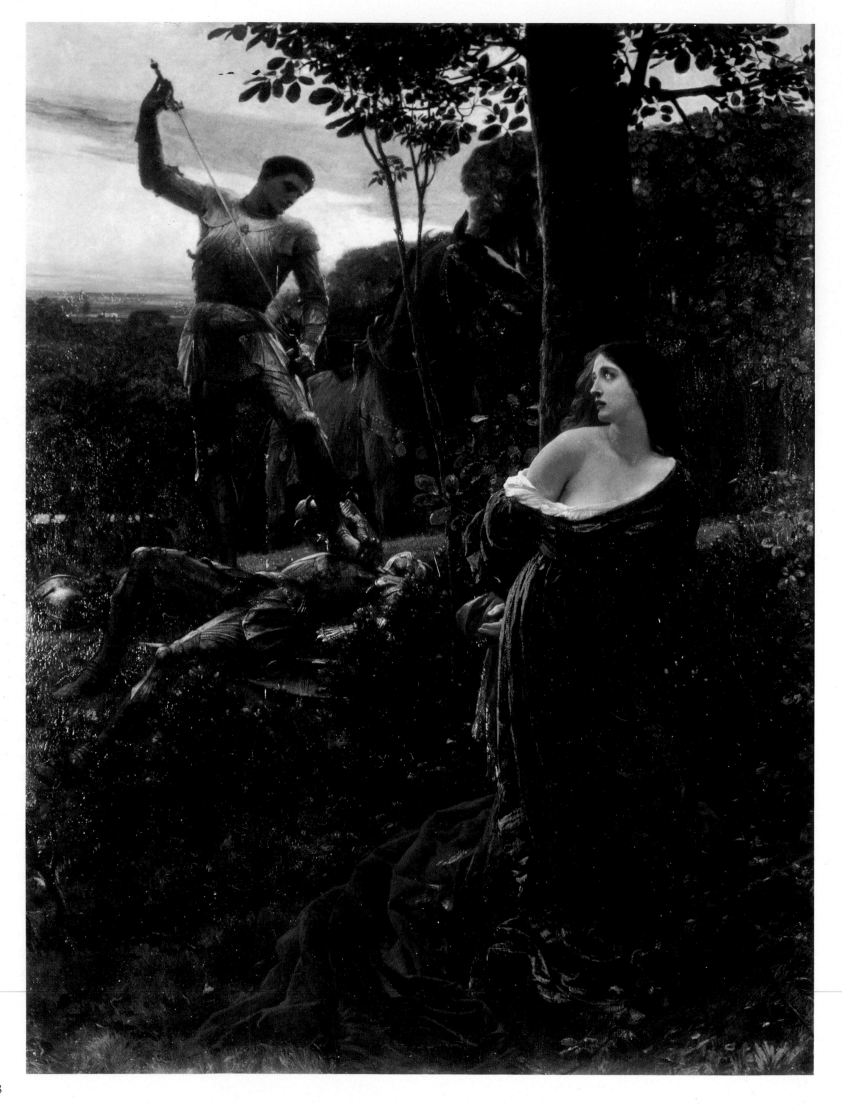

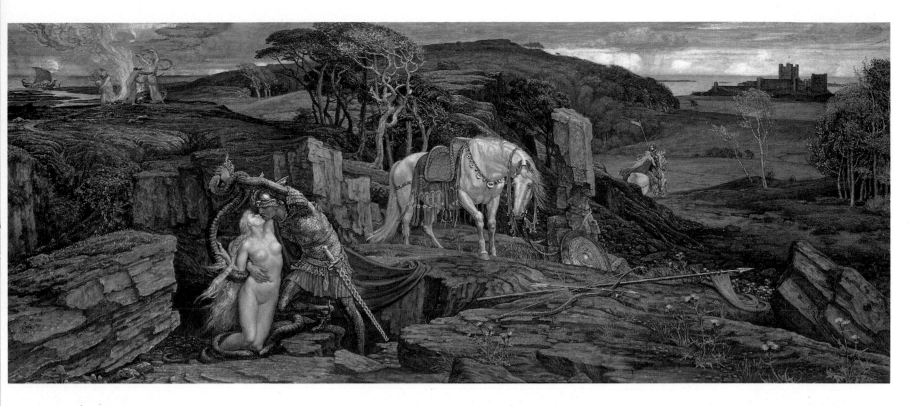

Walter Crane (1845–1915)
The Laidly Worm

1881
76 × 147 cm/29¾ × 57¾ ins
Private Collection

Crane was a great admirer of Burne-Jones, whose work he first saw at the Old Watercolour Society in 1865. In his autobiography he recalled what a deep impression Burne-Jones's pictures made on him: '. . . we had a glimpse into a magic world of romance and pictured poetry, peopled with ghosts of "ladies dead and lovely knights" – a twilight world of dark mysterious woodlands, haunted streams, meads of deep green starred with burning flowers, veiled in a dim and mystic light . . .' The description could very well apply to Crane's own romantic pictures of medieval subjects.

Sir Frank Dicksee (1853–1928)
Chivalry

c1885
Canvas 183 × 136 cm/72 × 53½ ins
Forbes Magazine Collection

Frank Dicksee came from an artistic family; his father Thomas Dicksee was an artist, as were several other relations. He entered the Royal Academy Schools in 1871, and exhibited his first picture there in 1875. Throughout the 1880s and 90s he painted historical, literary, biblical and allegorical subjects in a lavishly-costumed and richly-coloured style that earned him great success and popularity. *Chivalry* was commissioned by the Victorian engineer Sir John Aird, and exhibited at the Royal Academy in 1885. Later Dicksee turned increasingly to Society portraits.

the compositions somewhat static, but they have a remarkable richness of decorative effect. One of the first writers on Strudwick's work, surprisingly, was the young Bernard Shaw, who wrote an article about him in 1891 in the *Art Journal*, praising his 'transcendent expressiveness'.

Strudwick also worked for the painter John Roddam Spencer-Stanhope, a rich dilettante who had been, together with Val Prinsep, one of the young artists involved in the Oxford murals of 1857. Spencer-Stanhope eventually evolved his own very personal version of the Burne-Jones style, in which Florentine Renaissance painting plays a very large part. His pictures are always beautifully composed and highly decorative, if at times rather obviously derivative. Stanhope's niece and pupil was Evelyn de Morgan, wife of the potter and novelist William de Morgan. Like her uncle, Evelyn de Morgan had independent means, and therefore had no particular need to sell her pictures. They are consequently rather rare, and a great many belong to the de Morgan Foundation, which recently lent a group to Cragside, in Northumberland. These enable one to form a clearer idea of the highly individual style which Evelyn de Morgan developed. Her pictures are nearly all large, complex allegories, with practically no historical or even literary content. They are beautifully and richly painted, and their mystical atmosphere and vague allegorical titles have led to their frequent comparison with European Symbolism. English Symbolism is notoriously difficult to define, but it is certainly present in the work of many late Pre-Raphaelites, notably Evelyn de Morgan, and also Sidney Harold Meteyard. Meteyard studied in Birmingham, which was one of the last strongholds of Pre-Raphaelite influence, well into the twentieth century. Birmingham was the birthplace of Burne-Jones, so it is hardly surprising that his influence was very strong there. Meteyard's pictures reflect an obvious admiration for Burne-Jones, and also for the poetry of Tennyson. *The Lady of Shalott* was almost a cult subject among the later Pre-Raphaelites – Waterhouse, Holman Hunt, Byam Shaw, Grimshaw and Meteyard were only a few of the artists who painted it, some of them more than once. Meteyard's later pictures are mostly allegorical and symbolic figures, highly-wrought and beautifully coloured, in a style very close to that of Evelyn de Morgan. They too have been identified with the growth of Symbolism.

Another fervent admirer of Burne-Jones was Walter Crane, who has described in his memoirs the excitement of his first visit to the studio of the great man. Crane later became famous as a designer and book illustrator; his children's books, in particular, have been firm favourites in English nurseries ever since. He also painted a few fine

139

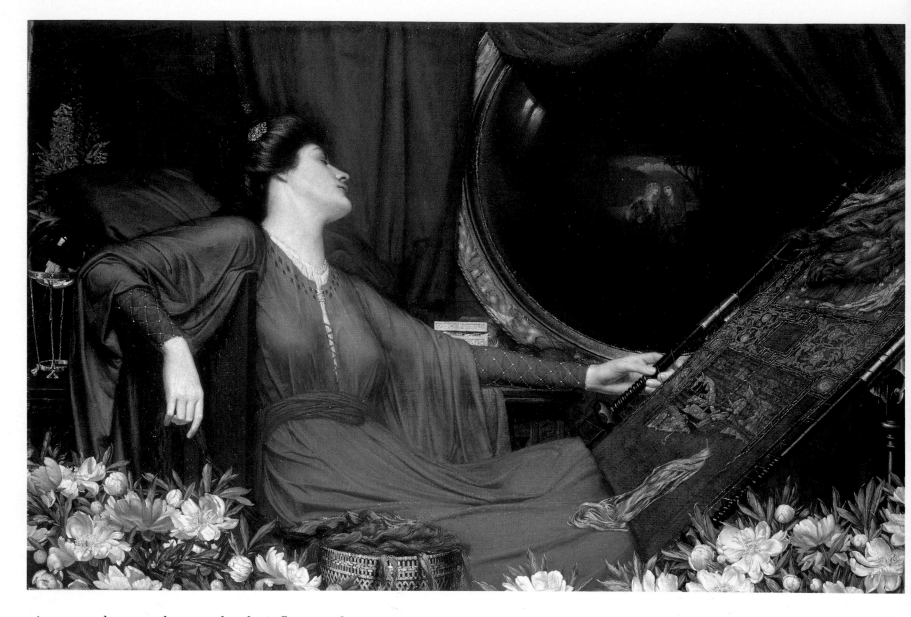

pictures and watercolours under the influence of Burne-Jones. Crane also became a close friend of William Morris, and like him, a Socialist. Many Pre-Raphaelite artists, such as Madox Brown, Crane and Shields were active in their support of Working Men's Colleges, and remained faithful to the left-wing political ideals that had been one of the original aims of the Brotherhood.

The list of other artists influenced by Burne-Jones is endless. Charles Fairfax Murray was one of the most interesting, as he also compiled an outstanding collection of the Pre-Raphaelites' work, a large part of which is now in the Pierpont Morgan Library, New York City, Birmingham City Art Gallery, and the Fitzwilliam Museum, Cambridge. Charles Hallé, who helped to found both the Grosvenor and the New Gallery, also painted allegorical figure subjects in the Burne-Jones idiom. Percy H. Bate, in his book *The English Pre-Raphaelite Painters*, published in 1899 and still a standard work of reference, lists many other artists as belonging to the Pre-Raphaelite school. Among these are the almost forgotten Matthew Lawless and George Wilson; he also lists George Dunlop Leslie, Valentine Cameron Prinsep, George Adolphus Storey, John Dawson Watson and Philip Hermogenes Calderon as showing signs of Pre-Raphaelite influence. Certainly isolated examples of their work can be cited as Pre-Raphaelite, but none of them can really be regarded as more than peripheral. Bate also includes James Tissot as a Pre-Raphaelite — a rather far-fetched claim which one cannot take too seriously, although Tissot did exhibit mainly at the Grosvenor, alongside Burne-Jones and Whistler. Bate fails to mention Frank Dicksee, who as a young artist, painted several fine pictures of Pre-Raphaelite inspiration, such as *Chivalry* (p. 138), a magnificently romantic picture with echoes of both Millais and Burne-Jones.

140

Sidney Harold Meteyard (1868–1947)
''I am half-sick of shadows'', said the Lady of Shalott

Signed and dated 1913
Canvas 76 × 114 cm/30 × 45 ins
The Pre-Raphaelite Trust

Meteyard was another of the late, romantic Pre-Raphaelite painters whose ideas derived basically from Burne-Jones, but whose poetic and allegorical style is more similar to that of Evelyn de Morgan. The poetry of Tennyson continued to inspire Pre-Raphaelite painters right up to 1914. Meteyard belonged to the Birmingham school of painters, which produced a number of interesting Pre-Raphaelite artists in the period from 1890 to 1920.

John William Waterhouse 1849–1917

Surprisingly, Bate also fails to mention in his book the one artist now regarded as the greatest late Victorian romantic painter after Burne-Jones – John William Waterhouse. This is probably because Waterhouse painted mainly classical and Homeric subjects, and Bate therefore classified him as a follower of Leighton. However, Waterhouse also painted subjects from Tennyson and Keats, such as *The Lady of Shalott* (below), which he painted three times, and *La Belle Dame Sans Merci* (p. 143). Also, most contemporary critics correctly observed that Waterhouse's style was a very individual and brilliant fusion of the classicism of Leighton and the aesthetic Pre-Raphaelitism of Burne-Jones. As such it is one of the finest achievements of late Victorian art, and no book on Pre-Raphaelitism would be complete without him. Waterhouse is a Pre-Raphaelite, but he is also a classicist – perhaps the only artist to have successfully reconciled these two opposing forces in late Victorian art.

If Leighton and Burne-Jones are both late Victorian dreamers, then so too is Waterhouse. His subjects are a typical Aesthetic mixture – classical, biblical, historical, Keats, Tennyson, Boccaccio – but his genius lay in the uniquely poetic and imaginative way in which he reinterpreted these familiar themes. For Waterhouse was much more of a realist than either Leighton or Burne-Jones. The same mood of

John William Waterhouse (1849–1917)
The Lady of Shalott

  Signed and dated 1888
  Canvas 153 × 200 cm/60¼ × 78¾ ins
  Tate Gallery, London

Waterhouse's first major picture in Pre-Raphaelite style. The choice of such a romantic Tennysonian subject – a stock Pre-Raphaelite favourite – may well have been inspired by the Millais exhibition at the Grosvenor Gallery in 1886, which Waterhouse is known to have seen and admired.

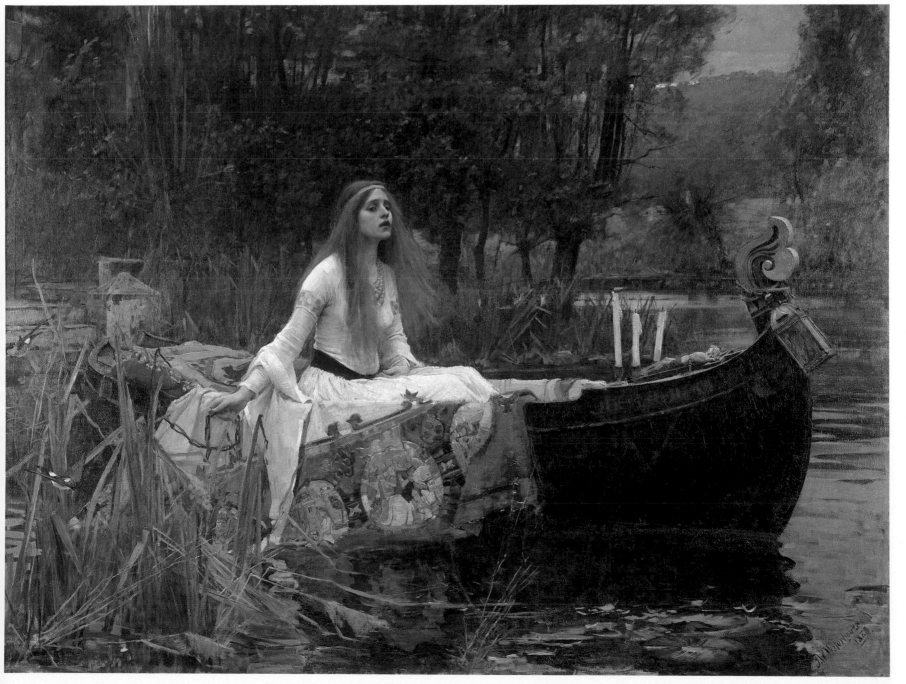

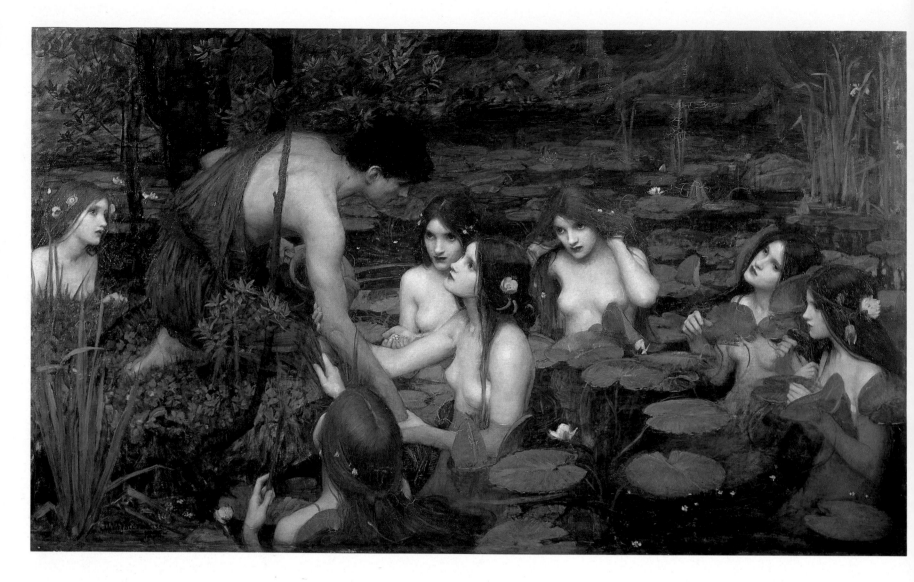

nostalgia and melancholy pervades all their work, but Waterhouse's nymphs and goddesses are real flesh-and-blood people, whereas Burne-Jones's are like beings from another planet. Looking at Waterhouse's *Hylas and the Nymphs* (above), we seem to have chanced upon a group of Victorian mermaids luring a shepherd to his doom in the depths of a mysterious, but very English forest. By contrast, Burne-Jones's *Mirror of Venus* or the *Perseus* series might be happening on the moon. The key to Waterhouse's style is this unique gift for combining realism and poetry.

In all Waterhouse's pictures the same romantic, dreamy mood prevails. Waterhouse was an artist who, once he had found his style, stuck to it for the rest of his career. Rather like Albert Moore, he had one song to sing, but he sang it very beautifully. Also like Moore, Waterhouse was a quiet and retiring man, not particularly ambitious for worldly honours. He followed the conventional path to success, becoming an Associate of the Royal Academy in 1885 and a full Academician in 1895. He lived a blameless and quiet life in St. John's Wood, happily married and not excessively tormented by nymphs or *femmes fatales*. He did not seem to care much for artistic factions, preferring to devote himself only to his work. Consequently, his art seems to reconcile many opposites – the classical and the Pre-Raphaelite, the realist and the poetic, the academic and the romantic. Waterhouse's ability to combine romantic subject-matter with a modern style earned him admiration from all sides, and during the 1880s and '90s his reputation rivalled even that of Leighton and Burne-Jones. After the death of Burne-Jones in 1898, Waterhouse remained one of the few admired and respected exponents of the late Pre-Raphaelite style. Between 1900 and 1910 he painted some of his finest pictures, mostly of classical subjects, and he continued to exhibit at the Royal Academy until 1916.

Waterhouse was born in Rome, and both his parents were artists. Many of his childhood years were spent in Italy, and he was to return there many times during

John William Waterhouse

Hylas and the Nymphs

Signed and dated 1896
Canvas 97 × 160 cm/38 × 63 ins
Manchester City Art Gallery

Hylas was squire to Heracles, one of the Argonauts. When they stopped on the island of Cios, Hylas went off in search of water, but was lured to his death by water nymphs. This picture is now Waterhouse's best-known work, and has become one of the key images of the *femme fatale* in late Victorian art. Waterhouse's style is a uniquely personal blend of fantasy and reality, and he is one of the few Victorian artists to paint the Greek myths convincingly.

La Belle Dame Sans Merci

1893
Canvas 112 × 81 cm/44 × 32 ins
Hessisches Landesmuseum, Darmstadt

Keats was always a favourite poet with Pre-Raphaelite painters, even from the very beginnings of the Brotherhood. In 1893 the poetry of Keats was again the inspiration of this very romantic and beautiful picture, one of Waterhouse's finest and most strongly Pre-Raphaelite works.

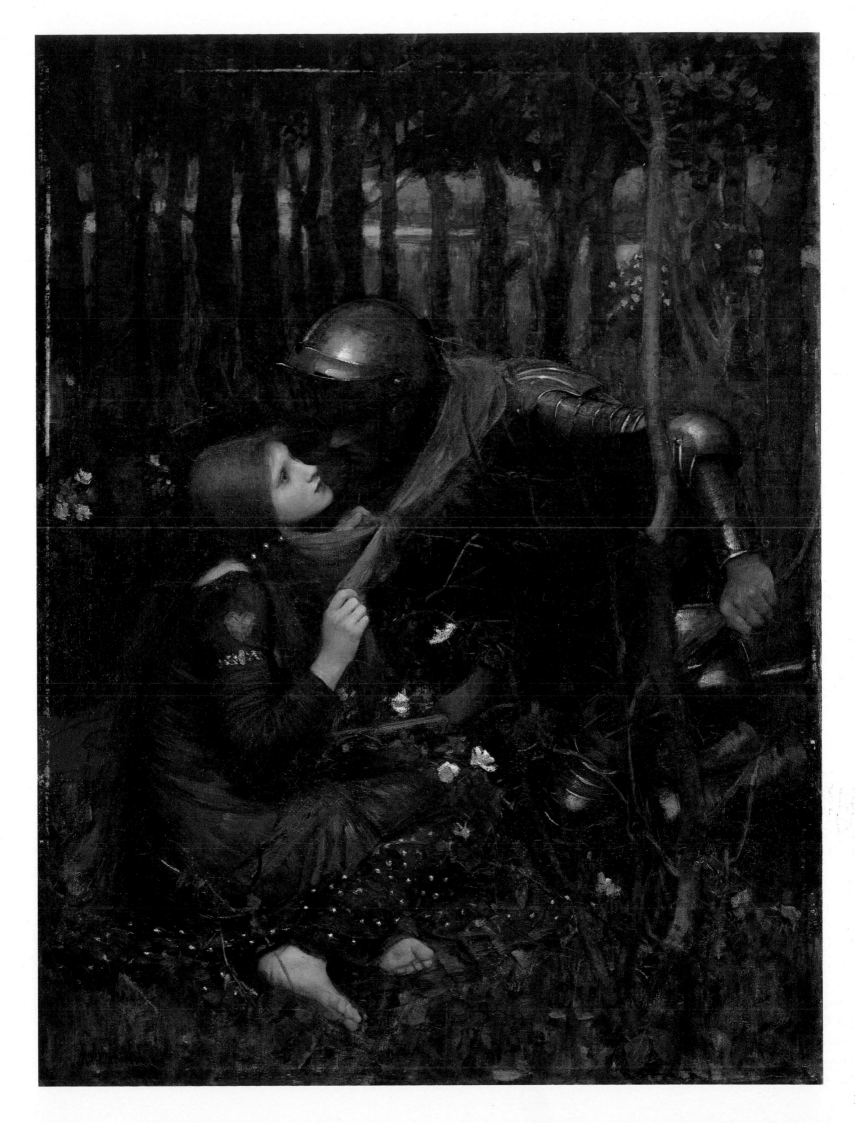

his career. His love of Italy is reflected in many of his early pictures, and also in his lifelong devotion to classical subjects and to the great traditions of Italian and European painting. The Waterhouse family returned to England, and in 1870 the young Waterhouse entered the Royal Academy Schools. The greatest influence on his early work was Lawrence Alma-Tadema, then at the height of his powers and popularity. Between about 1874 and 1885 Waterhouse painted a number of Roman scenes, which in their technique and concern for archaeological accuracy betray the Alma-Tadema influence. One of these, *Saint Eulalia* of 1885, earned him his election as an Associate of the Royal Academy. Then in 1886, he painted *The Magic Circle*, a dramatic picture of a sorceress, which clearly shows his personal style evolving. This was followed by the wonderful *Lady of Shalott* of 1888. This picture is painted in an exceptionally broad and strong realist style, and reflects Waterhouse's new involvement with Frank Bramley, Maurice Greiffenhagen and William Logsdail, all of whom lived in the same row of studios in Primrose Hill. But in spite of this interest in the plein-air realism of Bastien-Lepage and the Newlyn School, Waterhouse never wavered in his devotion to romantic and poetic subjects; not for him the peasants and fishermen of Stanhope Forbes or Frank Bramley. *The Lady of Shalott* already shows how Waterhouse could combine uncompromising realism with a poetic subject. Although he never painted in quite such plein-air style again, it left an indelible mark on his technique, and he continued to use the rich colours and broad impasto typical of the Newlyn School. Waterhouse's colours always have an iridescent and glowing quality, full of golds, yellows, purples and reds, and ideally suited to the poetic mood which his pictures evoke.

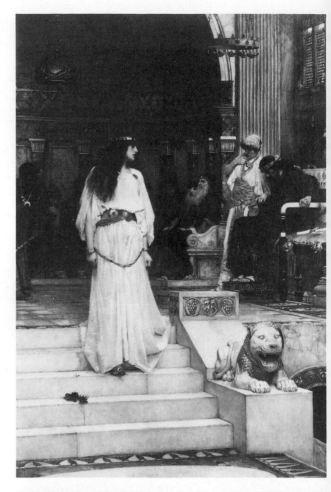

As Waterhouse began to develop his own distinctive style, and move towards more romantic and poetic subjects, he was already beginning to display a fascination with the *femme fatale*, that recurrent image of so much late nineteenth-century European art. As one might expect, Waterhouse's Circes and Sirens are not evil and destructive monsters like those of Gustave Moreau and the European Symbolists. Rather they lure and entrap their victims by their wistful beauty and mysterious sadness, as if they cannot help what they are doing, and rather regret it. This is evident in such pictures as *Circe Offering the Cup to Ulysses* of 1891, or *Circe Invidiosa* of 1892, but above all in the beautiful *La Belle Dame Sans Merci* of 1893. Here a typical Waterhouse enchantress gently draws the armour-clad knight into her fatal embrace, set in a landscape full of haunting mystery and beauty. The girl is the classic Waterhouse type, with long hair and a wistful expression on her face – the hallmark of the Waterhouse style. The picture vibrates with a delicate, haunting sensuality, and is set in a dark, overgrown wood. The figure of the knight is of course Waterhouse himself, increasingly obsessed by his own vision of womanhood. From the 1890s onwards, all Waterhouse's pictures are of women. Men appear only as victims.

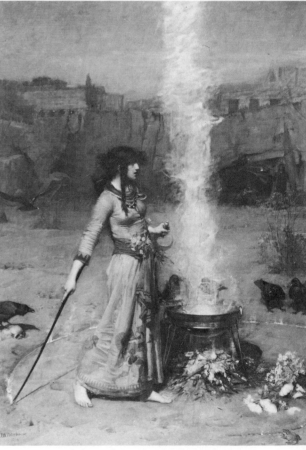

Waterhouse's creative genius reached its peak in the 1890s, and this decade was to produce many of his most memorable masterpieces. In 1891 he painted the large and extraordinary *Ulysses and the Sirens*, very little-known in this country, as it was bought for an Australian museum almost straight out of the Academy. It shows Ulysses and his men on board ship, threatened by the Sirens, who are depicted as huge birds with the faces of beautiful women. It is the only picture by Waterhouse which has a truly nightmarish, menacing quality, similar to that of the Symbolist painters. Much more typical of the Waterhouse mood is the now famous *Hylas and the Nymphs*, one of his best-known and most popular pictures, and a key image in late Pre-Raphaelite art. Here Hylas, the helpless male victim, kneels by a reedy pool, from which emerge seven beautiful, red-haired nymphs, all with that unmistakable 'Waterhouse look'. Several critics complained that the girls all looked the same, but this in no way detracts from the mysterious and poetic atmosphere of the picture, which is totally convincing. Although Waterhouse was an academic artist who worked from models in the studio, his imaginative gifts enabled him to transcend

Above: **John William Waterhouse**, *Mariamne*, 1887. Below: *The Magic Circle*, 1886.

144

John William Waterhouse
Ophelia

Signed, undated
Canvas 102 × 64 cm/40 × 25 ins
The Pre-Raphaelite Trust

Women in Pre-Raphaelite
pictures are either *femmes fatales*
or tragic heroines, and Ophelia
remained one of the most
popular images of the tragic
heroine. Waterhouse was greatly
influenced by Millais; he saw a
retrospective exhibition of
Millais' work at the Grosvenor
Gallery in 1886, and must have
known his *Ophelia*. But as usual,
Waterhouse has interpreted the
theme in a highly personal way.

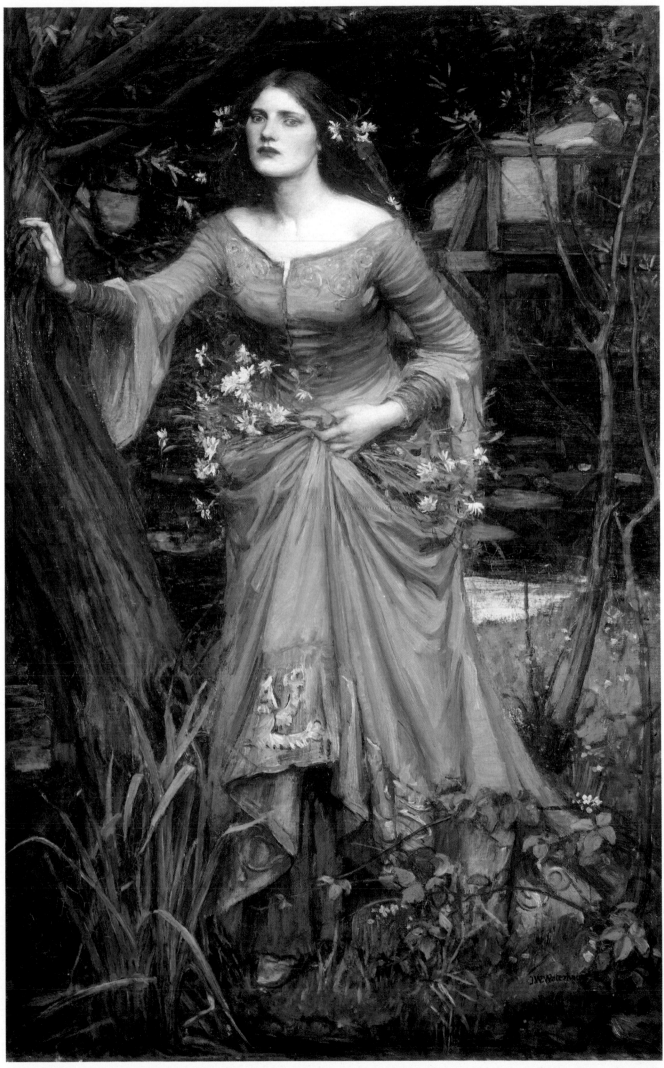

reality, and achieve poetry. Contemporary critics were united in their praise of the picture. The *Magazine of Art* thought it equalled 'the highest qualities of Sir Edward Burne-Jones at his most delightful period ... a spirit of real poetry pervades the canvas.' The *Art Journal* thought it 'a combination of the better attributes and intentions of Leighton and Burne-Jones'. During the 1890s Waterhouse was to paint many more beautiful pictures, such as *Ophelia* (p. 145) in 1894, *Saint Cecilia* the following year, and *Ariadne* in 1898. After 1900, he was to continue painting for another sixteen years, but was never quite able to recapture the mastery that produced such a succession of masterpieces in the 1890s. The essentials of his style were already established, and after 1900 his work represents a continued exploration of familiar themes. His style becomes, if anything, more refined, more decorous, and less dramatic. There is a striving towards prettiness, but it never degenerates into sentimentality, or cheap titillation, as it does in so many of his contemporaries. The *femme fatale* remains the central theme, as in *A Mermaid* of 1900, and the majority of his subjects are classical. The destructive power of woman is the theme of many of them, such as *Echo and Narcissus*, *Nymphs Finding the Head of Orpheus*, *Phyllis and Demophoön*, and many more. But there is no cruelty or bloodshed in any of these pictures, only the same wistful mood of vague longing and regret. The theme that appealed most to Waterhouse in his late years was that of Psyche, also a favourite with Burne-Jones. But he also painted another *Lady of Shalott* as late as 1915, and a scene from Boccaccio's *Decameron* in 1916, both traditional Pre-Raphaelite favourites. Works like these are among the last, faint echoes of Pre-Raphaelitism, a final homage to the spirit of the Brotherhood, founded over sixty years before.

By 1912 Waterhouse's health had begun to decline, and his creative powers with it. In 1915 he failed to send a picture to the Royal Academy for the first time in twenty-four years. He worked right up to the end, and his last picture, entitled *The Enchanted Garden*, was left unfinished. It makes a fitting epitaph, for what is the

Edward Reginald Frampton (1872–1923)
The Annunciation

Undated
Canvas 127 × 114 cm/50 × 45 ins
Private Collection

Frampton's highly decorative, exaggerated style is typical of the last phase of Pre-Raphaelitism, which extended well into the twentieth century. Other exponents of this style include Frederick Cayley Robinson and Robert Anning Bell.

John William Waterhouse, *Saint Cecilia*, 1895.

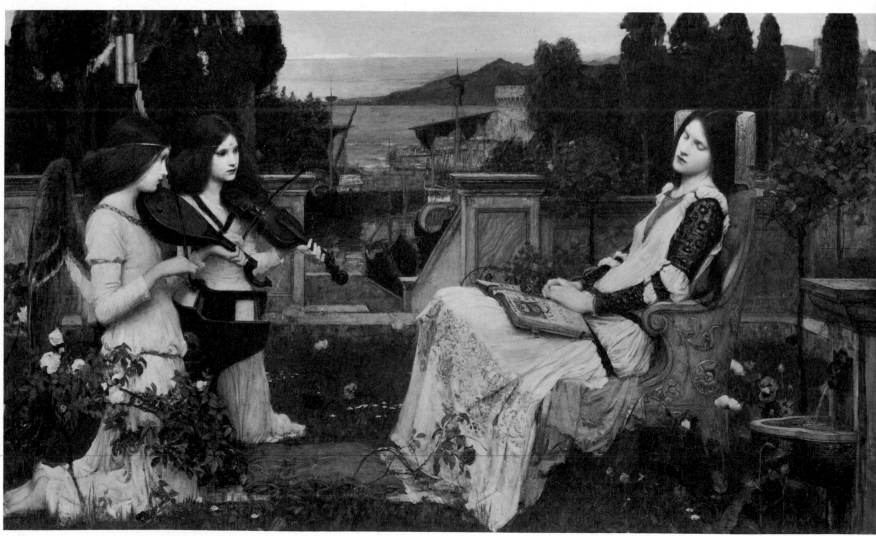

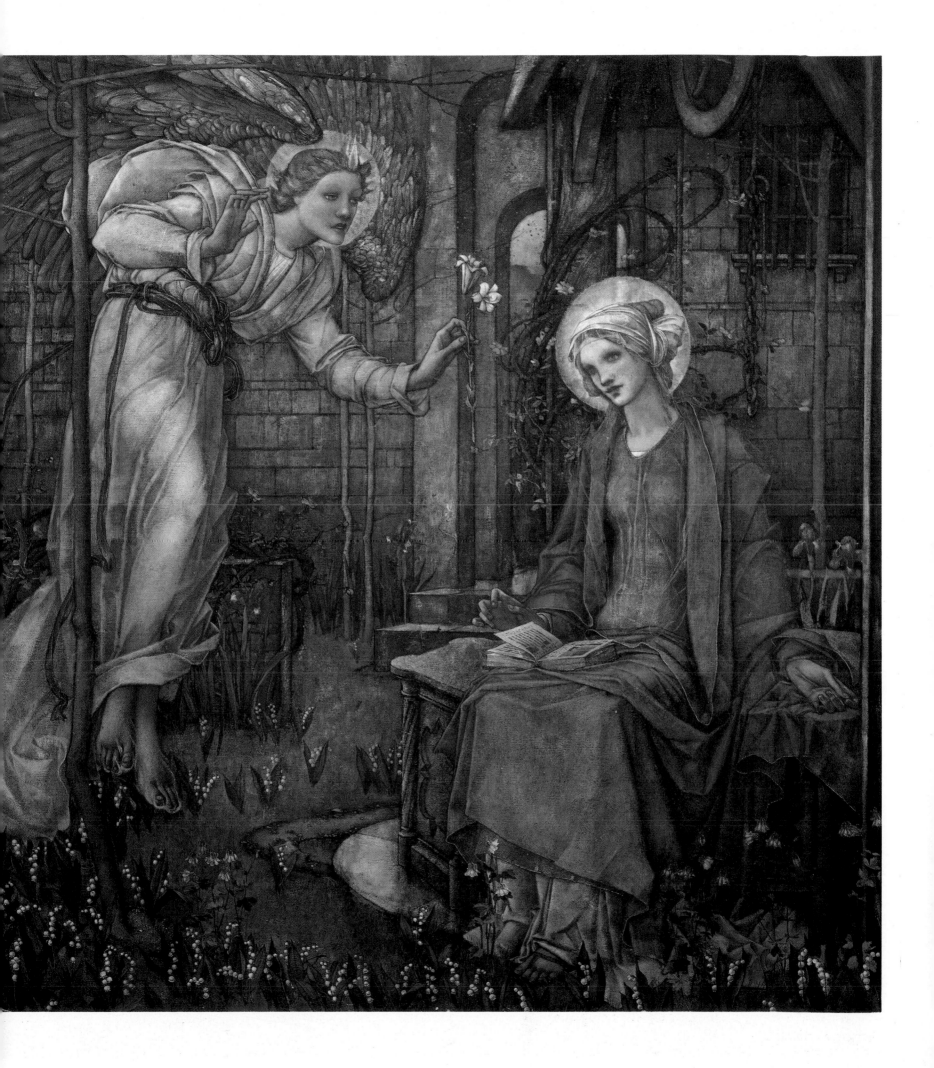

work of Waterhouse if not an enchanted garden? And yet we know so little about its creator. Of all the major Pre-Raphaelite figures, Waterhouse remains by far the most enigmatic. Nothing is known of his private life or his artistic beliefs, as no letters or diaries survive. His married life seems to have been happy, but one cannot help speculating about the identity of the mysterious and beautiful model who reappears so often in his pictures. She certainly plays as central a role in Waterhouse's pictures as does Jane Morris in those of Rossetti. But who was she, and what was her relationship, if any, with Waterhouse? It remains one of the few Pre-Raphaelite mysteries, and one that will probably never be solved.

The Last Phase 1890–1920

To the art critic, Percy Bate, writing in 1899, it seemed that the Pre-Raphaelite movement was still 'sweeping on', and widening as it went. He admitted, however, that the original aims of the Brotherhood had long ago been achieved, and that Pre-Raphaelitism in the 1890s was 'more diffuse'. By this time, Pre-Raphaelitism had become part of the very fabric of English culture, permeating into almost every branch of the arts. During the 1890s several of the great figures of the movement died – Millais and Morris in 1896, Burne-Jones in 1898, and finally Ruskin in 1900. The far-off days of the Pre-Raphaelite Brotherhood were already part of history, and Pre-Raphaelitism was becoming a vague and loose term, which in painting could be applied to any romantic or medieval subject, or *femme fatale* with red hair. Pre-Raphaelitism was still an ideal, a noble and heroic ideal, but it had already begun to blend imperceptibly into Art Nouveau and Symbolism; in the hands of Aubrey Beardsley it had become part of the decadence of the *fin de siècle*. Pre-Raphaelitism still retained its hold over the imaginations of many artists, both old and young, but it was becoming *passé*. The New English Art Club, founded in 1886, was by then attracting many of England's brightest young artists to the Impressionist cause, away from the Grosvenor and the New Gallery. In the Art Club in 1900, two young artists danced for joy when they heard of the death of Ruskin – to them it was as if a great and oppressive weight had been lifted off their shoulders. Roger Fry's revolutionary Post-Impressionist exhibitions at the Grafton Gallery were only a decade away.

The last Pre-Raphaelite artist of real stature was John William Waterhouse, but there were many other distinguished and talented painters who remained faithful to the cause. An artist very close in spirit to Waterhouse was Herbert James Draper, still a largely forgotten and underrated figure. Like Waterhouse he painted mainly classical mythology, but in a highly romantic and poetic style that has distinct affinities with both Burne-Jones and Waterhouse. His nymphs and goddesses have the same wistful, slightly simpering quality as those of Waterhouse, but at his best, Draper was a fine painter. Practically his only known work today is *The Lament for Icarus*, purchased by the Chantrey Bequest in 1898 and now in the Tate Gallery. It is only rarely on view, but is reproduced in most of the standard books on Victorian painting. Much better-known today is John Liston Byam Shaw, who developed a very personal and stylized Pre-Raphaelite manner of his own in the 1890s. Shaw was a great admirer of Rossetti, and many of his pictures are taken from Rossetti poems, such as *The Blessed Damozel* (p. 152). But Byam Shaw combined romantic Rossettian subjects, usually involving beautiful girls, with the bright colours and high finish of Millais and Holman Hunt. The only other artist to do anything comparable to this was Frederick Sandys, but Byam Shaw's pictures have a lyrical Art Nouveau quality, especially in the swirling and convoluted draperies of the female figures, which is quite alien to those of Sandys. Byam Shaw was also a distinguished book illustrator, and his numerous drawings and watercolours for books were usually done in the same brightly-coloured, elaborately romantic style as his paintings. The late nineteenth century was the golden age of illustrated books, especially children's books, and many Pre-Raphaelite artists made notable contributions in this field. The influence of Pre-Raphaelitism on book illustration is outside the scope of this book,

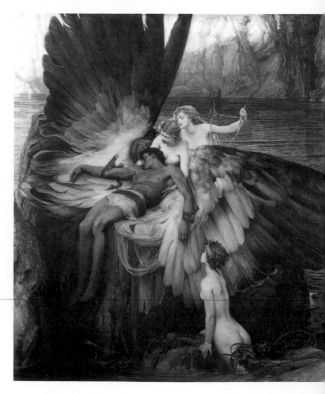

Herbert James Draper, *The Lament for Icarus*, 1898.

Eleanor Fortescue-Brickdale (1871–1945)
The Wise Virgins

Signed with monogram, inscribed on a scroll, and dated 1901
Two watercolours in one frame, upper panel 37 × 30 cm/14½ × 12 ins; lower panel 11 × 30 cm/4½ × 12 ins
Christopher Wood Gallery

The late Victorian period produced a fine school of artist-illustrators, of whom Eleanor Fortescue-Brickdale was one of the best. She illustrated many books, and also painted in oil and watercolour in a romantic, poetic style, derived mainly from Burne-Jones. Her pictures are often in sets of two or three panels, usually in frames designed by herself.

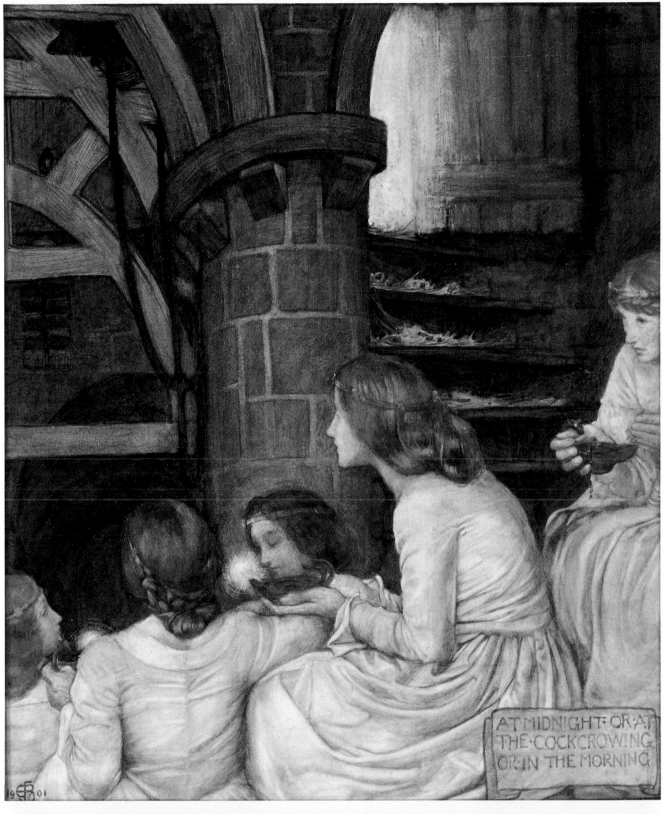

AT·MIDNIGHT·OR·AT
THE·COCKCROWING
OR·IN·THE·MORNING

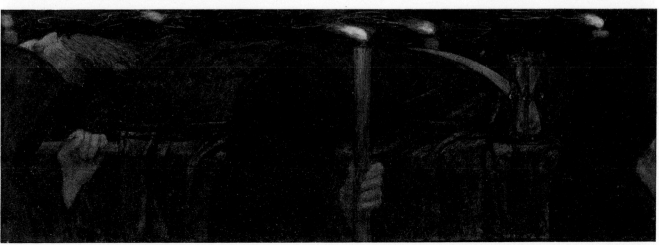

but in the work of such artists as Walter Crane, Henry Justice Ford, Edmund Dulac and Arthur Rackham, Pre-Raphaelite influence was widely disseminated, and continues to influence book illustration even today. Another of the many Pre-Raphaelite painter-illustrators was Eleanor Fortescue-Brickdale. Her early works, such as *The Wise Virgins* (p. 149), show the influence of Burne-Jones, but she was also a close friend and pupil of Byam Shaw, and her book illustrations are very similar in style to his. Another very influential illustrator was the short-lived Aubrey Beardsley, who was introduced to Burne-Jones by Oscar Wilde. As a result, Burne-Jones recommended Beardsley to the publishers Dent and Co. to illustrate an edition of the *Morte d'Arthur*. Beardley's illustrations, which horrified poor Burne-Jones, developed that streak of sensual decadence, which had always been present in the work of such Pre-Raphaelites as Rossetti and Simeon Solomon, into mannered and grotesque caricature.

Painters such as Byam Shaw, Draper and Fortescue-Brickdale continued the Burne-Jones tradition of involvement in decoration and design work. All of them were involved in mural decoration, stained glass, and many other activities. Through the Arts and Crafts Movement, and its many associations and guilds established towards the end of the century, the spirit of Pre-Raphaelitism was kept very much alive. One city with a particularly vigorous Pre-Raphaelite tradition was Birmingham, the birthplace of Burne-Jones. Here Joseph Southall, Charles Gere, Arthur Gaskin, Henry Payne and other members of the Tempera Society kept alive the twin Pre-Raphaelite ideals of romantic and poetic subjects allied to skilled

Thomas Cooper Gotch (1854–1931)
The Child Enthroned

c1894
Canvas 159 × 102 cm/62½ × 40 ins
Private Collection

Gotch painted many portraits and allegories of children, often of his own family, in which the idea of childhood is treated as something mystical, even holy. He is one of the few late Pre-Raphaelite artists whose work, like that of Evelyn de Morgan can be categorized as Symbolist.

Thomas Cooper Gotch, *Alleluia*, 1896.

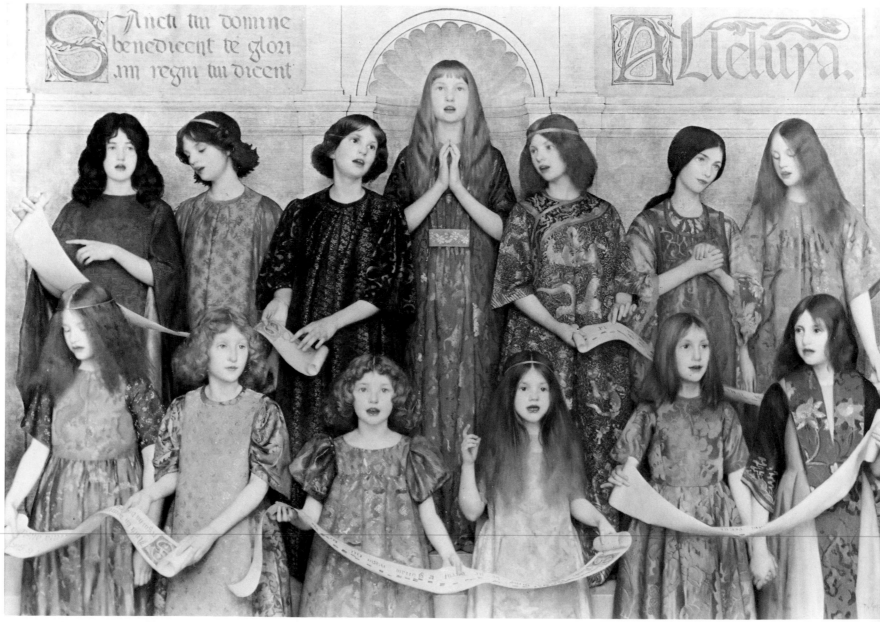

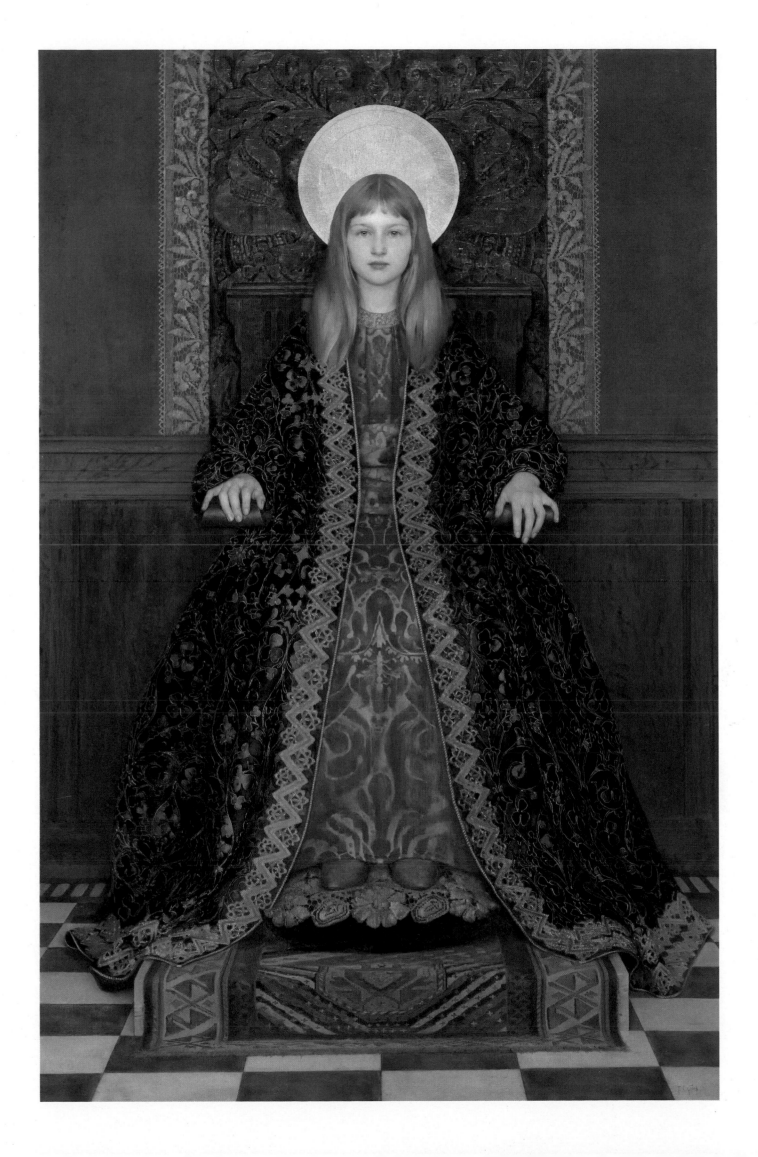

151

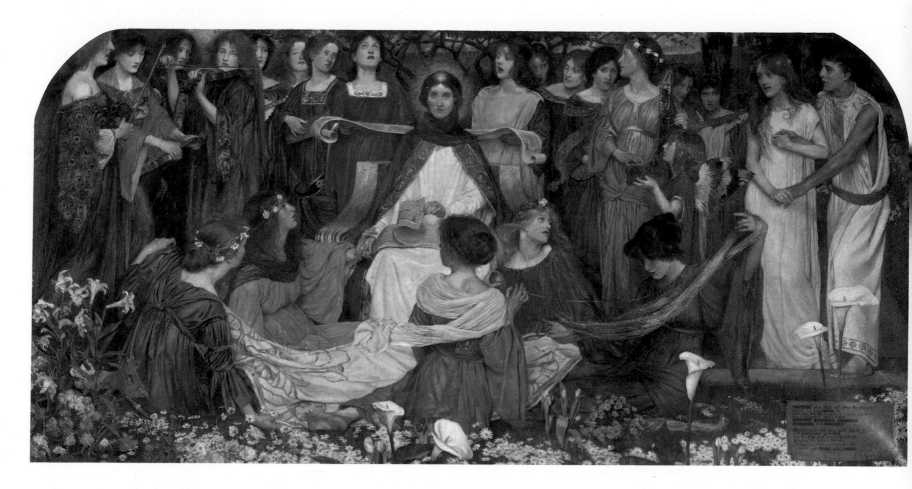

craftsmanship. Bate groups them together with various 'decorative' artists, such as Charles Ricketts, Charles Shannon, John Dickson Batten, Henry Holiday, Heywood Sumner, Anning Bell and the Rhead brothers. Bate also singles out Frederick Cayley Robinson as one of the most promising young Pre-Raphaelite artists. Robinson was a member of the Tempera Society, and his early works are mainly medieval subjects painted in a romantic, elaborate style that certainly owes much to Pre-Raphaelitism. Later, however, he fell more under the influence of Puvis de Chavannes, and his later work has a monumental quality that sets him apart from the other late Pre-Raphaelites.

Bate detected Pre-Raphaelite influence in the work of several other painters working in 1899. Among these are artists practically forgotten today, such as Gerald Moira, Walford Graham-Robertson, and Archie MacGregor, or artists who failed to fulfil the promise of their early works, such as Henry Ryland. Edwin Austin Abbey, an American painter, is also briefly mentioned as an artist coming under Pre-Raphaelite influence, particularly that of Madox Brown. This seems a rather far-fetched comparison, but we can agree with Bate more wholeheartedly about two other artists, Edward Reginald Frampton and Thomas Cooper Gotch. Frampton's highly mannered and decorative style combines Pre-Raphaelitism with the flowing line of Art Nouveau. He is the only equivalent, in painting, of Aubrey Beardsley, but without the decadence. To our eyes, more attuned to European painting of the late nineteenth century, the work of Gotch seems as much Symbolist as Pre-Raphaelite. Gotch was an unusual Pre-Raphaelite, inasmuch as he began his career as a member of the New English Art Club and the Newlyn School. Following a visit to Italy in 1891, he turned to more poetic and allegorical subjects, painted in an elaborate and hieratic style that reflects the influence of Italian Renaissance painting. As a result, Gotch's style is an intriguing mixture of influences, and he is one of the few late Pre-Raphaelites whose works can genuinely be defined as Symbolist. One of his most strongly Symbolist works is the often reproduced *Death the Bride*, which now belongs to the museum in Gotch's home town, Kettering. Bate might have mentioned in this context the Hon. John Collier, a fashionable late Victorian and Edwardian painter of portraits and psychological dramas of upper-class life. He also painted a

John Liston Byam Shaw (1872–1919)
The Blessed Damozel

Signed and dated 1895
Canvas 94 × 180 cm/37 × 71 ins
Guildhall Art Gallery, London

Byam Shaw was one of the most original of the late Pre-Raphaelite painters, who tried to combine romantic Rossettian subjects with the pure, bright colours used by the original Pre-Raphaelite Brotherhood. He was also a distinguished book illustrator, decorator and founder of the Byam Shaw School of Art.

The Hon. John Collier (1850–1934)
In the Venusburg (Tannhauser)

Signed and dated 1901
Canvas 243 × 168 cm/95½ × 66 ins
Southport Art Gallery

Collier began his career as a pupil of Lawrence Alma-Tadema, and ended as a painter of fashionable portraits. He did, however, paint a number of dramatic figure subjects, some of which have a Pre-Raphaelite flavour, especially his costume pictures of women.

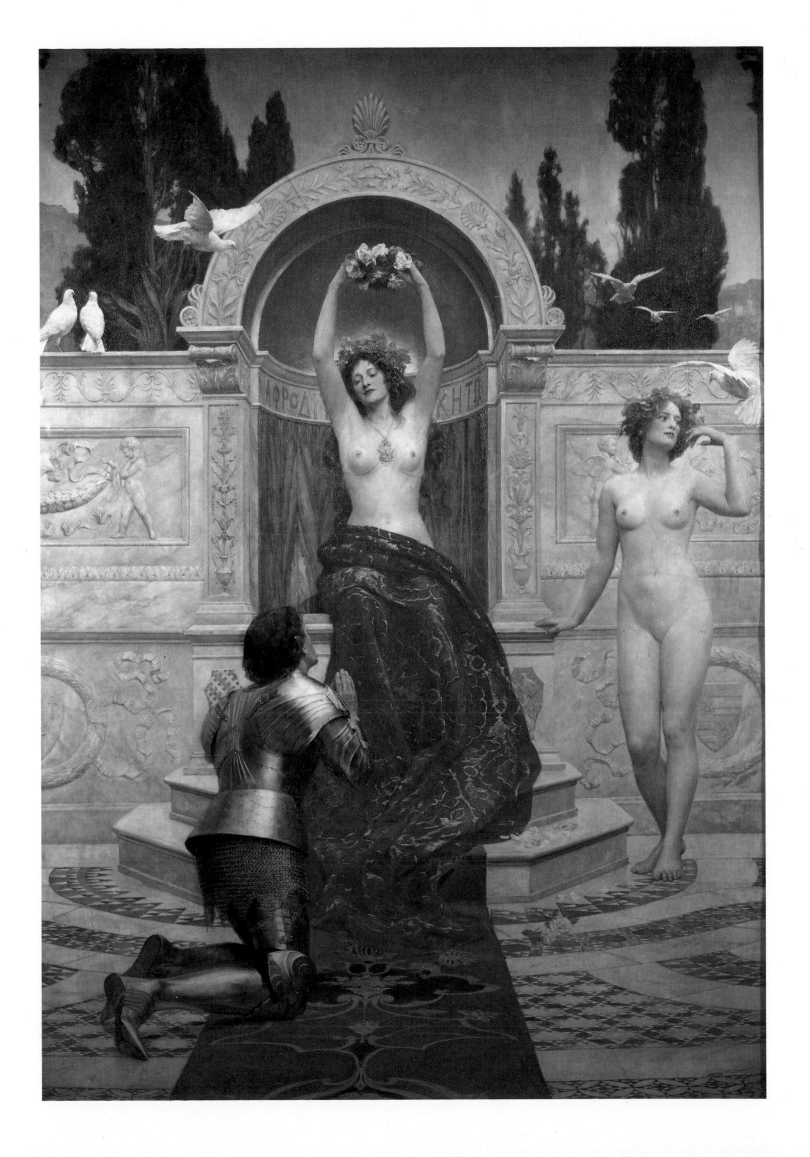

number of historical subjects, particularly costume portraits of exotic ladies, which show Pre-Raphaelite influence of a similar type to that of Gotch. Another artist to explore this particular vein was Frank Cadogan Cowper, one of the very last of the Pre-Raphaelites. His *La Belle Dame Sans Merci* (below), painted as late as 1926, is a romantic Keatsian vision that recalls Waterhouse, Burne-Jones, and even the very early days of the Brotherhood, and is an appropriate note on which to bring to an end this final phase of Pre-Raphaelitism.

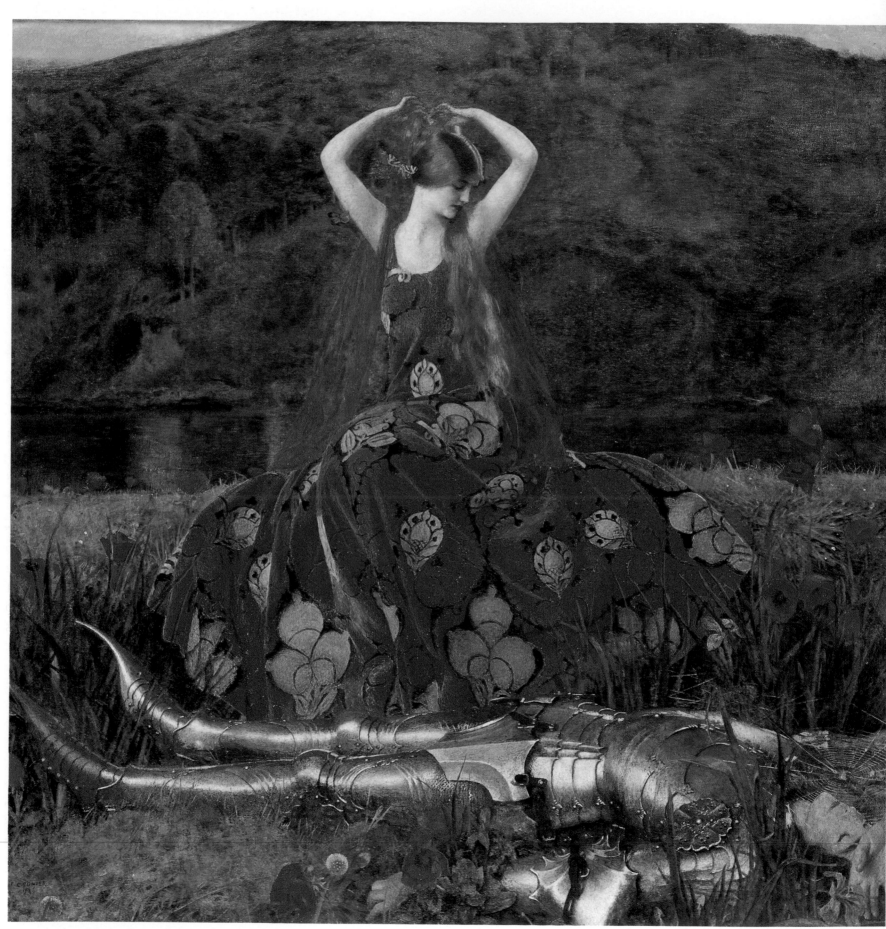

A Personal Postscript

Perhaps no school of art has suffered so much from changes of taste as the Pre-Raphaelites. During the 1920s and '30s a violent reaction against Victorian values and Victorian culture swept through artistic and intellectual circles. The advent of modern abstract art made Victorian painting particularly vulnerable to attack, and writers such as Roger Fry and Clive Bell devastatingly dismissed the whole of Victorian painting as contemptible and irrelevant. The Pre-Raphaelites, who epitomized so much of Victorian culture, suffered particularly from this critical reaction, and between the years 1920 and 1960 their fortunes reached an absolute nadir. Lytton Strachey and the writers of Bloomsbury had reduced the epithet 'Victorian' to a term of ridicule and abuse, and their legacy is still with us today. The adjectives 'Victorian' and 'Pre-Raphaelite' can still arouse fierce passions and prejudices, and many older writers still adopt a rather condescending tone when dealing with the Pre-Raphaelites. It has taken nearly fifty years to eradicate the accumulated prejudice against the Pre-Raphaelites, and for the present writer, studying art history at Cambridge in the early 1960s, it still seemed that English art stopped dead with Constable and Turner. Beyond them yawned the Victorian abyss, of which the Pre-Raphaelites were just another deplorable manifestation. If the Pre-Raphaelites were mentioned at all, it was only to be held up to ridicule, and instantly consigned to historical oblivion. Later in the 1960s, working in the picture department at Christie's, I observed that the occasional appearance of a picture by Rossetti or Burne-Jones was a subject for mirth, and their works were sold for derisory sums by today's standards. To admire them, or worse, to actually collect them, was considered a sign of eccentricity, even madness. I learnt that there were a few pioneering spirits studying and collecting the Pre-Raphaelites by this time, but it was still considered 'bad taste'. The whole weight of the artistic establishment supported the view that 'good art' had somehow disappeared in England in about 1830.

Now, twenty years or so later, the position has completely changed. A revolutionary change in English taste has come about in which museums, art historians, auction houses, dealers and collectors have all played a part. Like all fundamental changes in taste, it has been a long and hard-fought battle. Fashions in art do not change overnight; sometimes they can take a whole generation, and the Victorian revival can be said to have begun in the 1950s, gathered momentum in the 1960s, and come of age in the 1970s. Victorian art, in all its manifestations, is now avidly studied and collected once again, and the Pre-Raphaelites have been in the vanguard of the revival. Just as they suffered most when the critical reaction went against them, so they have now benefited the most when the pendulum began to swing back in their favour. In the last ten years, we have seen major exhibitions devoted to Millais, Rossetti, Hunt, Burne-Jones and Waterhouse. Interest in William Morris and the Arts and Crafts Movement has never been greater. The Pre-Raphaelite movement is now taught in schools and studied in universities; books, articles and theses appear almost every week, but in spite of the enormous quantity of Pre-Raphaelite literature, there is still a great deal more to be written. In the salerooms we have now seen Burne-Jones selling for six-figure prices. During the 1970s it even became fashionable for girls to look 'Pre-Raphaelite' again. It seems that we now live in a more romantic age, and it is possible to admire pictures of medieval knights rescuing damsels in distress without appearing ridiculous. The Pre-Raphaelite dream is something we can look back to with sympathy and understanding, and also share and identify with. The Pre-Raphaelite movement was a dominating force in English art for over fifty years, and it is once again part of the very fabric of English culture. At last it is possible to study Pre-Raphaelite art objectively and dispassionately, and appreciate it for what it is — perhaps the most fascinating and interesting school of art that England has produced.

Frank Cadogan Cowper (1877–1958)
La Belle Dame Sans Merci

Signed and dated 1926
Canvas 102 × 97 cm/40 × 38 ins
Private Collection, London

Cadogan Cowper can claim to be the very last of the Pre-Raphaelites, as he continued painting Arthurian knights and damsels in distress at the Royal Academy well into this century. Although the models and faces have a 1920s look, the mood of his pictures is still authentically Pre-Raphaelite. He also painted murals in the Houses of Parliament, and his *Saint Agnes in Prison* was purchased by the Chantrey Bequest.

Bibliography

The bibliography of Pre-Raphaelitism is vast and growing constantly. The best survey of it is William E. Fredeman's *Pre-Raphaelitism: A Bibliocritical Study* (Harvard University Press, 1965). The following list is therefore intended only as an introductory guide to the best general books on the subject and such biographies of individual artists as are available. Even so, many of these books are rare or out-of-print and will be found only in libraries. They are arranged in order of first publication.

GENERAL BOOKS

Bate, Percy H., *The English Pre-Raphaelite Painters: their Associates and Successors* (Bell & Co., London, 1899).

Marillier, Henry Currie, *The Liverpool School of Painters*, (London, 1904).

Gaunt, William, *The Pre-Raphaelite Tragedy* (Jonathan Cape Ltd., London, 1942).

Ironside, Robin, and Gere, John A., *Pre-Raphaelite Painters*, (Phaidon Press Ltd., Oxford, 1948).

Boase, T. S. R., *English Art 1800–1870* (Oxford University Press, Oxford, 1959).

Reynolds, Graham, *Victorian Painting* (Studio Vista, London, 1966).

Bell, Quentin, *Victorian Artists* (Routledge and Kegan Paul Ltd., London, 1967).

Maas, Jeremey, *Victorian Painters* (Barrie and Rockliff, London, 1969).

Nicoll, John, *The Pre-Raphaelites* (Studio Vista, London, 1970).

Hilton, Timothy, *The Pre-Raphaelites* (Thames and Hudson Ltd., London, 1970).

Fleming, G. H., *That Ne'er Shall Meet Again* (Michael Joseph Ltd., London, 1971).

Wood, Christopher, *The Dictionary of Victorian Painters* (Antique Collectors' Club, Woodbridge, 1971).

Staley, John, *The Pre-Raphaelite Landscape* (Oxford University Press, Oxford, 1973).

Wood, Christopher, *Victorian Panorama: Paintings of Victorian Life* (Faber and Faber Ltd., London, 1976).

BOOKS AND CATALOGUES ON INDIVIDUAL ARTISTS

Ford Madox Brown

Hueffer, Ford Madox, *Ford Madox Brown, A Record of his Life and Work* (London, 1896).

Walker Art Gallery, *Ford Madox Brown* (Liverpool, 1964).

Edward Burne-Jones

Bell, Malcolm, *Edward Burne-Jones, A Record and Review* (George Bell and Sons, London, 1892).

Burne-Jones, Georgiana, *Memorials of Edward Burne-Jones*, 2 vols. (Macmillan, London, 1904).

Harrison, Martin and Waters, Bill, *Burne-Jones* (Barrie and Jenkins, London, 1973).

Fitzgerald, Penelope, *Edward Burne-Jones, A Biography* (Michael Joseph, London, 1975).

Arts Council of Great Britain, *Burne-Jones* (London, 1975).

William Dyce

Poynton, Marcia, *William Dyce* (Clarendon Press, Oxford, 1979).

Arthur Hughes

National Museum of Wales, *Arthur Hughes* (Cardiff, 1971).

William Holman Hunt

Hunt, William Holman, *Pre-Raphaelitism and the Pre-Raphaelite Brotherhood*, 2 vols. (London, 1905).

Walker Art Gallery and Arts Council of Great Britain, *William Holman Hunt* (Liverpool, 1969).

Hunt, Diana Holman, *My Grandfather, his Wives and Loves*, (Hamilton, 1969).

John Everett Millais

Millais, John Guille, *The Life and Letters of Sir John Everett Millais* (London, 1899).

Walker Art Gallery, *John Everett Millais* (Liverpool, 1967).

Lutyens, Mary, *Millais and the Ruskins* (John Murray Ltd., London, 1967).

William Morris

Mackail, J. W. *The Life of William Morris* (Longmans and Co., London, 1901).

Henderson, Philip, *William Morris, his life, work and friends* (Thames and Hudson Ltd., London, 1967).

Dante Gabriel Rossetti

Rossetti, William Michael, *Dante Gabriel Rossetti: His Family Letters* (Ellis and Elvey Ltd., London, 1895).

Rossetti, William Michael, *Ruskin, Rossetti, Pre-Raphaelitism: Papers 1854–62* (G. Allen, London, 1899).

Rossetti, William Michael, *Pre-Raphaelite Diaries and Letters* (Hurst and Blackett, London, 1900).

Marillier, Henry Currie, *Dante Gabriel Rossetti: An Illustrated Memorial of his Art and Life* (George Bell and Sons, London, 1899).

Doughty, Oswald, *A Victorian Romantic: Dante Gabriel Rossetti* (Oxford University Press, London, 1960).

Grylls, Mary R. G., *Portrait of Rossetti* (Macdonald, London, 1964).

Fleming, G. H., *Rossetti and the Pre-Raphaelite Brotherhood* (Hart-Davies, London, 1967).

Surtees, Virginia, *The Paintings and Drawings of Dante Gabriel Rossetti 1828–1882: A Catalogue Raisonné*, 2 vols. (Clarendon Press, Oxford, 1971).

Royal Academy of Arts, *Dante Gabriel Rossetti* (London, 1973).

Nicoll, John, *Rossetti* (Studio Vista, London, 1975).

Frederick Sandys

Brighton Museum and Art Gallery, *Frederick Sandys*, (Brighton, 1974).

John William Waterhouse

Hobson, Anthony, *John William Waterhouse* (Studio Vista, London, 1980).

ART GALLERIES

Almost every major British art gallery contains some Pre-Raphaelite works, but the best collections are owned by the following museums and galleries:

Tate Gallery, London

Victoria and Albert Museum, London

Birmingham City Museum and Art Gallery

Manchester City Art Gallery

Walker Art Gallery, Liverpool

In the USA many museums have Pre-Raphaelite pictures, but the finest collections are:

Bancroft Collection, Wilmington Society of Fine Arts, Delaware

Fogg Museum, Harvard University, Cambridge, Mass.

Index

Colour plate and black and white illustration page references are indicated in *italic*.